Tim Bowden is an acclaimed oral historian, broadcaster, and radio and television documentary maker who for many years, as host of 'Backchat', was known as the voice of the ABC. He is the author of seven books including *Penelope Goes West, The Way My Father Tells It: The Story of an Australian Life, The Silence Calling: Australians in Antarctica, Antarctica and Back in Sixty Days* and *One Crowded Hour: Neil Davis, Combat Cameraman.*

penelope bungles to broome

TIM BOWDEN

For Maeve & Gordon,
with love,

[signature] (+ Ros)

ALLEN & UNWIN

28/2/01

For Nina Riemer, legendary editor and friend

Allen & Unwin
83 Alexander Street,
Crows Nest NSW 2065
Australia
Phone: (61 2) 8425 0100
Fax: (61 2) 9906 2218
Email: frontdesk@allen-unwin.com.au
Web: http://www.allenandunwin.com

National Library of Australia
Cataloguing-in-Publication entry:

Bowden, Tim, 1937– .
Penelope bungles to Broome.

Bibliography.
ISBN 1 86508 424 7

1. Bowden, Tim, 1937—Journeys—Northern Territory.
2. Bowden, Tim, 1937—Journeys—Western Australia.
3. Northern Territory—Description and travel. 4. Western
Australia—Description and travel. I. Title.

919.4104

Set in 12/15pt Caslon 540 by Midland Typesetters
Printed by Griffin Press, Adelaide
10 9 8 7 6 5 4 3 2 1

contents

Acknowledgements

First to Ros, thanks not only for still travelling with me in Penelope and through life, but for her companionship, wise counsel on the manuscript and on-the-road photography.

Special thanks to the Allen & Unwin team, in particular publisher Patrick Gallagher and senior editor Rebecca Kaiser (who were gracious about deadlines when the Bowdens had to move house mid-manuscript), designer Nada Backovic and publicist Syreeta Clarke. My editor Nina Riemer has now edited seven of my eight books and I thank her for her fortitude and always encouraging guidance.

Salutations again to film maker Steve Westh, whose excellent documentary 'The Grey Nomads' continues to haunt our memory banks and inspire camp fire conversations. Also our friends Greg Mortimer and Margaret Werner, of Aurora Expeditions, who introduced us to the magnificence of Kimberley coastal cruising.

Finally, thanks to all those nomadic travellers and outback Australians we met along the way who have contributed to this narrative.

Introduction

These days I travel with two women, Ros and Penelope. It has not always been so.

Penelope came into our lives in 1997 when Ros and I were planning a summer journey from Sydney to Margaret River and back, around the Great Australian Bight and across the Nullarbor Plain. Our then unnamed Toyota Landcruiser had been located in Tasmania. After careful thought (observing how other travellers camp and travel is always fascinating), we chose a camping trailer called a Jayco 'Flight', with an off-road chassis, to tow behind our newly-acquired second-hand Landcruiser. We first saw the Flight—the smallest of its breed—at a caravan and camping show at Rosehill in Sydney. In travelling mode, it towed handily like a high box trailer. To turn it into a happy home at the end of the travelling day, you had to wind up its roof and pull beds out at each end. The expansion of its interior space was quite dramatic. Ros was so impressed by the splendour of its layout—with beds, table, bench seats, fridge and stove—that she immediately dubbed it 'The Manor'.

Picking up on that, our genial Jayco salesman David Carrick shot back that we would now have to call our

Landcruiser 'Penelope'. I was not quick in twigging to the link with actress Penelope Keith and the popular British television series 'To the Manor Born', but Ros, having lived for most of her married life in a male household with me and our two sons (even our first dog was male), was entranced with the idea. As it happened, having a four-wheel-drive with a silly name was perpetuated by my book of our first camping and driving odyssey in the summer of 1997–98, titled *Penelope Goes West—On the Road from Sydney to Margaret River and Back.*

On that summer journey, we had to stay close to the coast to avoid being fried. Having not done any major driving and camping forays since the early 1980s, we were astounded by the numbers of fellow Australians (and overseas tourists) on the road. We were mindful of an excellent television documentary we had seen titled *The Grey Nomads*, charting the progress of a cross-section of the hordes of chronologically-challenged travellers ceaselessly circumnavigating the continent on Highway One. Not only did Ros and I meet them, we joined them.

In 1999 we set aside three months for our dry season Kimberley journey. The area was not entirely new territory to us. In 1982 we had hijacked our two sons Barnaby (10) and Guy (7) from school for a similar period when we drove in a venerable VW Kombi van with box trailer through New South Wales and north-west Queensland, via Boulia and Longreach, to Katherine before tackling the Gibb River Road with its creek crossings and boulder-strewn track from Kununurra to Derby, and then to Broome.

The Kimberley, with its grotesque, obese boab trees, red sandstone mountain ranges and dramatic land and light scapes enchanted us. We marvelled at the vastness of man-made Lake Argyle, fished for the elusive barramundi in sedate dry season streams and kept a wary eye out for crocodiles. The grey nomads were evident even in 1982, a clutch of them camped near the bridge over the Victoria River under shady gums in those bulbous 1950s style caravans where a hoop of plyboard was stretched over a frame. Most were pensioners, supplementing their tucker by catching barra from the river and saving up their pension cheques to cover petrol for the next move. They were raucously cheerful and full of life, joyously aware that geography and circumstance had blessed them with a life Riley would have envied. I kept them in mind.

By June 1999 my two female companions and I were ready to take to the road again. The plan was to drive from Sydney to Broome in two weeks—fast travel by our standards, but essential if we were to catch the big catamaran *Coral Princess* for a ten-day cruise up the Kimberley coast, exploring that majestic, fractured coastline with its twelve-metre tides and ancient red sandstone ramparts, before returning to Broome and resuming our more leisurely travel habit.

Our route to Broome was to be via Port Augusta (barely pausing for breath), up the Stuart Highway to Alice Springs, then driving the Tanami Track to Halls Creek. After the coastal cruise we planned to return to Halls Creek, drive in to the Bungle Bungle National Park (not in existence when we were last through) and head on to Kununurra on the Ord to prepare for the Gibb River Road.

After that we thought we'd give Penelope her head down into the Pilbara and the Mid West of Western Australia, questing for national parks and wildflowers and whatever else took our fancy. It would all be new country for us. That, surely, was what our kind of travel was all about. A quick sashay across the Nullarbor would bring us back to Sydney.

Penelope needed a little attention. Stiffer springs in the rear to cope better with extra gear on board and with the weight of The Manor's towbar. Having our tail higher in the air had the added bonus of giving us some rear vision over the top of the camper. We also gained a few centimetres in height through fitting narrower tyres, on split rims, to replace the squashy, wide radials that I had inherited with the car. I was advised that the fatter tyres were likely to have their side walls slashed in some of the limestone country we would be passing through in the Kimberley. There was also an advantage in having the same wheels and tyres on Penelope and The Manor.

After considerable thought, I fixed a three-quarter length roof rack to the Landcruiser. Ros always thinks I take too much of everything, and she is almost certainly right, but we would need to carry an extra tyre and tube. I also rigged up an awning from the passenger side of the roof rack which could be unfurled for shade at lunchtime stops and supported by a couple of tent poles and guy ropes. (It wasn't my most inspired thought. We didn't use it once!) Another completely unused item was a waterproof bag containing the side walls for the awning of The Manor. At least they were up out of the way. Because our journey would take us through central Australia in winter (where night temperatures can drop below zero degrees Celsius) before reaching the tropical dry season in the north, we had to take both cold weather clothing and light gear—another extra bag for the roof rack. As it turned out, the roof rack was particularly useful for carrying firewood: national parks these days do not allow wood to be gathered within their boundaries for quite sound conservation reasons, and popular camping places can also be short of firewood.

Inside Penelope, I took out the back seat and moved the cargo barrier forward to its second position just behind the front seats. Into this extra space went big fishing-style heavy plastic bins with essentials such as our wine cellar and deep storage for nonperishables like pasta, Asian spices, dehydrated peas, tinned fruit, canned ham and dried fruit. There was space between the cargo barrier and the front seats to slip in folding tables and two extremely comfortable collapsible chairs in small holding bags. The general cargo space easily encompassed a ladder (for getting up on the roof rack), camp oven, Coleman pressure lamp, a smallish three-way fridge (strapped down to stop it wandering about), two water containers and various boxes for boots, bush shower and other camping necessities—which included our historic Hong Kong wooden tucker box (complete with Chinese characters and preserved ginger stencil), its top doubling as a cutting board.

Two big sliding drawers built into the rear section provided easy access to tools, spare jack, tow rope, extension leads, tow ball and shaft (when not in use), snatch strap, shackles, extra oil, spare engine belts and hoses, our portable barbecue and two handles for erecting The Manor into camping mode. I only carry a modest tool kit because I am not very handy. Just about everyone else we meet off the beaten track is either more mechanically gifted than I, or a fully-fledged bush mechanic with a portable welding outfit. As Ros has noted, a raised bonnet lid in a camping ground is an open invitation for male bonding. Within seconds a cluster of faces is discussing the problem.

Our friends Graham and Shirley Taylor from Adelaide,

also occasional nomads, have noted this syndrome. Graham said he was constantly amazed at the way in which grey nomads pitched in to help each other. 'You only have to drag out the toolbox to find A. N. Other looking over your shoulder questioning the problem, and uncannily able to produce the 7/16th Whitworth ring spanner so desperately needed, but safe in your workshop in Adelaide.'

It was a dark and stormy night (I had to work that in somewhere) in Launceston, northern Tasmania, when Graham and Shirley pulled into a caravan park. Just as they did so, the left rear tyre of their Toyota Hiace camper subsided slowly and noisily. Not wanting to sleep on an angle—Graham is a big man—he decided to change the wheel, rain or no rain. But because the axle was so close to the ground, he needed two jacks.

'I sent Shirley off to another Toyota moored in a nearby bay,' Graham said, 'and she came back with their jack. As I lay in the mud and rain labouring in vain, Mr Toyota himself appeared offering to help.

'He joined me in the slush under the Hiace as we wrestled with the two jacks. His wife came over too, reminding him "not to knock himself out". She told Shirley that her husband was just out of hospital having had not one, but two, brain tumours removed.'

As Graham was digesting that news, she added, 'We've had a bad year. Just after Christmas he collapsed on me and had heart surgery with five bypasses'. Graham wondered if his Good Samaritan would emerge alive. But the job was done, and the Taylors saw their helper two days later in the north-west town of Deloraine, alive and well, and were able to thank him again. Graham said it was 'typical grey nomad support—he must have been in his late seventies'.

Two days before our departure date we retrieved The Manor—which is kept at boarding school out at the Jayco centre at Minchinbury near Sydney in between trips—and loaded it with linen, sleeping sheets, blankets, and our spare clothing kept in bins under the bench seats on either side of the table. We carried two rechargeable Coleman lamps for reading in bed. I had a longer cable made to carry 12 volt power from our auxiliary battery in Penelope to The Manor while in camping mode. It was difficult to keep cups, enamel plates and unbreakable drink beakers in any sort of order, because the small cupboards under the bench top with sink and stove were hinged and the whole assembly had to be folded over upside down during travel (signalled by a cheerful clattering crash every time) because doing so lowered the profile of the trailer for towing.

On the back bumper bar of The Manor were two extra jerry cans for fuel and water, and an extra gas bottle. We carried 130 litres of water when fully loaded—60 litres in the under-floor tank of The Manor, two 20-litre jerry cans, and one 10-litre container for daily use. This is not excessive when travelling in the waterless outback, particularly when so much of the bore water in places like the Pilbara is so hard and full of minerals that it's a wonder the tails of the cattle don't calcify into limestone and snap off.

I carried a Macintosh Powerbook 520C in the clothes locker of The Manor to access and send email from time to time—when we could get access to a phone socket. On occasions we found ourselves trying to explain to motel managers why we wanted to hire one of their rooms for ten minutes.

'Just to use the phone socket.'

'Oh really?'

To keep our daily diary I carried a Newton eMate, now sadly discontinued by Apple, but a handy little machine to take notes on and, from time to time, transfer them to the Powerbook. We do not have a mobile phone—which would not have worked from most of the areas we planned to visit anyway. For urgent messages I told people to ring my answering service in Sydney, which I paged into from public phones—yes, they still exist in outback places. There was even one at the Bungle Bungles. We could have hired a satellite phone at great expense, but as we were not planning solo crossings of the Gibson or Great Sandy Deserts and knew we could survive for at least two weeks on the food and water we were carrying if we broke down in isolation, we gave that a miss.

Ros, the official photographer, carried a new Minolta 600si with all kinds of amazing bells, whistles and electronic wizardry embedded in its chips, her previous Minolta 5000 as a back-up, and I had a pocket Olympus for handy holiday happy snaps. Ros took transparencies using Fuji Velvia film.

With Penelope fully packed and attached to The Manor in our Northbridge driveway, and a 5 am start planned, we fell into a fitful slumber, a bit like kids trying to get to sleep on the night Santa comes. I don't know why, but at 2 am I woke up wondering if Ros had packed our down sleeping bags. A startled squawk from my partner at 4 am, when I asked her, confirmed a very bad near miss.

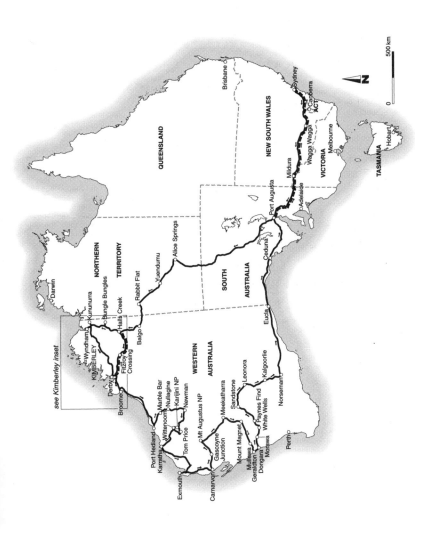

see Kimberley inset

KIMBERLEY

NORTHERN
TERRITORY

WESTERN
AUSTRALIA

SOUTH
AUSTRALIA

QUEENSLAND

NEW SOUTH WALES

VICTORIA

TASMANIA

Darwin

Kununurra
Bungle Bungles
Wyndham
Halls Creek
Fitzroy
Crossing
Balgo
Derby
Broome
Port Hedland
Karratha
Wittenoom
Marble Bar
Nullagine
Karijini NP
Newman
Tom Price
Exmouth
Mt Augustus NP
Gascoyne
Junction
Carnarvon
Meekatharra
Sandstone
Mount Magnet
Leonora
Mullewa
Geraldton
Dongara
Morawa
Paynes Find
White Wells
Kalgoorlie
Norseman
Perth
Eucla

Rabbit Flat
Yuendumu
Alice Springs

Ceduna
Port Augusta
Adelaide

Mildura
Wagga Wagga
Canberra
ACT
Sydney
Melbourne
Hobart

Brisbane

N

0   500 km

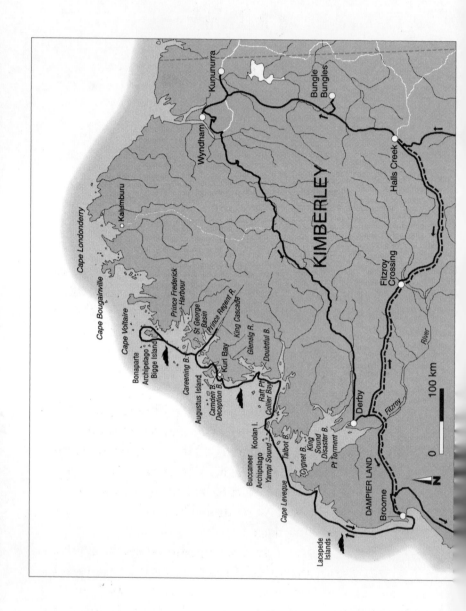

Cape Londonderry

Cape Bougainville

Cape Voltaire

Bonaparte
Archipelago
Bigge Island

Prince Frederick
Harbour
St George
Basin
Careening B.

Augustus Island
Camden B.
Deception B.

Kalumburu

Prince Regent R.

King Cascade

Glenelg R.

Doubtful B.

Kuri Bay

Raft Pt
Collier Bay

Koolan I.

Buccaneer
Archipelago
Yampi Sound

Talbot B.

Cygnet B.
King
Sound
Disaster B.
Pt Torment

DAMPIER LAND

Lacepede
Islands

Broome

Cape Leveque

Derby

Fitzroy

Fitzroy
Crossing

River

KIMBERLEY

Kununurra

Wyndham

Bungle
Bungles

Halls Creek

0   100 km

N

one

Assignation with Alice

There is a wonderful feeling of exhilaration on the first morning of a big trip, gear packed, fuel tanks full and the joyous realisation that unknown pleasures and adventures lie ahead—combined with the luxury of freedom of choice on the open road as to where you go and how long you stay there. As the clutch engaged, and Penelope and The Manor crept up our steep laneway at 5 am on that cold June morning trying not to make too much noise to disturb our sleeping neighbours, there was the gleeful realisation that we were leaving behind the daily routines of suburban living. This was quickly followed by periods of soul-searching and reflection—not of the wisdom of leaving— but pondering what items, essential or trivial, had been left behind. There is always something. At least it wasn't the all-important sleeping bags.

Getting away on a fine morning also raises the spirits. The red flush of dawn had us almost clear of the great Sydney sprawl, heading south from Campbelltown on the Hume Highway to connect up with the Sturt Highway at Yass, which would take us west over the Hay plains through

Wagga Wagga, Narrandera and Hay to our first overnight stop at Balranald. Still pumped up with the adrenalin of heading off, I slipped a cassette of our 'holiday song' into the player (on a major trip an almost daily occurrence that Ros calls 'morning prayers') and sang along with Harry Nilsson's rendition of 'Everybody's Talkin'' with its undeniably 1960s' ambience. Those who remember those years may recall the film *Midnight Cowboy* featuring a New York hustler, played by Jon Voight, heading south to Florida with his crippled friend (Dustin Hoffman), where—as the song so delightfully points out—life, the weather and just about everything else simply had to be better.

As we began the climb up into the Southern Highlands, cattle stood patiently in the frozen fields, waiting for the sun to thaw their pastures. But they only had a fraction of my attention. I had begun a king-sized worry. Ros says I always do this at the beginning of a trip. This time I was brooding about the roof rack. Why had I insisted on putting it on? When we finished our packing, there was more room in Penelope than I'd anticipated for some of the gear I had destined for the roof. The aerodynamic drag of a roof rack is considerable. They say it adds 20 per cent to your fuel consumption to tow a trailer. Maybe I should add another ten per cent for roof rack drag? So what about my fuel calculations? With main and auxiliary tanks holding 140 litres of fuel—plus another 20 litres of diesel from the spare jerry can—I had calculated we could safely travel 800 kilometres between re-fuelling points. I needed to get at least 400 kilometres from the main tank. But perhaps the roof rack had put paid to that.

Ros was looking out her window as the early sun threw long shadows across the countryside, blissfully unaware that I was nurturing a classic fret.

Bloody roof rack! With no head wind at all, we were battling to do 85 kph. Admittedly we were climbing, but what if we couldn't manage our cruising speed of 100 to 110 kph over long distances? A sudden flash of inspiration— maybe it wasn't too late to get rid of it? We could divert to Canberra and leave it with friends and repack. Or take it to Queanbeyan and leave it with the Jayco people there.

'Ros—' (tentatively).

'Yes?' (She knows that tone of voice.)

I advanced my arguments. They were not well received. What about our ability to carry firewood into national parks? I admitted that was a good point. And how could we possibly test fuel consumption when we were climbing over the Great Dividing Range? Point taken. Ros produced our travelling thermos.

'Would you like a cup of coffee?'

Perhaps she thought caffeine helped soothe lunatics. I sipped away and cogitated darkly on matters of fuel consumption and wind drag. Ros broke the long silence.

'OK, this is what we do. We can refuel at Wagga Wagga and then test the speed and fuel consumption of the main tank on the flat when we hit the Hay plains. If that proves a disaster—which I don't think it will—we can leave the roof rack somewhere in Port Augusta. We have to come back through there on the way back.'

What a woman. Sheer genius. I brightened up and began to enjoy the passing countryside again. And so it came to pass that we did manage to coax 400 kilometres out of the main tank, cantered along quite comfortably at

110 kph on the Hay plains, and forgot all about leaving the roof rack at Port Augusta.

To maximise the distances we could travel on our first two days out we had decided to stay in motels at Balranald and Port Augusta, and celebrate our first bush camp somewhere off the Stuart Highway on day three. I'd not given much thought to why Balranald was so named. It's the oldest European settlement on the Lower Murrumbidgee River, dating back before 1850, and the result of a homesick Scot, George James McDonald, the Commissioner for Crown Lands for the Lower Darling District, who dropped by in 1848 and thought the tiny settlement looked like his home village Balranald in the Outer Hebrides, for God's sake. I'm told that 'bal' in Celtic means abode, or village, of Ranald—the clan of Ranald. How McDonald managed to tie in the Outer Hebrides with the kangaroos, gum trees, resident Aborigines and inland plains can perhaps only be explained by copious libations of whatever moonshine was available at the time.

Balranald has also been a crossing point for many of the early explorers. Charles Sturt was the first European to pass by in 1830, during his exhaustive exploration of the Murray–Darling river system, followed six years later by Thomas Mitchell who, having demonstrated that the Lachlan River flowed into the Murrumbidgee, then went on to prove that the Darling River actually joined the Murray—which Sturt believed to be so, but had not actually seen.

The doomed duo of Burke and Wills crossed the Murrumbidgee by punt on 17 September 1860, and camped overnight on the river bank in front of the Balranald Inn.

Despite crossing the continent from Adelaide to the Gulf of Carpentaria, Robert O'Hara Burke must go down in Australian history as one of the more fat-headed explorers. He rushed off from the Coopers Creek camp in December with a party of four men, six camels, four horses and inadequate provisions instead of waiting for the bulk of his party who were making their way up from Adelaide to join him. It was the hottest time of the year, and they didn't make it back to Coopers Creek—on their last legs—until April the next year.

The story of their deaths by malnutrition and thirst is well known, and only one of the four, John King, survived by sensibly attaching himself to a group of Aborigines for a month until a relief party arrived. (King was originally a soldier in the Indian Army who had left India because of poor health! He later said of the Aborigines: 'They treated me with uniform kindness and looked upon me as one of themselves.') The Aborigines must have been puzzled by the inability of Burke and Wills to live off the land. Burke and his companions must also have wondered from time to time where the Aborigines got their food and water and how they managed to live. Was it a misplaced sense of British superiority that prevented them from making closer contact with other human beings who were clearly making a success of existing in that harsh country? Like Scott of the Antarctic (also an impetuous planner) in a different kind of desert, Burke took other, more sensible expeditioners like his deputy, William John Wills, with him to their deaths.

It's a pity today's travellers can't see more from the road of the rivers they are following. Often the only evidence of the river's presence is provided by the irrigated fields of bright green, newly-sown cereal and vegetable crops against the more subdued olives and browns of the native vegetation. You have to detour down side roads to see narrow ribbons of life-giving water that sustains life and agriculture in the Murray–Darling basin on a slow meandering journey to South Australia.

Travellers not on a tight schedule should allow time for detours. On our last foray along this route to Port Augusta (via Mildura and Renmark) we called in briefly to the town of Morgan in South Australia. We refuelled, bought a couple of dogs' eyes with dead horse (pies with sauce) for lunch at the first shop we saw, asked about the state of a then gravelled road to Burra, and took off. To our enduring travelling shame, we weren't even aware then that Morgan was on the Murray where the river sweeps around what is variously known as the Great Bend or the Great Elbow. Only 160 or so kilometres from Adelaide, it was once an important regional and communications hub, not only for river traffic, but as a railhead and port. In its heyday, towards the end of the nineteenth century, Morgan was the second busiest port in South Australia after Adelaide. This time we drove in further to a little park where we could overlook the river, ferry, charmingly restored buildings along the river front and remains of the railway station and wharves. While we had lunch we resolved to call in on our way back to do the Morgan Historical Walk, detailed in an excellent pamphlet put out by the local tourism association.

Although the vineyards along the Murray near Renmark were not looking their most attractive with the vines leafless and skeletal, we called in to a small winery to pick up a few glass receptacles of bottled sunshine—and the cheapest muscat we would find. We planned to meet up with Greg

Williams, Heather Messer and their two boys Todd and Ryan at Kununurra in a month's time. On our first meeting at Cape Arid National Park on the south-east coast of Western Australia, I had generously given Greg a bottle of muscat purchased from the same area at the startlingly low price of $2. Neither of us had high expectations of it, and when Greg did get around to sampling it he claims he put it to better use by topping up the brake fluid in the master cylinder of his venerable Toyota Landcruiser. The cheapest muscat on offer this time was $4.50 a bottle and we bought two—one to sample in the cold nights of the central desert and the other for Greg and Heather.

We had given Port Augusta short shrift on our previous visit. It was raining at the time and the mix of salt flats and muddy mangroves at the head of Spencer Gulf and sweep of scrubby desert wilderness stretching seemingly to infinity caused us to agree with the explorer Matthew Flinders when he came here on 13 March 1802. He wrote in his diary: 'Nothing of particular interest having presented itself to detain us at the head of the Gulf, we got under way.'

For the modern traveller, the view from Flinders' desolate vantage point now takes in the sprawl of Port Augusta's light industrial area, and the big chimney of the power station belching a great plume of smoke. I had written in my travelling diary that Port Augusta was one of those places that simply had to exist because of its geographical location, whether it wanted to or not. It was railhead, port, gateway to the north and a place all road traffic heading east or west across the continent simply had to pass through. Keeping my original ignorant dismissal of Morgan in mind, I was clearly in need of what the Chinese would call 'correct thinking' about the charms of Port Augusta.

Our friend Ted Egan in Alice Springs, all-round good bloke, singer and spinner of outrageous yarns, had recommended we stay at the intriguingly named Standpipe Motel in Port Augusta which, Ted said, had a brilliant Indian restaurant. We didn't mind 'doing ourselves nicely' because it was the last time we would sleep away from The Manor for the next three months—apart from our planned voyage on *Coral Princess*. Even though we were looking forward to camping again, it was a special occasion of sorts.

The original Standpipe Hotel was built in 1883, shortly after the arrival of water piped under Spencer Gulf to a pressure tower at Port Augusta West. Charles Chappel, the original licensee, saw the virtue in having another watering hole close by, and his hotel was strategically situated as a meeting place for travellers heading north or west. He erected the original 'standpipe' which was a pipe, like an inverted L (ꓶ) under which water containers could be filled up, or camels and horses washed. The pressure came from the nearby water tower. The hotel's licence lapsed in 1901 and after that the building was variously a private residence and a nursing home. Since the early 1980s the old hotel has been splendidly restored as a function centre, restaurant and bar with high, decorated ceilings and a superb collection of historic photographs dating back to the days when camels and their Afghan drivers were the only way of getting supplies to remote settlements and when a forest of masts and spars from the rigged ships at the port loomed over the town.

It was the shortest day of the year when we were there and we needed to buy fresh supplies for the beginning of our 'proper' camping. I was having problems with the battery of my eMate notebook computer which was not holding its charge. Fortunately Port Augusta had a Tandy electronics shop, and I hoped to get a charger which I could plug into the 12 volt bayonet point socket on Penelope's dashboard. The problem, I reasoned, was to find a charger with the right voltage, and computers can be tricky. That is how we came to meet Paul Wilson, the Tandy manager and long-term and enthusiastic resident of Port Augusta. He did not have the equipment I wanted, but suggested an even better idea. There was a converter available—perhaps in the sister shop in Alice Springs—which would convert 12 volt direct current to 240 AC current, thereby allowing me not only to charge up my tardy eMate with its existing charger, but also to run my bigger Powerbook away from mains power. A quick phone call to Alice Springs. Yes, they had one and would hold it for me. Now, how long were we staying in Port Augusta?

I confessed we were off the next morning. Paul was incensed. 'But there is so much to see here.'

He looked at his watch.

'The sun will be setting in about twenty minutes. You just have time to drive north to Yorkey's Crossing—that is right at the actual top of Spencer Gulf—and you can get some great photos of the setting sun lighting up the Flinders Ranges to the east.

'There's no time to talk further now. Just get in your four-wheel-drive and go. I'll come and see you at the Standpipe Motel tonight when you get back and we'll talk some more. Make sure you have a good look at the black-and-white historic photos in the bar of Port Augusta taken in 1900.'

He was absolutely insistent about this, and we drove off

obediently. We got to the crossing as the orange bowl of the sun dipped behind the hills to the west, and we saw its dying light highlight the rolling flanks of the Flinders Ranges to the east, just as Paul had described it.

We met up in the Standpipe bar as arranged, and had a good look at the historic photos on display. When I mentioned, over a drink, that I was interested in the 1802 visit by Matthew Flinders in his ship *Investigator*, Paul nearly exploded with enthusiasm. He had read Flinders' original journal of his Spencer Gulf visit and drawn conclusions based on his local knowledge. Flinders had seen a large mountain in the distance which he named Mt Brown (after his on-board botanist) and a party was sent off to climb it.

Mt Brown was approximately 30 kilometres to the east of Spencer Gulf, and Paul Wilson believed that a trick of the light made Mt Brown look at least half the distance away it really was—and Flinders' exploratory party miscalculated and had to spend a night out on the mountain. To put his theory to the test, Paul did the walk himself and spent a night on the mountain.

'I thought of how terrified they must have been looking back towards the Gulf, with the lights of Aboriginal camp fires glowing in the dark. They had no contact with the Aborigines.'

Paul's enthusiasm for Port Augusta and its surrounds was so infectious I felt I should sell up in Sydney and move there to live. After our succulent dinner of Tandoori chicken, garlic prawns and buttered narn I had completely revised my earlier ignorant impressions of Port Augusta. A lesson, surely, for spending more time exploring unknown places before passing judgment.

We pulled out of the Standpipe Motel's drive on to the Stuart Highway heading north at 7.15 am. Penelope's heater was pumping out welcome warm air on this cold but clear and sunny winter's morning. Unlike our view from Yorkey's Crossing the previous night, the low sunlight was now from the east, highlighting some distinctive flat-topped mountains to the west. Their table-tops stood above thick swathes of early morning mist looking for all the world like Antarctic tabular icebergs rising above a frozen sea. As Penelope's big diesel warmed to its work and our cruising speed slowly picked up to 100 kph plus, we drove through bands of mist through which the sun could be seen as a red glow, refracting at times to form miniature rainbows. It seemed a good moment for 'morning prayers' and a sing-along with Harry Nilsson. Wattles and the occasional desert oak were totally still in the windless air, with diamond points of dew sparkling on their thin fronds. We were heading north towards warmth and adventure.

Some Sydney friends had given us a set of audio tapes of some of Henry Lawson's short stories to while away the many hours of outback driving. Ros slipped the first tape into Penelope's player and produced some life-enhancing coffee from the thermos. I had not realised what a gloomy fellow Henry was. His stories were beautifully crafted, but almost invariably dark and desolate, about frightful things happening to battling people who were powerless against the dirty deals life had dealt them. My memory of the first story we heard that morning—and I may have telescoped some of the content of later stories—was about the sudden death of a young man in a droving plant, who drowned trying to get cattle across a flooded river. After he died, his companions realised they didn't really know him; in fact, they weren't even aware of his proper name. As he appeared a bit simple, they had given him a hard time in the way of the bush, with cruel practical jokes, which the young man had taken in good part. In his pathetic swag they found some letters to his widowed mother who was looking after his grossly handicapped brother, and totally dependent on the little money he could send home. The drovers took the hat around for his mum, and then buried the kid they'd been so nasty to in a lonely grave, without a proper burial service. I recall the story ended with the sound of the hollow thuds made by clods of hard earth falling down on the cheap wooden coffin.

We couldn't face the next story immediately, and drove in silence for about ten kilometres. The morning seemed less enchanting than it had been, and we both brooded on the sadness of what we had heard.

'Why do you think Penny and Malcolm chose these tapes for us?'

'Perhaps,' Ros said, 'it was to dampen our spirits in case of over-excitement, or to warn us of the dangers of the outback waiting for us.'

Nothing short of certain death, if the tenor of Henry's stories continued as they had begun. Over the next three months we did finish the tapes, but we had to pace ourselves. Not all the stories were redolent of utter despair, but even the lighter ones were less than optimistic about the human condition.

As it happened, Ros and I did not play spoken word or even music tapes very often (apart from morning prayers) during our long driving spells. We both like sitting and thinking, and taking in the passing scene. Even in the desert there is always something to see, hawks hovering

over unseen prey, wild flowers, changing patterns of vegetation, distant low hills, patterns of sun and cloud in the sky
and on the ground. As you get further north there are strings
of paddy melons (spawned from seeds brought in
by the Afghan camel drivers in their pack saddles it is
believed) lying beside the road in various stages of maturity
from striped dark green to gold and yellow. You have to
keep a wary eye out for wildlife, although kangaroos are not
such a menace in the daylight hours. Emus, though, are so
unbelievably stupid that they are quite likely to dash out in
front of you at any time of the day or night, and although
crows and some of the smaller hawks feeding on carrion by
the road are very savvy about cars and trucks, the majestic
wedge-tailed eagles by their very size are slow to take off
and pick up flying speed and sometimes get skittled right
beside their erstwhile dinner.

I recall being supremely irritated by an American journalist, newly arrived in Australia, who did a series of articles
for the *Sydney Morning Herald* some years ago on a trip to
Alice Springs and the red centre, hitching rides on trucks
and road trains. He thought the countryside on the way as
boring as bat shit, with nothing to look at. I wondered what
he was doing with his eyes. There is always something to
see in the bush. No desert is ever featureless. In our case
the Stuart Highway ran through desert country that was
reasonably lush with growth after recent rains.

We were looking forward to the first bush camp of the
trip. This is an aspect of outback travel that I regard as quin-
tessentially Australian—the luxury of pulling off the road
into the scrub, and just camping away from organised camping grounds or caravan parks, and other campers. Sadly it is
getting harder to do because of the extension of property

fences along the major highways, even in quite remote parts of the country. In the case of four-wheel-drive vehicles towing campers or trailers (most caravanners don't have the clearance to do this easily) it is best to pick a track someone has already made, to avoid further damaging the fragile countryside. Tyre tracks can stay etched on desert country for years. If possible, I like to put a barrier of trees between the camp site and the road—not to hide from gun-toting maniacs or marauding hoons—but to discourage other travellers from joining in. There is a regrettable herd mentality that cuts in when city dwellers take to the road. I have lost count of the times I've found a nice spot, only to hear the sound of an engine, and another camper nosing in to share the location.

'I do hope you don't mind us coming in here but we thought it would be safer.'

Safe from what, for God's sake? The chances of being shot and raped by a psychotic killer are so remote as to be dismissed and there is nothing in the Australian bush that is life-threatening, provided you don't step on a poisonous snake. Yet the fear of camping alone, for many, is palpable.

Before we left on our first driving and camping odyssey in 1974 with Kombi and trailer and infant son, I remember talking with a middle-aged caravanner in Melbourne who was a habitual traveller to Queensland's Gold Coast for the Victorian winter. I mentioned we were heading north. He said that we had to be very careful to note the differing dates of school holidays in the various states.

'Why?'

'That means that many of the caravan parks will be full and if you don't book ahead you might have to spend a night "out". In that case, if I were to see you camped by the side of the road I'd pull in and join you for security.'

I had visions of a kind of fortified camp on the Pacific Highway, with Indians circling the wagon trains. In his mind, caravan parks were zones of known safety in a hazardous and uncertain lawless outer world, but we try to camp 'out' as often as we can.

At 4 pm, with the sun already low in the winter sky, we started to look out for a camp site between Marla Bore and Cadney Homestead, north of Coober Pedy but still south of the Northern Territory border. Driving the Stuart Highway these days is such a luxury compared with the goat track we remembered in 1974. Then you could not lift your eyes from the uncertainty of the red, rutted road ahead lest you all but disappeared into a crater of talcum-powdered bulldust or burst a tyre in a savage pothole gouged out by semi-trailers or road trains. Today a smooth, wide bitumen strip allows both driver and passenger to admire the beauty of the desert, and the interplay of that wonderful central Australian light on the vegetation and the worn down, orange flanks of flat-topped hills that were once the ancient seabed—below which we were motoring.

The upgraded Stuart Highway, often banked high above the surrounding red desert, makes it more difficult to make impromptu exits, but with a four-wheel-drive and The Manor's high off-road chassis we could take liberties. Ros spotted a faint track off to the right, and we engaged four-wheel-drive and headed down the bank at an alarming angle to check out where one or two vehicles had gone before us. About two hundred metres off the road, and screened by low acacias, we found a ring of fire-blackened stones and enough room to establish our camp without disturbing or knocking down any more vegetation. (We

didn't use the stones. Our Port Augusta friend Paul Wilson
said they shouldn't be used, as the shale-like rocks in this
area often exploded like grenades when heated.)

It was a moment to savour, the first bush camp of the trip,
a time of unalloyed joy. It was always good but there was
something particularly delightful about doing it again after so
long, and in such idyllic surroundings. The sun was low in a
cloudless sky as I unhitched The Manor and connected to
Penelope's auxiliary battery with the three-metre extension
cord I'd had made for this trip. It only took us seven minutes
or so to wind up The Manor to its full height and pull out the
beds at each end, both supported by two metal rods. We
had planned a barbecue, and I dug a small trench in the
red sand to make the fire safe, and conserve firewood—
not that there was a shortage. The desert chill was coming
down so we put on warmer clothes and sat in our camping
chairs by the fire, a rum and lime juice in hand, as the chops
spluttered, the butternut pumpkin and potatoes in foil
baked slowly in the hot coals and the billy boiled.

After dinner—eaten outside as it was simply too
magnificent to do anything else—we made up the fire for
warmth, sat back with our mugs of coffee as the flames
flickered shadows on the nearby bushes and looked up into
the blaze of stars that only outback Australia can produce.
We soon spotted the familiar Southern Cross and the
nearby Scorpion with its wicked and distinctively curved
tail. The half waxing (gibbous) moon was not bright enough
to dim the mysterious depths of the Milky Way and we
knew from now on we would be familiar with the phases of
the moon in a way city dwellers are not. In fact, I calculated—not with any great brilliance—that the moon would
be in similar shape in three months' time when we were

driving home. Ros said she didn't want to think about that right now. We had demolished a bottle of red to mark the first night 'out' and decided to try a tot of the $4.50 muscat. It was not a good idea. Ros chucked hers into the bushes, and it is not like her to waste a drink. I drank mine and wished I hadn't. But we did sleep well.

With frost on top of The Manor and below zero temperature, it was challenging to clamber out of the warm cocoon of our excellent down sleeping bags that had so nearly stayed at home. On the road by 8 am, we were surprised by the number of hawks and huge wedge-tailed eagles feasting on the fresh carcasses of kangaroos presumably bowled over in the night by road trains and semis. With the low morning light of the rising sun, it was a photographer's paradise. Some of the eagles simply looked at us disdainfully as we drove by, so we managed to slow down and get some action shots of these big feathered flying machines getting airborne—as they did when we got too close.

Over the Northern Territory border we called in at the Endunda Roadhouse for fuel, at the turn-off to Uluru. It is always a busy spot, with a wonderful variety of camping rigs to marvel at. One I could not resist photographing was a huge bus—used by its owners as a caravan—towing a large trailer on which sat a substantial people-carrier van.

We planned to arrive in Alice Springs in the early afternoon for a reunion with Ted Egan and his partner Nerys Evans at Sinka-Tinny Downs, a five-acre block on the south side of the city and Heavytree Gap—that narrow gash in the MacDonnell Ranges through which all traffic, and the Ghan train, must pass to reach the city.

One of Ted's many terrific songs is titled *Characters of
the Outback*, and its author is indubitably one of them. Originally from Melbourne, from an extended Irish Catholic
family in which songs and singing were in the blood, Ted
dutifully abided by his mother's rules of upbringing which
involved learning to cook, ironing his own shirts and leaving
home at sixteen. Heading north essentially with adventure
in mind, he got it, becoming a cadet patrol officer at the age
of nineteen with the then Department of Native Affairs in
Darwin. That began his life-long association with Aboriginal people, the Northern Territory and its rambunctious
history.

Ted Egan is a modest man and doesn't talk much about
himself. He speaks two Aboriginal languages, and can get by
in a few more. In the 1950s in Darwin he started an Aussie
Rules football team, St Marys, composed principally of Tiwi
Aboriginal people from Bathurst and Melville Islands. This
brought him to the attention of Paul Hasluck, then Minister
for Territories, who encouraged him to join the Department
of Native Affairs in 1952. Ted has worked as a teacher in
remote communities like Groote Eylandt and, while raising
his own family, was superintendent of Aboriginal communities like Yuendumu in central Australia. He was
encouraged by the political scientist Colin Tatz (also in the
Territory under the auspices of Paul Hasluck) to study for
a BA degree, which he did by correspondence, studying at
night by the uncertain light of kerosene pressure lamps. It
took him ten years of part-time study and Ted told me he
should have been awarded a Doctorate in the management
and maintenance of Tilleys. Not unfond of a drink, and a
great collector of yarns, stories and songs, Ted has composed more than 200 songs reflecting the diversity of the

Northern Territory he has celebrated most of his life.

That is how we first met, when Ros and I came through Alice Springs in 1974 on our first big trip. I had been recording on tape the reminiscences of some retired drovers and ringers then living at the Old Timers' Home in Alice Springs. My cousin, John Hawkins, was the surgeon at the Alice Springs Hospital. Also a keen film maker, he was a good contact for meeting some of the pioneers—most of whom he not only knew, but had cared for medically. He showed us the rushes of a film he was editing about a canoe trip he had recently done on the Daly River. (He was one of the first canoeists to tackle the unexplored wild rivers of Tasmania's south-west wilderness in the 1950s and 1960s.) As a temporary soundtrack he was running three of Ted's songs, 'The Daly River-O', 'The Reluctant Saddler' and 'The Rock Named Uluru'. The songs were gutsy and powerful, evoking just the kind of feeling about the Northern Territory reflected by the yarns the old stockmen and pioneer women had been telling me on tape. John told me where to find Ted, who had just moved from Canberra to Sydney and was still working for the Department of Aboriginal Affairs.

Ted had no formal musical training, and accompanied himself on an unusual instrument—a Fosters beer carton, from which he coaxed the most amazing percussive effects. He said the best way to tune it was to drink the contents. We met in Sydney in early 1975 and discussed my radio project with the old-timers. That was the genesis of a radio documentary program titled 'The Top End—It's Different Up There' which went to air on ABC radio in *Sunday Night Radio Two*, presented by Margaret Throsby, during which Ted came into the studio with his beer carton. The taped excerpts of the old and not-so-old Territorians were interspersed with

my live interviews with Ted and his earthy, witty and inform-
ative songs accompanied on his trusty 'Fosterfone'. The
program was well received, and we became good friends.

In the late 1970s, Ted Egan and I travelled together
recording traditional Aboriginal music in the Top End and
the Centre of the Northern Territory. Then Ros and I
accompanied Ted to the Birdsville Races and recorded (in
the Birdsville Pub) the basic tracks for an LP with Ted on
his Fosterfone and with me adding a scratch ukulele accom-
paniment. Needless to say some professional musicians had
to augment this fairly basic effort later but, to our collective
surprise, *The Bush Races* put out by RCA did rather well. We
slept out under the stars in our swags on the banks of the
Diamantina River, and Ted introduced us to the delights of
station killed beef (laid out on the bonnets of our cars in the
cool of the night to cure), and the excellent bush libation of
rum, lime juice and water in enamel mugs—again cooled by
the night air with no refrigeration available.

Since 1983 Ted and Nerys have been living at Sinka-
Tinny Downs, building a remarkable house with rammed
earth walls and high ceilings, among native central
Australian trees and shrubs, and housing a great collection
of paintings, sculptures and carvings from the artistic
community of Alice Springs and from friends all over
Australia. For the last ten years they have been working
towards realising their dream of a feature film based on
Ted's ballad, 'The Drover's Boy'.

During the pastoral expansion into the Northern Territory in the last half of the nineteenth century, Aboriginal
tribes were decimated, their wells poisoned, and in many
cases their groups simply massacred. Because cohabitation
between European men and black women was forbidden

by law, some drovers dressed young abducted Aboriginal
women in men's clothing and took them along in the droving plants. The young women were excellent 'stockmen'
and drovers and, in some cases, despite the brutality of
their induction into their androgynous role, some very fine
relationships were forged, children born, and powerful
personal commitments made. Of all the songs Ted Egan
has written, he considers 'The Drover's Boy' the most
significant and important, and he has allowed me to include
the lyrics in this narrative.

THE DROVER'S BOY   *Ted Egan*

They couldn't understand why the drover cried
As they buried The Drover's Boy,
For the drover had always seemed so hard
To the men in his employ,
A bolting horse, a stirrup lost,
And The Drover's Boy was dead.
The shovelled dirt, a mumbled word,
And it's back to the road ahead
And forget about The Drover's Boy.

They couldn't understand why the drover cut
A lock of the dead boy's hair.
He put it in the band of his battered old hat,
As they watched him standing there,
He told them, 'Take the cattle on,
I'll sit with the boy a while,'
A silent thought, a pipe to smoke,
And it's ride another mile,
And forget about The Drover's Boy.

They couldn't understand why the drover and the boy
Always camped so far away,
For the tall white man and the slim black boy
Had never had much to say,
And the boy would be gone at break of dawn.
Tail the horses, carry on,
While the drover roused the sleeping men,
'Daylight, hit the road again'
And follow The Drover's Boy,
Follow The Drover's Boy.

In the Camooweal pub they talked about
The death of The Drover's Boy.
They drank their rum with a stranger who'd come
From a Kimberley run, Fitzroy.
And he told of the massacre in the west,
Barest details, guess the rest,
Shoot the buck, grab a gin,
Cut her hair, break her in,
Call her a boy, The Drover's Boy,
Call her a boy, The Drover's Boy.

So when they build that Stockman's Hall of Fame
And they talk about the droving game,
Remember the girl who was bedmate and guide,
Rode with the drover side by side,
Watched the bullocks, flayed the hide,
Faithful wife, never a bride,
Bred his sons for the cattle runs.
Don't weep . . . for The Drover's Boy.
Don't mourn . . . for The Drover's Boy.
But don't forget . . . The Drover's Boy.

Ros and I planned to spend at least three days in the Alice before tackling the desert route across the Tanami Track to Halls Creek and when we saw Ted and Nerys we wanted to know how the film was progressing. Getting a feature film up and running is a tough call, but we learned that Nerys had written the script and a director and cast had been chosen. Some general filming had been done— magnificent scenes of large mobs of cattle moving across the vast dusty red plains—and a set built on private property about fifteen minutes' drive south-west from Sinka-Tinny Downs. Ted drove Ros and me down to have a look at it, while he took some extra photos needed for publicity.

The set, with some buildings like the police station constructed in stone, is already part of an outback tourist experience organised by the owners of the property and will remain after the film has been made. Ted has had a stone-capped well constructed and also a water whip—a uniquely Australian invention where a system of pulleys and buckets, operated by a horse or camel walking back-wards and forwards on the one track, pulls up water from quite deep underground wells. It is almost certainly the only working whip in Australia.

On the way back to Sinka-Tinny (to do just that) Ted mentioned a surprise he had organised for us during a 'Derelicts' Lunch' the next day. At Sinka-Tinny Downs, 'Deros'' lunches are special occurrences which demolish the rest of the day and usually the night as well. He refused to be drawn on the nature of the surprise.

When the baronial-sized table (built of polished sleep-ers from the old Ghan train line) was set, bottles uncorked and lashings of delicious tucker unveiled, a curious vehicle drove in the front gate of Sinka-Tinny Downs—a hefty white utility with a double set of wheels at the back, a large white container on the tray, and with the whole ensemble topped by a large fibre-glass kayak with its nose projecting well over the bonnet. Out of it stepped Trish Sheppard and Iain Finlay, old friends whom we had not seen for many, many years. Both are prolific travellers and authors, but Iain's face and persona are probably best known through his involvement in the science-based television program 'Beyond 2000', and before that, as a compere of the ABC's television current affairs program 'This Day Tonight'.

It was a curious coincidence that Trish and Iain—also friends of Ted and Nerys—had recently taken off on an extended driving and camping expedition in northern Australia, unaware that we were doing the same thing until they met up with Ted in Alice Springs. There was much hooting and hugging. I had first met Trish and Iain during the America's Cup challenge at Newport, Rhode Island, in 1967. I was helping with the radio coverage for the ABC, and Iain—then a freelance—was coordinating the daily television coverage being sent out by satellite in the days when that technology was very new indeed. Their daughter Zara was then eighteen months old, and we shared a flat during the hectic yacht racing during which the Australian entry *Dame Pattie* put up a very good show against the New York Yacht Club and actually won one of the races.

More than any other couple I know, Trish and Iain had refused to let having children cramp their travel style. In 1976 when Zara and Sean were only ten and eight, the whole family set off on a 13 000 kilometre journey from Cape Town to Cairo, and wrote a book on their experiences, *Africa Overland*. It was clearly a risky journey, particularly with children, but it was not Sean or Zara who were most at risk: Iain nearly died of dehydration and dysentery while travelling in the back of a truck in the Sudan, in 40° Celsius-plus heat. A chance meeting in a mud hut at a roadside stop with a paramedic, who gave Iain an injection of atropine to help him retain fluids, undoubtedly saved his life.

Now with their children grown up, like us, Trish and Iain were delighting in the joys of the nomadic life—spendng even longer on the road this time than we were. By coincidence, we were heading up the Tanami Track at the same time. There was a great deal of uninhibited talk and reminiscence.

Two of the other guests could best be described as the 'grand dames' of central Australia. Mona Byrnes—a well-known and gifted painter who had been brought up by her Lutheran missionary parents with the Aborigines of the Hermannsburg Mission to the west of Alice Springs in the 1920s—was in crackling form. So was Daphne Calder, who had the leading female role in the classic Australian film *The Overlanders* with Chips Rafferty in 1946.

I had read the autobiography of Kurt Johannsen, Mona's brother, also brought up at Hermannsburg and who helped transform the transport systems of the outback by inventing the road train. The full story is in his memoir *A Son of 'The Red Centre'—Memoirs and Anecdotes of the Life of Road Train Pioneer and Bush Inventor of the Northern Territory of Australia*. Kurt was a self-taught, brilliant bush mechanic who could breathe life into and fix anything mechanical on wheels—or indeed off them. One of his inventions changed the dynamics of not only road transport in the Territory, but the entire cattle industry of the north. In 1947 Kurt worked out the mathematics of the length of the trailer bars linking up the three, sometimes four, trailers to a prime mover so they all followed the same track. His early proto-types could only travel at low speeds—40 kph—but quickly demonstrated to station owners that Kurt could get their cattle to market in terrific condition in a matter of days, instead of the weeks taken by droving them in the conventional way with inevitable loss of condition.

Kurt Johannsen was a legendary improviser. A spectacular example of his innovative genius occurred in 1950 when a couple of prospectors at Tennant Creek involved him in a bid to find Lasseter's fabled gold reef in the desert west of Alice Springs. Kurt had a Tiger Moth aircraft and, in great secrecy, he and prospector Jimmy Prince (who had a wooden leg) planned to fly west over the border into Western Australia. Flying by dead reckoning and local knowledge (there were no reliable maps), Johannsen decided to land on a claypan near Lake Hopkins to camp and refuel from spare jerry cans they were carrying. Unfortunately, when they took off the next morning, the wheels broke through a soft patch and the aircraft tilted up on its nose, breaking about 35 centimetres off each end of the single wooden propeller. Jimmy, who hadn't quite got his seat belt fastened at the critical moment, was thrown forward and bumped his head, exclaiming famously: 'Fuck the bloody aeroplane, the gold and everything else.'

They were in deep trouble as they had no radio and no one knew where they were. Kurt Johannsen considered trying to carve a new propeller with a tomahawk out of the twisted limb of a desert oak. But their first concern was water. Using one of the broken propeller ends as a shovel, Kurt went out into the middle of the claypan and dug down through mud and salt crystals for about a metre until he struck brine. Using two empty petrol jerry cans he constructed a primitive still to condense the salty solution into drinking water—managing to produce about six litres a day. This, he said later, 'made us both feel better'!

He then turned his attention to making a propeller. He trimmed down the rough edges of the broken blade with a small tomahawk, balancing it on a screwdriver. With the propeller reduced to about half its normal size, there wasn't much efficiency left. He stripped everything he could out of the aircraft to lighten it and, leaving Jimmy behind to await his return, tried a take-off the next morning, but the air was still and he couldn't even raise the Tiger Moth's tail off the ground. He waited for a breeze, and tried again. Taking a zig-zag path to avoid soft ground, Kurt opened the throttle—the engine screaming and revving at 1000 revs above its normal take-off rate—and coaxed the badly vibrating machine into the air. But he was only just managing to stay above the ground, not getting much higher than the tree tops.

Then he saw an eagle using a thermal and joined it. With the engine still howling at wildly unsafe revs, he managed to climb to 300 metres and headed for a camp at Mt Brown, 200 kilometres away, landing there with less than a litre of petrol remaining in his tanks. An air search was already underway, but no one knew where to look. Six days after leaving Jimmy Prince, Kurt Johannsen flew back (with a new prop) to pick him up. Jimmy told Kurt he was only going to wait another week, then make a mulga wood crutch and try to walk out—gammy leg or not. Kurt's jerry can condenser was still working perfectly. The broken and whittled propeller can still be seen in the Aviation Museum at Alice Springs.

That is the kind of pioneering stock our lunch companion Mona Byrnes sprang from.

In the course of a long and bibulous session, Iain Finlay and I talked about old friends, including Neil Davis, the combat cine cameraman who covered 11 years of front-line combat in Vietnam and Cambodia from 1964 to 1975. He was killed in Bangkok in September 1985 while filming an unexpected and rather unimportant coup in Thailand—something neither he nor his foreign correspondent friends would have expected to happen. Still, Neil himself said that you could always be unlucky, even someone the Cambodians called 'Mean Samnang'—the lucky one. Iain had worked in Southeast Asia in the 1960s as I had, and I reminded him of Neil's motto, which he wrote on the front flyleaf of every work diary he kept while in Asia. It said simply:

One crowded hour of glorious life
Is worth an age without a name.

He never knew where the quote came from, but liked it, and certainly lived its sentiments to the full. (It was actually written by Thomas Osbert Maudant some time during the Seven Years War of 1756–63.) Iain said he had a motto, too, like Neil Davis unsure of its origins, which he carried with him at all times and tried to abide by. He promptly extracted a rather tattered piece of paper out of his wallet to show me.

PERSISTENCE

Nothing in the world can take the place of persistence.
Talent will not; nothing is more common than unsuccessful men with talent.
Genius will not; unrewarded genius is almost a proverb.

Education alone will not; the world is full of educated derelicts.
PERSISTENCE and DETERMINATION alone are omnipotent.

Educated derelicts indeed! Disgracefully and indulgently, we derelicts did not finish our lunch until 10 pm—when the singing finally stopped.

We wanted to do a smidgen of touristing on our last day in the Alice. Ros was keen to visit the Olive Pink Reserve, on a small hill to the east of the Todd River, featuring a range of central Australian flora, much of it planted by Olive, a feisty anthropologist who lived and worked with desert Aborigines in the 1930s and 1940s. During her long life she fought bitterly with officialdom and male colleagues like T. G. H. Strehlow, C. P. Mountford, and the government anthropologist E. W. P. Chinnery who all tried to discredit her. After having been being refused a government permit to visit remote Aboriginal settlements in 1942, she simply moved out to a camp site at Thompson's Rockhole, near The Granites goldfield in the Tanami Desert, and stayed there for two years. After the war she moved back into Alice Springs, first camping and then living in a hut tending her bush garden.

One of her hobbies was to plant trees and name them after Federal politicians. If she didn't agree with what they were doing, she ceased to water their particular tree. Paul Hasluck, when he was Minister for Territories, felt that he must be doing something right when he saw his tree doing well on one of his visits to Alice Springs in the 1950s. Olive Pink, slight of build and of indomitable disposition, lived in Alice Springs until her death in 1975 at the age of ninety!

It is curious that tourist numbers have dropped off in Alice Springs in the last ten years or so. Many international tourists, particularly Japanese, fly directly to Uluru (Ayers Rock) and then either on to the east or west coasts—or Darwin—bypassing the Alice. There used to be cavalcades of coach tours rolling through, but in recent times the tourists who come by road tend to drive themselves—grey nomads like us. There are enough of them, fortunately, to sustain Ted Egan's evening outback show during which he tells outrageous yarns and sings a selection of his vast repertoire of bush songs.

Those who choose not to go to Alice Springs miss out on a very special part of Australia. Rich in history, with its Overland Telegraph Station celebrating the linking of Australia with the world through Darwin and the overseas cable in 1872, the Alice has much to offer. Its location alone is worth a visit, nestling among the MacDonnell Ranges which curve and snake across the landscape from east to west—tracks left by the great rainbow serpent of the Aboriginal Dreamtime. There is a special, translucent quality to the light in central Australia, unique to this area.

Those who do go to Alice Springs can now enjoy one of the world's great arid zone parks. Sir David Attenborough, commenting after a visit, said, 'There is no museum or wildlife park in the world that could match it. I thought it was superb, absolutely breathtaking, I have nothing but praise for it.'

The Alice Springs Desert Park opened in 1997 with a backdrop of the looming MacDonnell Ranges. The paths of the park lead the visitor through various desert habitats, from sand and desert through to lightly forested woodland.

Cleverly designed bird viewing areas allow a close-up look through glass at tiny finches and bee-eaters as well as more brightly hued parrots or larger curlews. The walkways lead you on to, and through, nocturnal houses where day and night are reversed for human pleasure as rarely seen marsupials like the Lesser Hairy-footed Dunnart, diminutive bilbies, spotted quolls, snakes and the improbably horned and camouflaged Thorny Devil lizards go about their nightly wanderings unconcerned about the human faces gazing at them. Whether it was a symbolic gesture of contempt or simply that it was unaware of our presence, one Tiger Quoll walked up to the glass separating it from gawping faces, turned around with its bum towards us and with great timing and finesse expressed a small, thin turd in our direction before scampering off.

Outside, in a small amphitheatre offering shade from the harsh desert sun, we waited for the advertised birds of prey display. There are two each day, and they are quite remarkable occasions. As we waited for the park ranger to do his stuff, various hawks and raptors with their cruel hooked beaks and beady eyes flew in and perched in nearby trees. It was like a scene from Alfred Hitchcock's *The Birds*. They certainly knew something was about to happen—food. As the ranger described the various species, the right birds flew in on cue to enjoy tidbits thrown up in the air to them. How they knew to arrive in the right order was beyond me. Commenting on one particularly fast predator, the ranger had a dead mouse (or something that looked like that) on the end of a piece of rope which he whirled around his head. A black kite swooped in and picked off the mouse at high speed in its talons. Tremendous entertainment.

But the piece de resistance for me was the small raptor

with feathery hocks like a miniature eagle which had developed a taste for emu eggs. Now emu eggs are big as eggs go, and if you have seen decorated ones, they have a shell which is as thick and tough as porcelain. The remarkable Black Breasted Buzzard was just a little fella, and the park ranger explained how it could not break the shell with its beak. So this ingenious bird had adapted itself to using a small stone as a tool. As we watched—and I must report that using real emu eggs would be ideologically unsound so it was a dummy egg with a goodie inside—the buzzard picked up a stone in its beak, reared up and dropped it on the 'egg' several times until it smashed it, ate what was inside and flew away. Stunning stuff, and I hope it appreciated its—of course—'raptorous' applause.

On our last night at Sinka-Tinny Downs we invited Ted and Nerys into The Manor for drinks and nibbles—a bit of a squeeze but time flies when you're having fun—and we realised if we didn't get on with our journey the next morning we might not go at all!

two

Tackling the Tanami

We thought we'd ease back gradually into travel mode as we only had 200 kilometres or so to drive to our planned first stop at the gateway to the Tanami Track, Tilmouth Well, which was advertised as a resort! It at least had fuel and a camping ground, which would do us. We had no plans for the golf or horse riding. So it was a leisurely 11 am before we nosed out the hospitable gates of Sinka-Tinny Downs to pause for a hamburger on the northern side of Alice Springs. A four-wheel-drive towing a businesslike off-road trailer pulled in beside us. Another couple, also seeking a fast food fix, were on the road as well and we chatted a bit about each other's camping rigs. Bill offered some valuable advice. He'd had the back window of his Nissan smashed by stones bouncing back off his trailer, and recommended some cardboard taped against the rear windows from the outside. We already had some spare sheets of rubberised material that would be perfect for the job, and decided to tape them on to Penelope's rear door windows that evening before we started to get serious about the Tanami.

His partner mentioned how lovely it was to be travelling in the comparative cool of winter. She had once driven to the Pilbara to see her sister for Christmas in 45° Celsius heat. When she wanted a cool shower, she was told to turn on the hot water tap. This was because the 'cold' water directly from the outside was too hot to bear. So the hot water was held in the switched-off tank—inside the house—until it cooled down. To make it hotter (if that was needed) you had to turn on the cold water tap!

The winter temperature, by day, in and around Alice Springs is a pleasant 25°, and I noted with some surprise (Penelope sports an altimeter) that as we drove north we were quite high above sea level, at 600 metres no less (which is as high as Canberra up on the Monaro). The rise is so gradual you hardly notice it. We had a good run during a sunny, still afternoon, through lightly wooded country, stopping to pile up a load of firewood on the roof rack in case we wanted to barbecue at Tilmouth Well—or some-where else for that matter. As we topped up our tanks at Tilmouth Well we spied a familiar white utility with a canoe on top. It was Trish and Iain, whom we thought we might see somewhere along the way. We made an impressive encampment when Iain unfolded a large tent from the back of his utility. The sides of the white box swung open to reveal drawers of gear (including his portable computer to keep track of his stocks and shares) and a handy kitchen bench with stove and three-way fridge.

When we went to the roadhouse to pay for our fuel we noted the dress rules for the restaurant which stipulated 'covered shoes'. Ros asked the woman behind the till (whose demeanour did not reflect total happiness at her life at Tilmouth Well) what that meant and she pointed to a bare-footed Aboriginal woman walking out the door and said, 'so that you don't look like that'. Oh dear. We decided to take our masked feet back to camp and eat in.

We did not barbecue because Iain and Trish are vegetarians but Ros cooked a vegetable curry, and Trish produced brown rice, lentils and salad. As we ate, a bevy of Port Lincoln parrots with their distinctive white necklaces and green livery bickered quietly over the right to drink from a dribbling sprinkler only metres from our dining tables, to be replaced seconds later by a raucous mob of pink galahs behaving in their usual larrikin way. After putting the world to rights over a couple of bottles of red and catching up on what our respective kids were doing or not doing, we decided to link up for the Tanami Track to Halls Creek. Then we planned to turn left for Broome, and Trish and Iain would go right to the Bungle Bungles, Kununurra and the Gibb River Road—which we would tackle later after our coastal voyage up the Kimberley coast on *Coral Princess*.

The next day's run was 400 kilometres, and the most tricky for fuel because we had to coincide with the opening times maintained by the proprietor of the fuel outlet at Rabbit Flat. Even if we filled up our tanks 100 kilometres further up the track at the Aboriginal settlement of Yuendumu (which we both did), if we didn't top up at Rabbit Flat the next available fuel was at Halls Creek, 450 kilometres further on and right on the edge of our range, particularly if we did any side trips, or struck rough going.

Rabbit Flat opens for fuel and basic supplies from Friday to Monday only. There are stories abounding about the eccentricities of the proprietor Bruce Farrands who, with his French wife Jacquie, has been the Squire of Rabbit

Flat from 1969. Why he wouldn't serve fuel during the week had yet to be determined, but it was already Monday and we needed Bruce. We also hoped to camp nearby, because Rabbit Flat is a small island of freehold in an ocean of Aboriginal land. If Bruce wouldn't allow us to camp that night, we would need permission from the Aboriginal council concerned and we weren't sure how to go about getting it at that late stage.

The weather was clear and cold with a light breeze as we tackled the Tanami—in company with just about every kind of vehicle you could name from battered Kingswoods and Falcons on their way between Aboriginal settlements to ponced up four-wheel-drives with and without campers. We all deferred, of course, to the kings of the outback roads, the mighty road trains. You can see them coming about five kilometres away because of the great plume of dust that rises above them. The drill is to pull right off the road and give them all the room they need. Ros tried to get a photograph of them bearing down, with just the chrome and glass of the prime mover gleaming marginally ahead of the great brown cloud that envelops the three following trailers. You hope that rocks thrown up by the great double wheels don't break your windows as it thunders past. Then you wait for the dust cloud to dissipate so you can see where the road is again.

The Tanami Track is hardly a track any more. There are badly corrugated sections from time to time, but the route is in the process of being tamed. It was an unexpected shock to arrive at a section that had been sealed, with work continuing on that project eventually to provide an all-weather—well almost—link between Alice Springs and Halls Creek. The qualification is the wet season, which can cause the major rivers and even lesser water-courses to burst their banks and run wild, stopping travel—sealed roads or not—for weeks at a time. We were glad of our four-wheel-drive capability when we passed through the sections of the track being prepared for sealing where big rocks and banked dirt piled high on the road caused some thoughtful moments.

Contrary to expectation, the great flat bowl of the Tanami Desert is not bare, but covered with the ubiquitous spinifex, scrubby vegetation and some reasonably substantial acacias. I'm told that even light cover peters out by the time it joins the edge of the Great Sandy Desert to the west. I remembered a story told by a friend of mine and his wife who had driven the Tanami about ten years before in a venerable Land Rover. Ed claimed only two mishaps. He and Joan ran out of tonic water for their evening g & ts —apparently the Rabbit Flat store didn't run to tonic water. The other minor disaster was to break a tail-light by backing 'into the only tree on the Tanami'. Bit of artistic licence there, I thought. You could break a tail-light every twenty metres or so over most of the Tanami if you worked at it. Perhaps there had been lots of good rain in the intervening years.

About fifty kilometres south of Rabbit Flat we passed the Granites Goldmine, which our guide book said we could visit, but 'keep out' signs indicated otherwise. Gold was first discovered on the site in 1900, but its remote location and lack of water meant that only relatively small quantities of gold were recovered until 1973 when North Flinders Mines applied for exploration licences. After eight years of negotiation with the Western Australian Government and the traditional Aboriginal owners, a cooperative venture was set up with the Walpiri community and by

1986—the first year of modern operations—some 60000 ounces of gold were recovered. By 1992 this had grown to 120 000 ounces, and it is now a considerable operation employing from 150 to 200 people, most of whom commute to Alice Springs by air.

We reached the turn-off to Rabbit Flat by 3 pm. The road sign must be one of Australia's most remote, pointing south to Alice Springs (599) and north to Halls Creek (451). At the base of the sign was the carcase of a smashed sedan, so creamed it was difficult to work out its pedigree. With wheels missing, boot lid stuck up at a crazy angle, and the sides grossly dented, it must have rolled a few times before dying at that strategic point. I hope no one died in it.

The Farrands' Rabbit Flat homestead is only a couple of kilometres off the Tanami Track, set in a grove of large trees, with a rusty steel platform supporting some battered fuel tanks with gravity feed to an ancient bowser. Reputed to be the home of the most expensive fuel in Australia, I was surprised to see diesel listed as 60 cents a litre—but soon realised that you had to double that because the dial couldn't register $1.20 a litre. (Good value before world oil prices went beserk in 2000!)

But where was Bruce? Ros made a beeline for the toilets and I wandered aimlessly around the front of the homestead, among the hibiscus bushes. I jumped as a roar of greeting came from the bearded Farrands, who had appeared from nowhere, and who asked me if I wanted fuel. He came closer and peered at me thoughtfully. Television, I found out later, had only been at Rabbit Flat for the last ten years and Bruce had been a keen watcher.

'Hey, I know you—you're that fellow that used to do "Media Watch" on the ABC.'

'Ah, well no, that was the rather more follicly challenged Stuart Littlemore. I used to do a program called "Backchat".'

By this time I could see the outline of a canoe on top of the hibiscus bushes, and realised Iain Finlay and Trish Sheppard had arrived. Bruce must have felt that Ray Martin was about to step out of the next four-wheel-drive, which pulled up behind Iain. After a flurry of fuelling, Bruce asked us all to come inside for a cuppa. We were ushered past the small grill and narrow counter at the front of the shop, and into the homestead behind. Jacquie greeted us warmly. She is tiny, and as forceful and feisty as only an unreconstructed Parisian Frenchwoman can be—her heavily accented English had not a trace of an Australian twang after more than thirty years in the outback. Edith Piaf, eat your heart out.

Bruce met Jacquie in 1969 when she was an *au pair* at Mongrel Downs Station. She has been at Rabbit Flat ever since. Iain and Trish knew more about the Farrands than we did. Somehow this tiny woman had given birth to strapping twin boys! Over a cup of tea, Bruce told us that the doctor who had advised Jacquie during her pregnancy had neglected to tell her she was having twins in case she panicked! Bruce said that he should have realised that anyone who lived in a place like Rabbit Flat would be most unlikely to panic. In any case, panic was a luxury that couldn't be indulged in as the twins arrived early and unexpectedly and Bruce had to help with the delivery. Even as Jacquie went into labour they both thought there was only one baby, and then discovered there were two. After their bush upbringing both boys joined the Australian army.

Over the years Bruce has featured in a number of television documentaries and television magazine items, and

I suspect has rather relished his demonised reputation as an outback eccentric. He told us the reason they closed on Tuesdays, Wednesdays and Thursdays was to get some semblance of family life—otherwise they would be on the go from dawn till midnight seven days a week, with business not only from passing travellers, but the Aboriginal settlements and the nearby Granites gold mining operation. Although it was Monday night, Bruce allowed us to camp in the Rabbit Flat camping area—and I noticed that we were not alone. There was obviously a bit of a softy lurking behind that fierce beard and gruff manner.

I thought some of our camping neighbours were using a generator—one of my pet hates. But it was a battery-powered compressor, pumping up a mended tyre. The bloke told me he had blown two radials that day. We heard all kinds of horror stories about tyres. Iain had been told to keep his tyres soft, at around 35 psi off the bitumen and around 40 psi on the tarmac. On the other hand, the 'experts' who serviced Penelope in Sydney had recommended tyre pressures of 50 psi for all conditions. So far so good.

There was, though, a casualty of the corrugations in our basic equipment. The plug and socket connecting our three-way fridge in the back of Penelope had been damaged by moving cargo. Iain (being Iain) instantly produced a spare from one of his drawers in the side of his truck-with-absolutely-everything and connected me up again. But the blasted fridge would still not work. We could do nothing about it at Rabbit Flat. It would probably have to wait until we got to Broome. Still, there was always the fridge in The Manor, and the essential chilled ale at the end of the day was not in peril as yet. Camping, as Ros is wont to remark, 'is not about deprivation, but indulgence'.

We were keen to visit the Aboriginal settlement at Balgo, just inside the Western Australian border, having heard splendid reports of an art centre there. While in Alice Springs we had managed to phone one of the art coordinators, Erica Izett, and ask if we could call by. Erica and her partner Tim Acker had not long been at Balgo and the Warlayirti Artists Cooperative and said they would be delighted to see us. Was there anything we could bring? Erica made polite disclaimers but, when pressed, said fresh vegetables and fruit were hard to come by in the desert, so Ros and I had organised a box of greens. Iain Finlay and Trish Sheppard had heard about Balgo too, and decided to join us.

The dot paintings of the Australian centre have been a relatively recent development, following the introduction of acrylic paint to some settlements in the early 1980s. Since then the distinctive designs and brilliant colours of the respective 'dreamings' of individual artists have achieved worldwide acclaim. In recent years some Aboriginal artists have been experimenting with more impressionistic work—like the canvases painted by one of the most distinguished desert painters, the late Emily Kngwarreye.

Most desert paintings draw on the landscape—from a bird's eye perspective—to relay information about watercourses, rock holes, sand hills and claypans as well as symbols of the Dreaming which can be expressed through concentric circles, animals, body markings—even weapons and other implements. The high prices of works of well-known artists in the Australian market and overseas have put enormous pressure on some of the painters—often paid in hundreds of dollars compared with the thousands of dollars commanded for the same paintings by the dealers

and the international market. As sharing is built into the
Aboriginal culture, few artists keep much of the money
they get. There have been some scandals too, involving
disputed work where relatives and friends have prepared
canvases later signed by one of the known 'names'. While
it is not uncommon for more than one artist to work on a
single painting, some of the desert communities have had
to deal with some unfortunate incidences of fraud.

The Balgo community is 30 kilometres to the west of
the Tanami Track over a reasonable red dirt road trenched
down into the soft sandy country. Originally Rockhole
Station, it was purchased by the Catholic Church in 1934 in
the hope that the mission there would provide a transi-
tional stage for Aboriginal people moving from the nomadic
desert lifestyle to the undoubtedly more sinful European
ways of Halls Creek. Neat white-painted stones marking
out the entrance road in front of an impressive stone church
greet the visitor—a vista that has probably not changed
much in more than half a century.

The Balgo community supports 450 people these days
but the main settlement was not immediately visible. We
drove towards the airport and missed the art centre before
turning around and trying again. An amiable bearded
Aboriginal bloke, his slight frame almost lost inside a big
overcoat, gave us directions. We realised later he was one of
the Warlayirti Artists Cooperative's most distinguished
artists, Helicopter. Helicopter who? Just Helicopter. He was
so called because, as a young boy, he was brought into Balgo
from the desert in a helicopter and that was the first time
anyone at the mission had seen him. The name stuck.

The art centre was a big airy building with a wide
verandah at the end and down one side. Aboriginal artists

were busily painting on large and small canvases. Inside
there was a kaleidoscope of brightly coloured paintings
displayed on the walls, and in stacks of canvases without
frames. Erica Izett and Tim Acker were busy arranging
paints and fresh canvases for arriving artists and cheerily
told us to grab a cuppa. The place had a wonderful atmosphere. Some resident artists—mostly middle-aged women—
preferred to paint in a group sitting on the floor chatting
to each other as they worked. Others worked alone, with
fierce concentration, adding the distinctive dots that filled in
the personal designs they had chosen. We noticed Helicopter had hunkered down on the verandah outside with a
big half-finished canvas with a couple of dogs to keep him
company.

We had time to look over some of the finished work.
One canvas, hung on the wall with a spotlight emphasising
its vibrancy, was delightfully impressionistic, with great
swathes of orange, brown and yellow delineating water-
holes, bush tucker and sand dunes. The artist, Elizabeth
Nyumi, a 52-year-old Nungurrayi woman, was not in the
centre at the time. Iain and Trish were also taken with her
work, and were looking closely at one of her larger canvases.
Tim and Erica explained later that Elizabeth is one of the
emerging Balgo artists and is starting to command high
prices. We gulped when we were told what her paintings
were selling for, but we were so impressed that we began
to consider being extravagant. After all, we would be
supporting the art centre, wouldn't we?

Well aware of the scams that have clouded the reputation of some Aboriginal desert dot paintings, the Warlayirti
Artists Cooperative has a process of authentication of
the artworks which is most impressive. Each painting is

photographed and a stamped certificate of certification issued with the details of the artist, including age, traditional area, tribal grouping and language.

I asked one young woman whether she had any paintings I could see. Gemma Galova, in her early twenties, shyly drew my attention to several of her works. One I found particularly pleasing. It was a conventional dot painting with concentric circles occupying most of the canvas —except that in the centre was a bold drawing of a magnificent frilled lizard, with its mouth agape and frill extended in full confrontation mode. Gemma told me that the frilled lizard was her totem. She had not long been painting, and her work was moderately priced. I told her I would buy the lizard canvas, and she seemed pleased. When I told Erica Izett later what I had said to Gemma, she was delighted.

'It will give her extra confidence to keep going. I think she has a lot of talent, and selling a picture at this time in her career will give her a big boost.'

The Elizabeth Nyumi painting was irresistible, and credit cards were waved. I saw Trish and Iain in similar mode. We asked that the framed painting be unstretched so we could carry both our canvases in a tube. Ros slept with the paintings every night for three months, as they travelled on her bed during the day.

Tim and Erica (who turned out to be vegetarians) were delighted with their box of greens from Alice Springs, and asked us to lunch at their house. On the way Erica took us out to the edge of a bluff which had a superb view over the surrounding country—the beginning, she said, of the 'Kingfisher Dreaming' which ran in a line from Balgo all the way to Uluru. The Catholic mission used to be down on the plain, but shifted up on to the higher country in 1940—probably because of better bore water. We climbed down a rickety wooden ladder into a cave where a nun had meditated and lived in seclusion for several years in the late 1940s. Her bible, the ledge used as an altar, and several other artefacts were still where she had left them.

Over lunch (we tried to go easy on the lettuce and celery) Tim and Erica told us that the Balgo artists had put $100 000 of their own money into finishing the art centre building, which had been partly built for years. It is clearly a most successful enterprise, but the general situation of the settlement is vexed. We learned later that in many ways the community represents the dilemma faced by other remote Aboriginal settlements—admirable projects like the art centre, radiating cultural pride and commercial success on one side, contrasted with certain parts of the settlement considered unsafe for visitors because of social breakdown, alcohol abuse and petrol-sniffing by adolescent and even younger kids who are bored and desperate.

Later when I met Steve, in charge of job placement at Balgo, I commented that there didn't seem to be many people about.

'That's because the dry season is a great time to travel. About 300 of our 450 population are away visiting friends and relatives in other communities right now. Most of them have gone to Alice Springs—but that can't be mentioned at the moment because someone called Alice died a few weeks ago.'

In some communities, Aboriginal custom forbids the use of the name of a dead person for varying periods of time after their death.

The sun was low in the afternoon sky by the time we

tore ourselves away from Erica and Tim's hospitality. It was later than we thought, because we had crossed into Western Australia and had lost an hour. Tim had told us that Sturt Creek was a good place to camp, but we had at least 100 kilometres to drive to get there, and choosing a camp site in the dark is best avoided. We made it by dusk, and had our camp established and a fire lit when a huge full moon rose behind the trees as the flesh-eating Bowdens cooked steaks and Trish and Iain barbecued vegetable patties. We broke out a bottle of French cognac from Penelope's deep storage to celebrate meeting up with Trish and Iain in such a remote place after so many years. Ros heard a loud slurping sound—other than our own— and shone a torch across the creek to illuminate the bulk of a huge black bull that had come down to the water to drink. A good camp, Sturt Creek.

Next morning Ros remarked at breakfast that it was 30 June, the end of the financial year. Sturt Creek seemed the best place to be, and even Iain, who follows the stock exchange and his portfolio keenly from afar by computer, agreed. We would only have one more day travelling together before going our respective ways at Halls Creek. But first we planned to visit Wolfe Creek Crater, the fourth biggest meteorite impact crater in the world and one of the most perfectly formed. It was quite close to Sturt Creek, and was a spectacular formation with a classically circular rim and a flat interior which has filled up with sand over the million years since the big chunk of extraterrestrial rock slammed deep into the earth's crust. It wasn't discovered until 1947, when it was spotted in an aerial survey. The Aboriginal people knew about it, of course, and called it *Kandimalal*. It marks the spot where one of two rainbow snakes came out of the ground. The tracks that the two snakes made across the desert are marked by Sturt and Wolfe Creeks. We took some fruit and cool drinks in our day packs and walked up onto the rim, and down onto the floor of the crater which is 900 metres wide and has a ring of greener trees and shrubs in its centre.

Then it was on to the last, badly corrugated section of the Tanami Track. Iain was running low on fuel and thought he might need to borrow a funnel from me to decant from a jerry can if he didn't quite make it to Halls Creek. So he led the way on the understanding that if he did need my funnel, he would stop and I would catch up. As it happened, it would have been better if I had gone first.

Corrugations, even quite bad ones, are better if you can maintain a speed of around 80 kph. Not long after we left Wolfe Creek Crater, The Manor seemed to be hard to pull. Ros sensibly suggested we stop to see why, and a very flat tyre on the driver's side seemed a convincing reason. Now was the time to see if my tyre-changing arrangements worked. This was our very own first flat tyre on Penelope or The Manor. The good news was that we were on a hard, flat and level gravel surface. The spare tyre mounted in front of The Manor is much easier to get at than the Land-cruiser spare under its rear which demands a degree in mechanical engineering to wind down using a jointed handle through a slot near the back bumper designed by a sadist. Keyhole surgery would be simple by comparison.

The hydraulic jack was easily got at, thanks to the sliding equipment drawers in Penelope's cargo area, and there was no great drama in changing the tyre. Which was just as well as Iain had decided he had enough fuel to press on to Halls Creek, and absolutely no vehicles came by during the hour it took me to change the tyre. There is an inevitable feeling of vulnerability when you break down in a remote place.

Fifty kilometres short of Halls Creek, the flat, feature-less Tanami Desert country changes dramatically to low, red, rocky hills and spinifex dotted with small eucalypts, and dry creek crossings every kilometre or so. The terrain positively screams 'Kimberley'. Ros and I shook hands ceremonially as we turned temporarily right to Halls Creek, and the unfamiliar quiet hum of tyres on bitumen replaced the rattle and bangs caused by the rocks and corrugations of the Tanami Track. Trish and Iain had waited for us at the junction with the Great Northern Highway—and then realised we had been delayed for some reason. They went the 16 kilometres on into Halls Creek to refuel, and were coming back to look for us when we saw them. That was not hard. A white kayak on top of a truck was a dead give away.

Before we camped, I was anxious to get the flat tyre fixed and Halls Creek has a big tyre place, Baz's Tyres. Baz was not short for Bazza, nor was the proprietor a home-grown Australian. Central European origins I guessed, but neglected to ask him. Baz was contemptuous of the tyres I did have, and said the casualty was beyond repair. I happily shelled out for a new one, of similar size, and asked Baz what had caused the flat. He wasn't sure. I told him that I had been advised to run on tyre pressures of 50 psi at all times.

Baz was incredulous. He was one of those nuggetty men of action who never speak more softly than a shout.

'Hey, who told you that? I don't care. Bloody good for my business that kind of advice. Hope your friends keep telling people that!'

So what tyre pressures would he recommend? Iain Finlay was right after all. Around 35 psi off the bitumen and 40 psi on. I did just that and had no further tyre troubles.

It was our last night in tandem with Trish and Iain who were heading east to the Bungle Bungles while we were to go north-west to Broome. We treated ourselves to a celebratory dinner at the Halls Creek resort, no less, demolished some pasta and red wine and made plans to have a post-trip reunion (with photos) in Sydney later in the year.

There was a blustery and cold easterly wind behind us as we headed off to Fitzroy Crossing, positively humming along at 110 kph. The last time we travelled this road in our Kombi (with trailer) in 1982 we were heading east, into the prevailing wind, and making such heavy weather of things I could not even stay in top gear! The road was unsealed then and not in good shape. We had camped in a creek bed 100 kilometres east of Fitzroy Crossing and a friendly passing water truck driver said he would have a look at the engine for me. He diagnosed a burnt out valve, which kyboshed our plans for the Tanami Track to Alice Springs. The only light moments recorded in the old diary for that night were comments from our youngest son Guy, then aged seven.

'Mum, I wish I was a kite hawk.'

'Why is that Guy?'

'So I could poo on people's heads.'

Guy also had a penchant for rows over nothing in particular—often when he was tired. So in our windy, dusty, creek bed camp, with his mechanically challenged father worrying mightily about how we were going to get back to

Katherine on three cylinders, he complained bitterly—and according to the diary, long into the night—that he had never had or been offered any of our wedding cake from our marriage seven years before he was born! He was lucky to survive the night.

Fitzroy Crossing was fairly basic in 1982. The only camping ground—if you could call it that—was behind the noisy pub, which is why we chose the creek bed out of town. These days, grey nomads and other travellers camp in great style on grassy lawns and under shady trees on the banks of the Fitzroy River camping and caravan park. But you have to get in early. By 3 pm, on any day in high season, the place is as full as a Catholic school. We were in early enough to make camp and then do some sightseeing, driving sixteen kilometres to Geike Gorge National Park, a spectacular 30- metre-deep slash that runs for fourteen kilometres through an ancient limestone barrier reef, once part of the continental coastline.

Back at the camping ground, I noticed our caravanning neighbours sitting out on the grass in their camping chairs and gazing intently at a spot under a small tree that was not only close to the access road, but directly on the main thoroughfare to the toilet block. Some pixilated Greater Bower Birds had chosen that busy spot to build one of their elegant bowers and strut their stuff only metres from traffic and people. They took no notice of the human activity, nor did they seem at all fussed by an old dog tethered only a lead's length from them. As I understand it, bower birds build their nest somewhere else: the bower is constructed by males solely to attract females. In this case they had decorated the bower with bits of blue plastic and some shiny bibs and bobs I couldn't quite identify. John and

Carol Turner, in the caravan behind us, said they had put out a couple of five cent coins which disappeared very smartly. As we watched, and camera shutters snapped, the posturing and prancing bloke bower birds went through their dances and display. They didn't seem to be having much joy from the opposite sex—not while we were watching anyway. It was quite charming and bizarre with so much human chaos going on around them.

After dinner I chatted with John Turner. It is always intriguing to find out why people travel. He and his wife had been on the road for a couple of months, and had no firm plans to go home. John was retrenched from his job at a power station near Newcastle, in New South Wales. He was only 51, had started with the power station as an apprentice and had never worked anywhere else. He wouldn't be able to access his superannuation until he was 55, but was far from depressed about his situation. A multi-skilled tradesman, he was excited about the possibility of changing his career, maybe even starting his own business. He'd already knocked back some job offers. Meanwhile, he was seeing something of Australia for the first time and having a ball. I had the impression that Carol wasn't quite as enthused as he was about the camping life, but was certainly giving it a go.

We decided to get into Broome a day earlier than planned to give us time for some make and mend. Ros was worried about a grating noise she said she could hear in The Manor's wheel bearings, and thought the whole camper needed a once-over from an expert before we tackled the Bungle Bungles and the Gibb River Road. I was not so concerned, but it was better to be sure than sorry.

'Let's try another Henry Lawson story,' said Ros. It was a mistake. Henry's lugubrious description of sodden swaggies eking out a desperate existence in the water-logged world of a cold New South Wales outback winter seemed particularly inappropriate to the bright sunshine and clear skies surrounding us, and we switched off the tape. I remember reading somewhere that Henry Lawson was afflicted with chronic melancholia. I believe it.

Broome was booming—it was smartening itself up eighteen years ago when we last visited. Now as we drove across the mud flats towards the centre of the city the midday sun gleamed on the corrugated iron roofs of the shops and supermarkets of the reconstituted modern Chinatown, edged as it always was by the green fringe of mangroves on the old harbour front, where some 400 pearling luggers once lay on their sides on the mud waiting for the great, ten-metre tides to float them alongside the wharves and jetties. Tourists now go to Broome all year round, but the winter dry season is high season, with cara-van parks and hotels bursting at the seams. We had to book three months in advance to have any chance not only of getting a site, but of having Penelope and The Manor stored for the two weeks we would be on the big catamaran *Coral Princess*, exploring the Kimberley coastline.

Broome 1900—what a town! Its main activities were pearling, drinking, fighting and unbridled licentiousness ... every shade seemed to be represented in its segregated coloured settlement: its Javanese, Japanese, Chinese, Filipino, Malayan, Egyptian and Indian inhabitants were indeed a motley assortment. In Broome, the pearlers were the undisputed kings, dominating its unruly cosmopolitan population.

The man who wrote that should have known. Not only was he there, but he was also a pearling master—Arthur Bligh.

I thought it more than faintly appropriate that the man who discovered the Kimberley (in European terms) and first reported the existence of pearl shell was William Dampier who, in the late seventeenth century, began his career as a pirate and a buccaneer. Broome, the town that really grew around the pearling industry from 1883, was a swashbuckling frontier town that has only relatively recently become respectable. Some would say it still hasn't.

I was amused to discover—considering Broome's importance—that the Governor of Western Australia, F. N. Broome, who should have been pleased when the Surveyor General John Forrest honoured him by naming the town after him, wasn't flattered by this honour, and wrote to the Colonial Secretary in Britain that the town 'was likely to remain a mere dummy town site, inhabited by the tenants of three graves . . . my present idea is to have the name cancelled'.

Forrest was not amused when this got back to him, as one of the three graves was that of his brother Matthew, who had shared many of the great exploration patrols, through and around the Kimberley, that opened the region up for pastoralists in the late nineteenth century.

There is no doubt that Broome's most colourful period was around 1900. The local aristocracy, if it could be so described, centred on the pearling industry. Without pearl shell and pearls, Broome would simply not have existed. Master pearlers and their families had big houses with servants, and their women attempted to keep up with the latest European fashions. Dressing for dinner must have been a sticky business in humid, hot Broome. The most distinguished buildings in town were the telegraph station and the cable station built in 1889, the year the cable linking Australia with eastern Java was brought ashore. (The first attempt to connect Australia with Europe by cable through Darwin and the overland telegraph line failed repeatedly from 1871 on as the cable had been laid over a volcanic seabed. Eventually a second cable was brought in via Broome.)

By the turn of the twentieth century, the rich beds of pearl shell stretching along the coast from north of Broome right down to Exmouth Gulf were being harvested by luggers and divers. The workers, recruited from many cultures, were segregated into a shanty town. The Asian quarters sprang up where the mangroves had been cleared from the shore. In later years the Sun Picture Theatre used to be surrounded by water on three sides during high tides, and patrons had to splash their way to dry land after the movies. The Chinese and Japanese controlled the economy, and gambling, opium smoking and sly grog shops operated happily and openly with the police regularly paid off to ensure that everything ran smoothly.

An American, Senator S. Smith, visiting Broome in 1902, said the shanty town was the most mixed collection of nations, creeds, languages and races he had ever seen, and any visitor might be excused for thinking that a small portion of Asia had been detached and grafted onto the side of Australia:

> The houses, mostly built of corrugated iron, and covering not more than 20 acres, were huddled together in an apparently inextricable jumble. The narrow crooked lanes reminded one of Singapore, with flags, banners and strange legends floating from bazaars, houses, stalls and shops.

Another visitor, told that every nation in the world had a representative in Broome, asked to see an Eskimo. He was promptly introduced to 'Klondyke' Tommy, an Innuit sailor who had drifted in from a Yankee whaling vessel, and settled down to rear a large half-caste family. Sumo wrestling and bouts of ju-jitsu were regular entertainments, but the main recreations were drinking in sly grog shops, gambling and, of course, sex. The Japanese even imported geisha girls to staff their brothels.

Some of the pearlers were remittance men from good English families. There were three James. 'Long' James, a flamboyant ex-Cambridge man, combined pearling with gun-running as a very profitable sideline. In the 1890s, old ex-army muzzle-loading Lee Enfield guns were available in Western Australia at ten bob each (a dollar in today's terms). Long James would ship them to rajahs in the spice islands where he would get from ten to fifteen pounds each for them. If the local war lord couldn't pay, Long James cut the value out in native labour which he brought back to Broome to sell to other pearlers as crew and divers.

'Gentleman' James was a polished operator who was well liked. His forte was smuggling Chinese into Australia at two rates—seven pounds a head for those landed anywhere in the Admiralty Gulf area and likely to be killed by the Aborigines, and twenty pounds a head for passengers who had to be landed in more civilised areas at greater risk to him. On one occasion he was running south with some of his twenty-pounds-a-head illegals when a customs boat hove in sight. Gentleman James ordered his four Chinese passengers to be locked up in a water tank, but an overzealous crewman screwed down the airtight manhole cover and suffocated all of them. Gentleman

James went to gaol in Fremantle after that debacle.

'Blackguard' James came from South Africa. He was a parson's son, but his claim to fame was his tongue and ability to swear—he was recognised as having the most vicious and fluent array of oaths and filthy language ever known. When he was in full verbal flight he had the curious habit of dropping to his knees—a doubtful acknowledgment of his pious origins. Blackguard James was one of the few Europeans who collaborated with the Japanese community in some shady commercial schemes.

A sad legacy of the hazards of diving for pearl shell was also seen in the shanty town area. In 1911 one observer wrote that the town abounded with cripples, victims of shark and crocodile attacks—but these crippled people were 'quite pleasant sights', said the visitor, compared with the human wrecks in all stages of paralytic helplessness, 'sitting outside their shacks, bodies unbelievably twisted, stiff and cold as frozen mutton, their features grotesque masks and in their eyes a look so pitiful that even the case-hardened Irish pearling masters would cross themselves as they slipped past these human wrecks'. The paralysis, of course, was the result of the 'bends' when bubbles of nitrogen formed in their bloodstream when they worked at considerable depths for too long, or were brought to the surface too quickly in their diving suits.

Colourful tales of this wild era in Broome are many, but I am duty bound to include the splendid story involving a West Indian called Con Gill who arrived in Broome around 1900. Gill was a loner, whose constant companion was a cockatoo he had raised from a fledgling. The cockatoo always followed him about, muttering and swearing. The bird had a great vocabulary in Malay and English and used to sing haunting Creole lullabies while Gill was sweeping out the bar. The cocky was also a heavy drinker—very fond of whisky and rum. When he drank, his language became even more abusive. The cockatoo used to fly over the houses of the town and, it was said, eavesdropped on conversations. Con Gill used to add to this belief by repeating conversations only the parrot could have supposedly heard.

Gill was also feared for his prowess in voodoo. When a European pearl shell packer called Brian Taylor heard he had been hexed by Gill, he tackled him about it. Gill reputedly said:

> Brian, you've got it all wrong. One time I had a row with another man over a half-caste woman, and I put a chicken-bone on his door-step with a bit of Voodoo to it, and his son got killed and his lugger sank and his wife went mad, all in a few weeks—but I don't harbour any resentment now.

The cocky's most famous escapade took place on Christmas Day 1924, when one thousand pounds in bank notes disappeared from the desk of a pearler who had borrowed it to pay his Japanese crew. The police were brought in with black trackers, and everyone who could have had access to his house was searched, but the money was not found. Gill's cockatoo took a great deal of interest in all this, walking about on the roof of the house offering his own comments. Then someone noticed that the bird had a roll of notes in his beak wrapped in an elastic band. A ladder was put against the side of the house, and there was a lot of 'Come here cocky, nice cocky, pretty cocky' and so on. A policeman climbed up on the roof with a biscuit, but cocky didn't want a biscuit and flew off with the money.

Everyone thought Gill had it, but that could not be proved. Another loan was raised and the crew was paid. Two years later when the guttering of the local pub was cleaned before the monsoon rains, remnants of shredded bank notes were found in the cockatoo's nest in a Bougainvillea overhanging the roof. Some of the numbers of a few of the notes could be made out and the bank paid out on them. Gill and his cockatoo's reputations for voodoo and mystery were greatly enhanced.

There are big beds of pearl shell from Exmouth Gulf, north of Broome and at various locations right round the Gulf of Carpentaria to Cape York. But the biggest and most easily reached are off the north-west coast from Exmouth to Broome. One of the factors which led to the discovery of these pearl shell beds was the enormous tides, which range from six metres at Exmouth to a phenomenal twelve metres at King Sound. So, twice a day, huge areas of tidal flats were exposed and so were the shells—the most prized being the silver or gold-lipped pearl oyster *Pinctada maxima*. Dead shells could be collected along the beaches, but the living shells produced the best mother-of-pearl. A lucky by-product, of course, were the pearls themselves, formed when pieces of grit, or even biological irritants, caused the oyster to coat the invading unwanted foreign matter in its flesh with layers of smooth nacre. Those pearls that formed within the oyster itself were round, or pear-shaped; other pearls formed in the shell itself were known as blister pearls.

The demand for pearl shell for ornaments, buttons and jewellery was boosted by a change in European women's fashions from 1850. Commercial pearling began in Western

Australia in 1861 when James Turner, on board the Fremantle vessel *Flying Foam*, gathered 910 shells and 150 pearls in the vicinity of Nickol Bay near Cossack, south of Broome. Later, Turner engaged Aborigines to dive for pearl shell in shallow water from dinghies. They were very good at it, but the use of their labour was quickly abused, with unscrupulous pearlers turning to 'blackbirding' and hijacking Aboriginal men (and women) from areas far from the pearling grounds, and keeping them as slave labour. Many, mourning the loss of their traditional lands and tribal community, simply sickened and died. European pastoralists were also hostile to their Aboriginal labour being poached by the pearlers. Nevertheless, by 1873 more than eighty boats were operating off the coast south from Broome.

In the early 1870s the Western Australian government banned the use of Aboriginal labour in the pearling industry and so began the influx of Asian labour that led to the extraordinary shanty town in Broome. These were rough years, with massacres, mutinies and murder commonplace, as well as pearl stealing. The rewards could be rich. Australia's largest natural pearl, the Star of the West, was found off Broome in 1917. It was a drop-shaped pearl and weighed 6.48 grams. It was sold in London for six thousand pounds.

The distinctive pearling lugger was developed for its ability to lie, undamaged, on the hard sand during the enormous tides of the region, and to support dry-suit diving operations. Pearling has always been a risky business. Cemeteries in Broome, Darwin and Thursday Island contain the bodies of scores of divers who died from the bends in the late nineteenth and early twentieth centuries. But sharks or paralysis were not the only dangers. The north of Australia is a wild place in more ways than one. In 1899 a cyclone off Cape York Peninsula wrecked 50 vessels and 300 men were lost.

Fortunately Ros and I were taking to the high seas in the calmest, most opportune time of the year. We would leave, not from the old harbour near Chinatown, but from the new deepwater jetty at the end of the Broome peninsula.

We were booked into Tarangau Caravan Park at Cable Beach where there is now an international-standard resort and smart new caravan parks mushrooming nearby. Tarangau was our style of park—small, with plenty of trees for shade, backing on to some bushland with scrub turkeys pecking about companionably. The Blenkinsop family, who run it, do so in a relaxed and pleasant way. We discovered that Peter Blenkinsop, a silver-haired ex-navy Vietnam veteran, was also going to pilot *Coral Princess* out of the deepwater port when we left on our Kimberley coastal odyssey—a nice coincidence.

After picking ourselves an attractive shady spot we started to harbour evil thoughts about the scrub turkeys. They have a relentless, utterly unchanging call that sets your teeth on edge. Not that I would have done it myself, but I noticed Peter Blenkinsop's son-in-law move them away from his workshop by the simple expedient of firing a slingshot at them. The turkeys got the message. Unfortunately they came back to us, to be joined by some moth-eaten looking peacocks and hens with their squawking calls, which at least have a bit more variation than the turkeys' maddening metronome-regulated glurking.

A swim at Cable Beach seemed a good option. After so much inland driving it was strange to see families sitting under striped umbrellas beside the vivid blue-green water so typical of this part of the world. The tide was almost full, so there was not far to walk. One enterprising entrepreneur had a set of lockers on wheels, which he towed up and down the beach with a four-wheel-drive as the ten-metre tides rose and fell. Later we watched the sun set, and argued gently whether we had or had not seen the legendary green flash that is supposed to occur at the instant the sun dips below the distant, watery horizon.

three

Cruising with the Ancient Mariners

The Kimberley is ancient—almost unimaginably so. It is even older than the rest of the exceedingly venerable Australian continent, which it bumped into catastrophically some 1830 million years ago. What is now the Kimberley was then part of a northern continent drifting south and featuring a spine of mountains of Andes proportions. This tectonic clash produced enormous upheavals in the earth's crust, triggering great eruptions of magma—molten rock—some of which burst to the surface in volcanic eruptions. The mega-collision buckled rocks into great folds still visible today, or pushed them deep in the earth's crust where they were mineralised by the extreme pressure and heat.

This collision of continents also lifted the oldest rock formations up and tilted them, leaving the Kimberley trademark—red ramparts of sandstone along the fractured coastline—lying back on an angle and investing the rocky headlands and escarpments with a faintly jaunty air. When these cataclysmic events took place, life on earth had only just begun in the form of primitive multi-celled creatures swimming in the warm, shallow seas.

Erosion over many millions of years has gouged deep gorges in the tough, mineralised sandstone, which has split along fault lines like gigantic rough hewn stone blocks seen in Inca ruins. But no human hand has shaped these vast Kimberley monoliths. Over the millennia the Kimberley has been compressed, eroded and split by the primeval forces of cold, heat, pressure, wind and rain to create natural rock sculptures—particularly headlands and bluffs.

The coast is so deeply indented and difficult to get to that there are very few access roads. Even visiting the coastline from the sea is fraught with difficulty as the daily twelve-metre tides churn in and out of vast inlets and drowned valleys making navigation extremely tricky—and dependent not on the time of day or night, but always on the ebb and flow of these great and powerful tidal forces.

Ros and I would be visiting the Kimberley at its most benign time, the southern winter and the northern 'dry' season, when the winds are gentle, the nights cool and the days temperate. While Europeans tend to think of the region as having wet and dry seasons—'wet' from December and 'dry' from about May—the Aborigines of the north-west Kimberley divvied up the seasons of their volatile region into seven:

Yirma (May–August)
Winter, or more accurately the dry season, when the south-east winds blow steadily. Grasses and spinifex are burned to encourage new growth to attract game. A pleasant time of the year with plenty of food and when ceremonies are held.

Yuwala (September–November)
Hot and dry with the rivers drying into pools. A difficult period. Most root crops have been gathered.

Djaward (late November–December)

Hot and unsettled weather with the approach of the rainy season. Sudden storms with thunder and lightning are common. Many of the edible fruits have ripened so food is plentiful.

Wundju (January–February)

The wet, with heavy rain falling almost daily—a miserable period. The rivers are flooded and the ground is waterlogged. Root crops from the dry season are rotten and sour. Hunting for game sustains life, but the rain makes it difficult to hunt. People build bark shelters or live in caves. Sickness is common.

Maiaru (late February–March)

This season is sometimes called 'autumn' because some leaves fall from trees. Rains ease, but food is still scarce.

Bande manya (April)

Everything is ripening. The first of the new season's root crops mature, ending the lean months of the wet season.

Goloruru (late April)

The end of April—the season when the south-east trade winds begin to blow, heralding the dry. More root crops reach maturity.

Even in peaceful *Yirma* there were hidden dangers. We would not be able to swim anywhere in either the inviting tropical sea or big rivers because of salt-water crocodiles and sharks, and we would have to keep our eyes peeled for venomous snakes on land. The Kimberley can never be taken for granted in any season.

We had time for a day's bumbling about in Broome before *Coral Princess* arrived to take us on our coastal odyssey. Ros, a ferocious tourist at times, brushed aside my weak exhortations about 'when we were going to have time to read our books'.

'You can read books at any time, but while we are in interesting places I want to see them,' she said.

As it happened, the repetitious glurking of those wretched scrub turkeys was a powerful incentive to leave camp. So we drove to the lighthouse at Ganthaume Point, where there are carnivorous dinosaur footprints which were imprinted into the sedimentary rock 120 million years ago but are a long way out from the point and only visible at very low tides. As the tide was high when we arrived, it was pleasing to see the Broome authorities had thoughtfully placed concrete casts of the footprints on dry land. (One of the real prints was cut out of the bedrock by a thief but fortunately was recovered several years later in Sydney, and the culprit charged.)

On our way back to Broome we drove past Reddell Beach, named after a pearling captain who was murdered by his own crew in 1899. It is entirely possible that he wasn't a very nice man. The Japanese cemetery, now well tended, is a vivid reminder of the casualties of the early pearling industry. There are 919 Japanese buried there—140 of them killed in the cyclones of 1887 and 1935, but the majority having died of the 'bends'. The graves are marked by rough rock pillars, inscribed with Japanese characters. We saw the cemetery in the late afternoon, the graves bathed in the soft warm light of the setting sun. The restoration of the cemetery was organised by a Japanese politician, Kazuo Tamaki, in 1983. We were both glad we had stopped to see it. It is impossible not to be moved by the experience.

The Broome Museum has a splendidly eclectic collection —one of the most recent outdoor exhibits being a wooden Indonesian fishing boat captured by the Australian navy for fishing within our territorial waters. Indeed the vessel was restored using the skills of the apprehended Indonesian sailors who were let out of gaol to do the job! Inside the museum there are many artefacts and photographs of Broome's pearling heyday, including a full dry diving suit, circa 1900, and of course plenty of pearl shell and pearls, from blister to cultivated.

One room displays photographs and mangled equipment from the disastrous Japanese raid on Broome in 1942. Broome had become a vital staging and refuelling port for thousands of World War II refugees fleeing from Indonesia—then the Dutch East Indies. It was also an air base for bombers, and a haven for flying boats, processing as many as 57 aircraft a day. But not on March 3, 1942. In Japanese terms it was a great day out. Seven Zero fighters from the Japanese navy suddenly appeared over the town and in sixteen minutes, destroyed twenty-one flying boats and other aircraft. Seventy people died. Broome had no defences save a few machine guns (with no ammunition) and Lee Enfield .303 rifles. (Wreckage of some of the Catalinas can still be seen at very low tides.)

The museum is run by volunteers. The collection is displayed in a way that can best be described as unexpected, but this adds to its charm, and we spent a few happy hours there. It has the original piano used to provide musical sound effects for the silent movies played in Broome's famous outdoor Sun Picture Theatre. Just inside the door is a decorated plaque on which is inscribed:

The heart that forgives an injury
Is like the perforated shell of a mussel
Which heals its wounds with a pearl.

Very lovely, wouldn't you say? It almost engendered warm feelings about those infuriating, glurking scrub turkeys which were still scratching about and making their perpetual noises when we got back to camp. Sitting under the trees having a cuppa we saw another nomadic couple of our own vintage approaching with a bottle in hand. Colin and Marilyn were from Tasmania and were touring about in a very smart camper that looked like a small A-frame house when erected. In Kununurra they had met our friends Greg Williams and Heather Messer who knew we would be in Broome. To continue the tradition of giving each other crook bottles of cheap plonk, Greg had asked Colin to present us with a bottle of 'ruby red' muscat if he saw us. This was a tradition that needed to be kyboshed. I made a mental note to speak to Greg about a moratorium—permanently—when I saw him next.

Coral Princess was due to sail the next day. We snugged down Penelope and The Manor to leave them with the turkey obbligato for ten days while we swapped our camping life for shipboard luxury with laundered sheets, our own cabin and table service. It seemed disloyal, but we hardened our hearts.

Our ship was dwarfed by the huge Broome jetty, lined with road trains full of steers about to leave for Indonesia and the Middle East as part of the live cattle trade that has saved the beef industry of the far north. Once there were meatworks in Broome, Derby and Wyndham. When we were last in the area in 1982, the muddy, tidal waters in Wyndham were fouled with carcasses and offal and the happiest crocodiles north of the Tropic of Capricorn. Those abattoirs are no more, and the nearest meat processing works available to Kimberley meat producers are in Katherine or Perth—expensive options. Walking along the jetty was hazardous. Nervous steers with their bums pressed against the slatted sides of the cattle trucks tend to projectile ... I won't go on. But there were some near misses. One way or another we were all being loaded on to ships. At least Ros and I were coming back.

A vintage Kimberley dry season day showed off the deep water port in its best dress, the blood red rocks of the shore contrasting with an electric blue sea. The lean, lanky frame and cheerful freckled face of Greg Mortimer beamed at us under a mop of red hair from the top deck of *Coral Princess* as we boarded on the high tide. Later the gangways would drop down, deck by deck, linked to stairways and connecting platforms from the jetty as the tide went relentlessly through its ten-metre cycle. Greg is one of Australia's best climbers. He and Tim McCartney-Snape were the first two Australians to climb Mt Everest in 1984 and six years later Greg and two companions successfully tackled the world's next highest mountain, K2, technically more difficult than Mt Everest and referred to by Himalayan climbers as 'the toughest mountain on earth'. (At 8511 metres, K2 is only 300 metres lower than Everest.)

In 1988 Greg Mortimer celebrated Australia's bicentennial in his own inimitable style. He joined a small band of climbers who sailed to Antarctica in a yacht and were the first to climb Mt Minto, at 5200 metres one of the frozen continent's highest peaks. During the Mt Minto expedition Greg fell in love with Margaret Werner, the vessel's indomitable cook, who produced gastronomic miracles from her tiny, lurching galley even in the stormiest conditions.

As the eleven members of the expedition headed back to Australia from the Ross Sea in their improbably named yacht *Alan & Vi Thistlethwayte* (named after the expedition's generous sponsors) the vessel's overworked diesel engine snapped its tail shaft and caused a change of plan. While they were sailing towards New Zealand (to take advantage of more favourable winds in the tempestuous Southern Ocean) Greg had plenty of time to think about adventure travel and how to get tourists to Antarctica.

In 1992, Margaret and Greg (now in partnership personally and professionally) began chartering Russian icebreakers to take tourists to Antarctica, working through World Expeditions, and in 1996 formed their own adventure travel company, Aurora Expeditions. This company specialises in polar voyages in the Arctic and Antarctic and off-beat destinations as diverse as the Silk Road in western China and Pakistan or remote coastlines like the Kimberley.

Greg has now been to Antarctica more than 60 times, leading tourist expeditions on Russian ice-strengthened ships. Being the man he is, he has introduced a degree of adventuring not normally part of the Antarctic tourist circuit. Each year, as part of his summer polar program, he runs a special climbing and kayaking voyage to the Antarctic Peninsula, leaving from the southern tip of South America. Those who wish to can climb an iceberg, canoe among the pack ice, basking whales and ubiquitous penguins, and scale unclimbed peaks. There are so many of these on the Antarctic Peninsula (around 1000 metres) that if you are the first to climb one, you can name it!

Ros and I have been to the Antarctic with Aurora Expeditions and Greg Mortimer, but we have not climbed or named any virgin mountains so far. I was a guest lecturer on Antarctic history after I wrote *The Silence Calling— Australians in Antarctica 1947–97* and presented 'Breaking the Ice'—a six part television documentary series on Australians who live and work on the frozen continent, and which has been broadcast a number of times since it was first aired on ABC Television in 1996. On *Coral Princess* I was to lecture on warmer climes—the history of the Kimberley from the first European interaction with it, early contacts with Aboriginal people and the exploration of its jagged coastline and interior river systems.

'You'll find the Kimberley trip a familiar routine—it's very like Antarctica,' said Greg as we went to the bridge to meet the captain of *Coral Princess*.

'Climate's a bit warmer, isn't it?'

Greg chuckled. 'Certainly is, but think about Antarctica for a moment. It's a big, remote coastline which can only be visited by ship. There are no roads to speak of. We go ashore—just as we do in the Antarctic—in small boats and spend time ashore in spectacular locations. We'll even see some humpback whales—and follow them for photography, as you've already done in Antarctica. You'll have to substitute sea eagles for albatrosses.'

Greg explained that he selected the Kimberley as an adventure tourist destination not because it was Australian, but because he and Margaret had scoured the world map for big isolated coastlines where people seldom visited.

'The Kimberley was in the top seven. It provides a remarkable look at the bare bones of the earth in an incredibly ancient and stable land mass.'

In an increasingly populated world, the Kimberley is a bastion of wilderness. Most of it is reserved for nature conservation or as traditional Aboriginal land. Covering 1.09 million square kilometres, the Kimberley is smaller than South Africa but larger than Egypt. Yet its permanent human population is only about 30 000, about 35 per cent of whom are Aborigines.

As in Antarctic cruising, *Coral Princess* passengers were welcome on the bridge at any time—unless the ship was leaving or entering port with a pilot, or during moments of tricky navigation. This was a wonderful privilege, and I didn't tire of taking in a captain's eye view of the voyage, day and night. The flying bridge was a great vantage point—unlike Antarctica without the hazard of frostbite but where sunburn was more likely.

It was all first names on *Coral Princess* and our skipper, another Greg, introduced me to Captain Jason.

'Two captains?'

'Yes,' explained Captain Greg, a tall young man who didn't look old enough to me to be in command, but then again policemen and soldiers seem to me barely out of their teens these days.

'I'm taking over from Captain Jason, who has been skipper until this voyage. He'll be keeping an eye on me to make sure I don't run aground.'

Captain Jason couldn't say much because he was welcoming the pilot on board, our caravan park proprietor Peter Blenkinsop, now looking very nautical and official in his whites with gold epaulettes. He winked at me and began to look over his paperwork. I felt it was time to get off the bridge.

During the cheerful chaos that characterises leaving port on the first day of a cruise, we bounced on our firm and comfortable beds in the en suite cabin (in staff quarters in the port hull of the catamaran, not quite below the water-line, but almost), stowed some gear and wandered about exploring the various decks as our fellow passengers milled about trying to find their cabins. We met Cyril and Enid Gorely who had a cabin deep in the port side hull near us. Cyril was over 80, and there was a very steep stairway to negotiate. Ros and I had a momentary concern that he might find it difficult until we saw Cyril and Enid scamper up and down with enviable agility.

There was another Antarctic parallel—the number of passengers. Greg Mortimer charters small Russian ships in Antarctica which carry about fifty passengers. This is a good number, because you can get to know everyone during the short voyage and getting ashore is less complicated than from ships with over 100 souls. Because of her modest size, *Coral Princess* too can worm her way into channels and inlets unavailable to conventional cruise ships.

We had 48 passengers on our big catamaran and clearly most of us were not in the full flower of our youth. A later survey revealed an average age of 64.4—and it would have been even more geriatric if Alana, the teenage daughter of Gillian and Alex Awramenko, had not drastically skewed our venerable average down. There were no Zimmer frames in evidence though. We had some remarkably nimble octogenarians who would later shame us younger sexagenarians by leaping up cliffs and walking us into the ground on field trips.

Not only did we have two captains, but three voyage leaders! Greg Mortimer, our official leader, was being understudied for later voyages by Mike Cusack, also an adventurer, who has seen more of the Kimberley than most. He and his partner Susan lived in isolation for a year, building their own shelter and living off the land, taking part in a survival exercise organised by Dick Smith's *Australian Geographic* in the bicentennial year 1988. They were selected from a highly competitive field of 500 couples who volunteered to do the same thing. I looked forward to hearing more about their adventures, not only during Mike's formal lectures, but over the bar and dinner table.

Then there was the resident voyage leader of *Coral Princess*, Mark Buckingham, a fit young man in his early twenties, who cheerfully adapted his duties to look after and skipper our excursion boat, *Explorer*, a high speed aluminium barge which could seat us all and burn along at 25 knots or so powered by two big outboard motors. *Explorer* was carried across the stern of *Coral Princess* suspended from two solid looking davits, and was lowered into the water when required for our daily adventuring. There were also a couple of Zodiacs, inflatable craft with powerful outboards similar—yet another polar link—to ones I'd experienced on Antarctic voyages.

We ancient mariner passengers—forgive me, Alana—met one another at our first dinner on board, a splendid seafood banquet of oysters, crabs, prawns and lobster expertly prepared by our chef Adam, who also looked as though he'd just left school. There was much animated talk as we began to get to know our fellow expeditioners. Name tags are a blessing, but as usual on any voyage I've been on, they become scarce within hours of being issued. There were several familiar faces. Fred Westwood, a friend from Tasmania, was on board having heard Ros and me enthuse about the voyage. And I spotted Joan Turner whose son Pip, a helicopter pilot, had flown me for many stimulating (and sometimes hairy) hours in Antarctica from 1989 to

1994. Perhaps his adventuring spirit came from his mother. I also discovered that Mike Richardson, foreign correspondent for the *Herald Tribune* based in Singapore whose byline I had read for many years, and his wife Amanda were with us. As *Coral Princess* speared her twin bows north through the tropical twilight, Voyage Leader Greg announced that we should change our watches to ship's time, one-and-a-half hours behind Western Australia, and actually Northern Territory time. It was, he explained, a kind of out-of-area daylight saving so we could make better use of the longer days during our Kimberley coast explorations.

No need for an alarm clock—it was enough for *Coral Princess* to drop her anchor and heavy chain. We awoke abruptly at Pender Bay on the north-western side of the peninsula known as Dampier Land, after the first English visitor to set foot on Australian soil. The low lying land we saw from *Coral Princess*, with sparse scrub stretching back to the horizon, is fairly typical of the northern reaches of the west coast of Australia. The Dutch navigators who stumbled on it, or were wrecked on its rocky reefs, wrote less than enthusiastically about it. Unlike the lush tropics of the Dutch East Indies it seemed to promise them little—not even the water so urgently sought by far-ranging sailing ships.

William Dampier arrived off the Kimberley coast in 1688 on board a little ship, *Cygnet*, which was really a privateer. This was not so much a voyage of discovery but of exploitation. The only reason its captain (not Dampier) had come south was to avoid the risk of careening the ship in the Dutch East Indies where a passing Dutch frigate might have taken advantage of a temporarily stranded English ship lying on its side having its bottom cleaned. As the Dutch would have been well aware, the Englishmen would have knocked off any of their ships that came their way. The crew of *Cygnet* understood that the land south of the Arafura Sea was seldom visited because the Dutch knew of its bleak reputation—a granite plateau, no rain forest, and none of the tropical lushness of the Spice Islands.

Dampier, an extraordinary adventurer, was actually hitch-hiking his way around the globe in a variety of ships, most of them up to no good. After some buccaneering in the West Indies and Panamanian coast, he joined a rough band of pirates on *Cygnet* to cross the Pacific. In the Philippines he took part in a successful mutiny after which the captain was put ashore. A man named John Read was placed in charge, and after some raiding on the coasts of China and Taiwan, *Cygnet* sailed for the East Indies. We don't even know Dampier's status on board, whether he was part of the ship's crew or a paying passenger.

Fortunately for posterity, this compulsive traveller was also an acute observer and diarist. During the ten weeks *Cygnet* moved among the islands of the appropriately named Buccaneer Archipelago, several landings were made on the Kimberley coast. Dampier described it all in his journal—and has given us the first contemporary accounts of meeting Australian Aboriginal people. He also described the flora and fauna and even made sketches of what he saw. (Dampier's diary was so important to him that when he eventually escaped from the motley bunch on *Cygnet* a few weeks later by swimming ashore on the remote Nicobar Islands—almost midway between the tip of Sumatra and Sri Lanka—the only thing he carried with him was his diary sealed in a bamboo tube with wax.)

Had the crew of *Cygnet* landed at Pender Bay there would have been no obvious pointer to fresh water. But as

48 eager late-twentieth-century travellers headed into the shallow waters towards a shelving beach for our first landing, we only had a short walk of several hundred metres across the sand dunes to feast our eyes on the unexpected body of fresh water that is Pender Lake. Ringed by screw pandanus trees, some producing their knobbly, red, rather putrescent smelling fruit, the lake is an astonishing oasis in the sand dunes, teeming with bird life including ibis, swans, grebes, ducks, black cockatoos, corellas and honeyeaters as well as the more formidable sea eagles and whistling kites.

Big estuarine crocodiles, our guide No. 3 Voyage Leader Mark told us, were known to amble across the dunes to the lake, their tracks clearly visible in the sand. We only saw the more reassuring, small squiggly wriggles of lizards and goannas, and the paw prints of small marsupials. One curiosity we were shown was the flower of the birds-beak rattlepod, which looks like a tiny green bird complete with beak and furled wings, about three centimetres long. It is also terribly toxic, particularly to horses, which get the staggers and die if they eat it. Some of us humans already had the staggers from struggling over the soft sand banks. Greg Mortimer (who is also a geologist) alerted us to the red outcrops of tertiary sandstone, in Kimberley geological terms formed only yesterday—65 million years ago—in contrast to the ancient quartzite sandstone of the rest of the Kimberley.

Not surprisingly, Aboriginal people have always lived around Pender Lake, and still do in a settlement to the north. Greg's eagle eye spotted some middens, where the wind had blown sand away to expose piles of trochus shells and even some stone tools. He recognised the distinctive quartzite sandstone which, unlike the local variety, was more than 2000 million years old, and obviously traded in from the east Kimberley by Aboriginal people thousands of years ago. We left the still sharp stone chips lying on the sand, glinting in the harsh sunlight where the long gone Weedong Lake community had last used them. Perhaps the next passersby would not see them. We benefited from a delightful accident of sand, wind and timing that made a deep and lasting impression on all of us fortunate enough to be walking with Greg at that moment.

Dampier gave us the first written description of the Australian Aborigines. He described them as 'the most miserablest People in the World', which has not endeared him to today's Aboriginal people well used to being denigrated by white Europeans. However, there is evidence that Dampier was no racist. When he finally left *Cygnet* and swam ashore to the Nicobar Islands it was because he did not agree with the way his captain was mistreating native people—and he wanted no part of that. He was more interested in observation and comparisons. When he wrote his book, he compared the Australian Aborigines to the Hottentots of Africa—whom he had not seen while he was in Australia. (Perhaps his publisher had told him to gild the lily a bit.) He wrote starkly about what he saw, in the light of his own experience:

> They have no Houses, or skin Garments, Sheep, Poultry, Fruits of the Earth, Ostrich Eggs &c., as the Hodmadods [Hottentots] have. And setting aside their Human Shape, they differ little from Brutes. They are tall, straight-bodied and thin with small long Limbs. They have great Heads, round Foreheads and great Brows. Their Eyelids are always half closed, to keep the Flies out of their Eyes, they being so troublesome here that no fanning will keep them from coming to one's Face . . .

Dampier is the first observer of the 'great outback salute' and the pernicious and ubiquitous Western Australian bush fly that will not only invade every human orifice, but accompany food into the mouth if given half a chance. Nothing has changed on the bush fly front in over 300 years.

> They have great Bottle-Noses, pretty full Lips and wide Mouths. The two Fore-teeth of their Upper jaw are wanting in all of them, Men and Women, old and young, whether they draw them out I do not know. Nor have they any Beards . . . They have no sort of Clothes, but the piece of the Rind of a tree, tied like a Girdle about their Waists, and a handful of long Grass, or three or four small green Boughs full of Leaves thrust under their Girdle to cover their Nakedness.
>
> They have no Houses, but lie in the open Air without any covering, the Earth being their Bed and the Heaven their Canopy. Whether they cohabit one Man to one Women or promiscuously, I did not know, but they do live in Companies of 20 or 30 Men Women and Children together.

Landing on a small island near Cape Leveque—not far from where *Coral Princess* anchored at Pender Bay— they surprised a large group of about 40 Aborigines who, in the circumstances, could not escape. Dampier was still expecting to find villages, or some kind of dwellings. (Later he confused ant hills in the distance with the kind of conical mud huts built by Africans.) At first the Aboriginal men threatened the Englishmen with their spears, but after a gunshot was fired into the air, everyone ran away, the children 'squeaking and bawling', but when it became obvious that the strangers meant no harm, there was at least amicable contact:

After we had been here a little while, while the Men began to be familiar, and we clothed some of them, designing to have some service from them. For we had found some Wells of Water here and intended to carry 2 or 3 Barrels of it aboard. But as it was somewhat troublesome to carry it to the Canoes, we thought to have got these Men to carry it for us. And therefore we gave them some old Clothes: to one an old pair of Breeches; to another a ragged Shirt; to the third, a Jacket that was scarce worth owning, which would have been very acceptable at some places where we had been. We put them on them, thinking that this finery would have brought them to work heartily for us. And having filled our Water and small long Barrels . . . we brought our new Servants to the wells, and put a barrel on each of their Shoulders for them to carry to the Canoe. But all the signs we could make were to no purpose, for they stood like Statues without motion, and grinned like so many Monkeys, staring one upon another. For these poor Creatures do not seem accustomed to carrying Burdens, and I believe that one of our Ship-boys of 10 Years old would carry as much as one of them. So we were forced to carry our Water ourselves. They very fairly put the Clothes off again, and laid them down as if Clothes were only for working in. I did not perceive that they had any great liking for them at first. Nor did they seem to admire anything that we had.

It is worth remembering that these were the first written observations ever made about Australian Aboriginal people. Dampier could not have known that the men never did any manual work except hunting. And he was also the first to note that Aboriginal people cared little for the trappings of European civilisation.

During lunch *Coral Princess* headed out towards the Lacepede Islands, also rich in history. They were sighted by the French explorer Nicolas Baudin, on his voyage of discovery in 1801, who named it after a celebrated French naturalist, Count Lacepede. But he did not land. Indeed the cautious Baudin stood well out to sea and did not land anywhere in the Kimberley area to the intense fury of a bevy of naturalists and scientists he had on board his ship *Le Géographé* who were itching to explore and collect specimens in this new land. The French, like the British, were interested in getting their slice of geographical action in and around the Great South Land. Although Baudin did not lay a glove on the north-west coast of Australia, it did not stop him, as Alasdair McGregor noted in his excellent book *The Kimberley—Horizons of Stone*, 'littering the coast with Gallic names'. I have already mentioned Cape Leveque and the Lacepede Islands. Baudin is also responsible for Joseph Bonaparte Gulf, Cape Bougainville, Cape Voltaire and many more. He kept going all the way down the coast. There is a Cape Rabelais in South Australia. I wonder what happened there? Perhaps a good time was had by all . . .

There are four low, sand-covered islands in the Lacepede group, now a nature reserve which provides sanctuary for many sea birds, including an estimated 18 000 pairs of brown boobies, 3000 pairs of frigate birds, as well as oyster catchers, egrets, pelicans and waders. The endangered green and flat back turtles breed on its beaches and the waters are bursting with marine life. Dugongs, stingrays, sharks and shovel nosed rays inhabit the shallow waters around the islands. It was a wonderful zoo, and after being delivered on shore by the trusty *Explorer* we wandered along the beaches occasionally photographing nesting birds and their chicks—particularly the big white fluffy boobie chicks which looked uncannily like something out of 'Sesame Street'. The Lacepede Islands pulsate with life.

It's a hard life. Penelope and The Manor in dry season camping mode,
Kennedy Range National Park, Western Australia.

Snug inside The Manor on a frosty Central Australian evening, the author resorts to
Antarctic beanie and red wine to spark inspiration for the daily diary.

Singer, song writer, author, teller of outrageous yarns and all-round good bloke,
Ted Egan, on the film set of *The Drover's Boy* south of Alice Springs.

Warlayirti Art Cooperative artists of the Balgo community, Western Australia,
are producing some fantastic desert paintings. Artists at work are Bridgid Mudgedell
(*Rock Pool Dreaming*) (right), Elizabeth Gordon (left), observer Ros Bowden and
a local drop in.

The dust trail of a road train on the Tanami Track can be seen from five kilometres away. Best to stop, pull over and live.

Rabbit Flat is undeniably a long way from anywhere—and this car is unlikely to get there.

(Left) Splendid *Kimberley Bauhinia* pods gleam red against the pale spinifex and look like flowers from a distance. (Right) Remote caravan parks are a hive of entrepreneurial activity.

The ebb and flow of the Kimberley's ten-metre tides, banded on these rocks, dictated our daily program and coastal visits.

At the end of each adventuring day, our trusty excursion boat *Explorer* returned us to the sanctuary of *Coral Princess*.

Slightly nervous thrill-seeking author in a rubber Zodiac prepares for a close encounter with the huge tidal surge banked up behind the cliffs of the famed 'Horizontal Waterfalls' of the Kimberley coast.

The ancient red rock ramparts of the Kimberley coast can only be fully appreciated from the sea.

Big Bird eat your heart out. This booby chick Ros photographed on the Lacepede Islands seemed straight out of Sesame Street.

Explorer delivers its venerable tourist adventurers to Camden Harbour under more pleasant circumstances than the unfortunate Victorian settlers in the summer of 1864.

Mouthless Wandjina spirit figures still guard their country in a cave in the hills behind Raft Point, Kimberley coast.

Historic graffiti of the splendid kind—the boab tree at Careening Cove has preserved Phillip Parker King's inscription: HBMC [His Brittanic Majesty's Cutter] MERMAID 1820.

Elegant Amanda Richardson prepares to join her fellow passengers in a croc-free pool we climbed up from the Prince Regent River to enjoy.

Fish leap out of the waters around the islands, and the green turtles constantly raise their reptilian heads to look about them with a faintly quizzical air.

The Macassans used to visit the Lacepedes at the end of the eighteenth century, camping there while they searched the coast for the prized delicacy, bêche-de-mer, sometimes called the sea slug, which they dried in the sun. They preferred to camp on islands as they were more easily defended against angry Aborigines seeking to avenge the theft of their women.

But it was all that valuable accumulated bird poop that attracted European attention in the middle of the nineteenth century. The guano reserves were eyed off by a Yankee adventurer in 1876. Because the Lacepedes were outside the twelve-mile limit, which was then where international waters began, legend has it that the American claimed the islands for the United States. When an Australian mining company started to remove the guano, the American consul in Melbourne requested that Washington send a warship to the islands to 'safeguard American property'. No action was taken.

We were to be sailing through the many islands of the Buccaneer Archipelago during the night. They were named after Dampier, of course. And my fascination with this journalist/pirate/explorer/collector continued.

When Dampier's book *A New Voyage Round the World* was published in London in 1697, it not only became a best-seller—three editions were printed in the first few months—but was translated into several European languages. And it had far-reaching implications. It alerted the British Government to the existence of the great south land and could be said to have triggered Britain's great colonial expansion of the eighteenth and nineteenth centuries.

Largely as a result of the book, the British Admiralty became enthusiastic about new discoveries and commissioned Dampier, former pirate and buccaneer, into the Royal Navy. He was given command of a rather down-at-heel little frigate, *Roebuck*, with orders to explore the southern continent, not just the north-west, but the east coast as well. Unfortunately for Dampier, *Roebuck* had rotten timbers, and not enough crew to work the ship properly—50 sailors instead of the required 70. The fitting out process dragged on so long that Dampier was not able to set sail until January 1699, instead of three months earlier as planned. This was to have serious consequences.

The voyage was a disappointment to all concerned. Dampier, for all his accomplishments, was not a good Royal Navy captain. Discipline on *Roebuck* was poor, and it was not a happy ship. He sailed around the Cape of Good Hope, made his landfall on the west coast of Australia at Shark Bay and sailed north to Lagrange Bay, some 100 kilometres south of Broome, where he landed to try to take on water and game if he could find any.

This time his contact with Aborigines was not so benign. He landed at Lagrange with ten men carrying cutlasses and muskets, and the Aborigines they tried to contact ran away. Dampier wrote in his journal that he wanted to 'catch one of them, if I could, of whom I might learn where they got their fresh water'. The Englishmen dug down into the sand to try to find fresh water, which angered the blacks who may have thought they were seeking the turtle eggs they regarded as their property. There was a clash during which one of Dampier's party was wounded by a spear, and one Aborigine was shot and also wounded. All Dampier managed to get was some brackish water. He did collect specimens while he was there, diligently took them back to the British Museum and was the first to note the presence of pearl shell in the area. The monument to Dampier in Broome should really be at Lagrange Bay, because that was the closest the English explorer ever got to the future Broome.

Sadly for Dampier, his voyage as an official captain of the Royal Navy was deemed a failure. After leaving the Kimberley coast he sailed to New Guinea but had no chance of exploring the east coast of Australia because *Roebuck* was in such a dreadful state—in fact she sank before they got back to England. Had the Admiralty not been so stingy in its choice of ship and tardy in fitting it out, Dampier might have carved a far larger niche in the history of the discovery of Australia. If he had been able to sail three months earlier as originally planned, he would have taken the Cape Horn route and may have found the fertile east coast of Australia more than half a century before Captain Cook. But the irrepressible Dampier shrugged off this brief flirtation with the Royal Navy and returned to his roving and freebooting life—during which he sailed to the other side of the world no fewer than five times, and circumnavigated the globe three times. But unlike most of his brother pirates, he seemed to be motivated not so much by gain and greed as by the joy of discovery.

I realised that we had approximately as many souls on *Coral Princess* as William Dampier had had on the leaky *Roebuck*. But our air-conditioned cabins with en suites would have been unimaginable luxury for seventeenth-century sailors, crammed together in dark, foetid surrounds with an occasional bucket of salt water on deck being the only washing facility available. Limited fresh water for drinking inevitably turned green in the casks and tasted foul. We have heard a lot about scurvy devastating sailors on long voyages, but there was also dysentery, tuberculosis, typhus and lesser complaints, as well as uncomfortable afflictions like boils and fungal skin diseases. Whatever your neighbour in the next hammock had, you undoubtedly picked up. Homosexuality was an acknowledged by-product of so many men being packed in together below decks.

Standing on the bridge as *Coral Princess* slipped through narrow channels between the Buccaneer Islands and the Kimberley coast, I saw the ghostly green light from the radar screen light up the face of No. 2 Captain, Jason. He looked serious but relaxed on the night watch—as well he might with all the navigational aids available to him, not only radar, but a global positioning system locking on to orbiting satellites that continually gave our position to within a metre's accuracy. Although we did have charts, on which our position was plotted with dividers and rulers in the time-honoured way, the operational map before the skipper's eyes was electronic, a pulsating cursor representing the ship's actual position on the map as we entered the narrow Yampi Sound between the mainland and Cockatoo and Koolan Islands.

Dampier would have been navigating essentially as seafarers had done since the thirteenth century—largely by guess and by God. The maps he had access to would have been exercises in wishful thinking by distant and ancient cartographers who believed in a southern continent as some kind of global balancing act. There were no detailed maps of the northern regions of Terra Australis in

1699—the extent of the southern continent was yet to be discovered. The Dutch navigated their way to the Spice Islands and back to Europe by custom as much as anything—a combination of using favourable winds and calculating their latitude from the sun, moon and planets.

Three centuries before the birth of Christ, early geographers had divided up the globe into lines of latitude—parallel concentric lines circling the globe—and longitude—curved lines crossing the lines of latitude and meeting at the poles. The astronomer and cartographer Ptolemy had plotted them on his maps by AD 150.

In Dampier's day, using a primitive measuring device called a cross staff—like a Christian cross with the crossbar furthest away—the seafarer could calculate the angle between the sun and the moon when both were visible. (Squinting into the sun in this way did terrible things to the observers' eyes, and eventually blinded cross staff navigators if they did it too often.) Navigators sometimes tried to use an astrolabe, but they were impossible to manage usefully on a heaving or pitching deck. Dampier would have had a magnetic compass for direction finding, but nothing was known then about magnetic variations, not only at different areas of the earth's surface, but those generated by the ship itself. (These problems were not tackled until the 1800s, when Matthew Flinders addressed himself to the anomalies—conducting experiments in magnetic variations when he was trying to navigate past, and also chart, the seemingly never ending limestone cliffs of the Great Australian Bight in 1802.)

Dampier would have calculated his speed by the time-honoured method of the log, a line with a weighted piece of wood at the end, divided by knots tied every 51 feet, which unrolled as the vessel moved forward, and a sandglass used as a timer while the number of knots that passed through were counted. The amount of line which ran out in a given amount of time, usually half a minute, was translated into nautical miles per hour. ('Knots per hour' are still used as a measure of speed at sea.) All these procedures were rough and ready when translated into dead reckoning.

The big missing link in early navigation was the ability to calculate longitude. As we know by modern Global Positioning Satellite devices (now so sophisticated they can be hand-held) you need an accurate measurement of latitude AND longitude to plot your position on the earth's surface. The problem with longitude was that it was inextricably linked with time. The navigator needed to know the time at an agreed place—either his home port or an agreed standard like the Greenwich meridian—and also the time on the ship at that very same moment. These two clock times then allow the navigator to convert the time difference into a geographical separation. The problem was not solved until ship's chronometers were developed to keep time accurately enough to allow reliable longitude calculations to be made, an advance not achieved until the nineteenth century.*

This meant that Dampier and his contemporaries had nothing to rely on when exploring a foreign coast, apart from their eyes. Unexpected storms or hidden reefs could end their voyages catastrophically, and often did. The VOC

---

* The remarkable story of how the self-taught English clockmaker William Harrison invented a sea-going clock and solved the longitude problem forever has been beautifully written and portrayed in *The Illustrated Longitude—The True Story of a Lone Genius Who Solved the Greatest Scientific Problem of His Time*, by Dava Sobel and William J. H. Andrewes, published by Fourth Estate, London, 1999.

(Vereenigde Oostindische Companie)—generally known as the Dutch East India Company—was first formed in 1602 and was the driving force behind the powerful Dutch trading empire with interests in China, Taiwan, Japan and, principally, the Indonesian archipelago. The company prospered despite appalling losses and held sway for two-and-a-half centuries. For every four ships that left Holland, only three were expected to return.

On *Coral Princess* our expectations were more optimistic. But when sailing these waters with all modern comforts and navigational certainty, I couldn't help thinking of those early explorers who needed their fair share of luck and good fortune to simply survive.

Clusters of lights on our port bow were a surprise to passengers on the bridge—although Captain Jason expected them to be there. Cockatoo Island was intensively mined for iron ore by BHP until 1986, and Koolan Island was only recently closed. Some 31 million tonnes of high grade iron ore were extracted from Cockatoo Island between 1951 and 1986. Restoration work on the huge open cut rock faces is still going on.

The dawn brought further evidence of commercial exploitation of this remote coastline—the farming of cultured pearls. These days colourful pearling luggers and pressure-pumped dry diving suits with those bulbous glass-fronted helmets have given way to more prosaic practices. The remote deep waters of Kimberley inlets are used as nurseries for baskets of the large gold-lipped oyster *Pinctada maxima*, each one of which has had a small polished sphere 8.5 millimetres in diameter (made from Mississippi pigtoe mussel) inserted into its innards. If all goes well, the compliant *Pinctada maxima* begins coating the irritating invading foreign body with layers of pearl nacre. After several months the shells are pulled up to the surface in their net baskets and X-rayed to see if the implant has 'taken'. It needs about two years to grow a commercial pearl. The only evidence the visitor sees of pearl farming is strings of buoys arranged in a semi-circle. Below each buoy is suspended a net bag presumably full of highly irritated oysters.

Those who tend the growing pearls are also irritated by the presence of outsiders. There are only two categories of visitors here—tourists or poachers. The Paspaley Pearling Company is the biggest operator in Kimberley waters and its tenders constantly patrol the buoy lines, not only cleaning and tending the shell, but keeping a close eye on the security of the multimillion dollar crop. Skulduggery is not unknown, and there were no friendly waves from the pearl workers on their barges as we roared up the still green waters of Talbot Bay in our two Zodiacs and the trusty 48-seat *Explorer*. Smoke from dry season bushfires was so thick they could barely see us anyway and there are no tourist tours of the closely guarded cultured pearl operations.

We were on our way to one of the Kimberley coast's most remarkable natural spectacles, the 'horizontal' waterfalls. The higher reaches of Talbot Bay are contained by 'gates' of red granite cliffs, only fifteen metres or so wide, through which the whole mass of water in the upper basin has to pass. Our timing was perfect. The twelve-metre tide had turned as we arrived, and was falling far faster than the trapped sea water could escape through the narrow gorge. The waters rushing out were backed up behind the narrow opening at least two metres higher than the foaming, swirling waters our excursion boats were battling on just to stay within a hundred metres of this explosion of natural power. The more intrepid (and that included just about everyone) took turns to transfer from *Explorer* into the Zodiacs and ride right up into the jaws of the 'waterfall' in the capable hands of No. 2 Captain Jason and No. 3 Voyage Leader Mark as the tough inflatables twisted and bucked in the white water and spray of this unique, truly horizontal waterfall. The annual profits of Mr Kodak and Mr Fuji soared in these hectic and remarkable minutes of exhilaration and awe.

If anything, the smoke had thickened as we passed the cultured pearl farm, but unworthy thoughts about using that as a screen to take a closer look at what was suspended under the buoys were quickly dismissed. Further demonstrations of mighty Kimberley tide power were still to come. After lunch we piled back into *Explorer* to power through the narrow entrance to Walcott Inlet, which encloses an enormous body of contained water 30 kilometres long and 11 kilometres wide. That water, like the horizontal waterfalls of nearby Talbot Bay, has to drain in and out four times a day. The area is pristine wilderness, although the Western Australian Government did some tidal-powered hydro-electricity experiments at the entrance during the 1960s. We couldn't see any traces of this, so they must have been modest. One surmises that an immediate problem would have been what to do with the power if they did generate it, so far from any sizeable population centre or industry.

The powerful twin-outboards on *Explorer* pushed us through the narrow opening of Walcott Inlet into the more serene backwaters. It was just as well we were on 'ship's time' as the sun was low on the horizon, shining dimly through the thick smoke haze and making the ramparts of

Kimberley sandstone even more blood red than usual. Someone spotted a sea eagle's nest in a dead tree near the shore, and Mark stopped the engines while we floated in silence. There must have been young in the nest because the two parent birds were fishing. As we watched, one of these great birds swooped down, only a hundred metres from us, and snatched a fish with its great talons from just beneath the surface of the dark, marbled waters. Forty-eight expeditioners sat speechless at this rare glimpse of a scene wildlife film makers would trade their eye teeth for. And this was only our second day of Kimberley coasting.

four

Kimberley Kaleidoscope

We woke early to warm darkness and joined our fellow passengers for an early breakfast as the high cliffs of Steep Island were gradually revealed in the growing light. The island looks like a loaf of bread thrown out into the bay. We were anchored just off Raft Point, between Steep Island and the red cliffs of the mainland which are fringed by green mangroves, bordering a small semi-circular beach. The vista brought to life a slide Mike Cusack had shown us the night before while talking about the early Aboriginal occupation of the area. The fragrant aroma of bacon and eggs reminded us of another association with tucker at this beautiful place. Apparently Steep Island was used as a place of initiation for boys. Their mothers and relatives used to feed them by putting food on wooden rafts and pushing them out for tides and currents to take to the island.

The early start was needed to take advantage of the cool part of the morning for our climb up behind the beach at Raft Point into the hills to see a superb rock gallery of Aboriginal paintings, not often visited because of its isolated location. The climb was steep, up a roughly delineated track winding through stunted gums struggling for survival in the stony Kimberley ground, but providing weird and wonderful sculptured shapes. An occasional boab tree added to the surreal surrounds with its bloated bottle-shaped trunk and bare upper branches clawing at the sky. There wasn't much chatter among the climbers as most of us were fighting for breath. Everyone was determined to get to the caves, high on the ridge above us. Already certain individuals were emerging as climbing enthusiasts. Alex Awramenko was not only a fanatical fisherman but a super-fit walker who bounded up the sharp slope on his long legs as though rocket assisted. He had worked out that there might be more fishing time on the beach while the slower members of the party worked their way up and down from the caves. Neil Tuffley, an older man but admirably fit and agile, was not far behind him. Accredited mountaineer Greg Mortimer moved along the line of climbers, miraculously on hand to lend a steadying arm to older and inexperienced walkers at crucial moments. He wasn't even puffing, despite doing the equivalent of the climb three times.

Pushing through the scrub and long grass we approached an overhang and were completely unprepared for the magnificence of the gallery that was suddenly revealed on the roof and walls of a large cave about four metres up the cliff face. A shiver ran up my spine as I saw for the first time, other than in photographs, the great white Wandjina spirit figures outlined in red ochre, drawn on the rock surfaces two and three times larger than human scale. The heads of the Wandjina figures are surrounded by added rings of white ochre which were said by the controversial Swiss-born author Erich von Daniken in *Chariots of the Gods* to represent space helmets and therefore to be clear evidence of earthly visits by aliens. Had he bothered to ask the Kimberley Aborigines (or research what anthropologists and rock art experts have written about their beliefs) he might have spared us his UFO-related nonsense. Aborigines believed the Wandjinas were ancestral beings, makers of the land, sea and human beings, and also spirits of the clouds. They controlled the weather, hence the halo of clouds around their heads. When each Wandjina came to the end of his time on earth, Kimberley Aborigines believed, he was transformed into a painting which also embodied his actual spirit.

To be in the presence of the Wandjinas, in a setting like Raft Point, was a profoundly moving experience. People in our party instinctively spoke in hushed voices as they might have done if they'd been in a cathedral or church, which in Aboriginal terms, we were.

Wandjina faces have eyes and noses, but no mouths. Aboriginal mythology provided a perfectly reasonable explanation for this. Wandjinas embody the rain as well as thunder and lightning. If they had mouths they would release unrelenting rain on to the land. In essence the Wandjinas are all powerful, controlling the fertility of humans, animals and the regeneration of all life through their mastery of the seasons, storms and the spirit world.

Some of the Wandjinas in the cave had bodies, others were just heads—a common depiction I was to find out as we visited more rock art sites. They were also surrounded by animals, big dugong-like creatures but with Wandjina-style heads, and fish. We also saw what appeared to be older drawings, in darker red, depicting slender human figures or squid-like creatures which in many instances had been painted over by the artists who had created the spectacular

Wandjinas. It was my first glimpse of the mysterious 'Bradshaw' paintings, considerably older than the Wandjina art, and named after the explorer Joseph Bradshaw who first discovered them in 1891. Both Wandjina and Bradshaw rock paintings are unique to the Kimberley, but utterly different in style and appearance.

The antiquity of the Bradshaw paintings is still in dispute, but the analysis of the mud of a wasp's nest built over one of them gives the painting a minimum age of 17 000 years! I found the Bradshaws utterly captivating, and was from that moment determined to find out more about them. We were going to areas of the Kimberley by *Coral Princess* and later by road with Penelope and The Manor where there were prime rock art sites to be seen—if we could find them. Ros came to wonder at the persistence of my Bradshaw obsession as the trip progressed, but humoured me as she generally does.

The whole concept of the human presence on the Australian mainland is extraordinary. When we think of past civilisations like that of ancient Egypt, 3000 years seems a long while ago. But the distinguished archaeologist Dr Josephine Flood has an arresting image and metaphor for the human presence in Australia, generally agreed to be at least 40 000 years and arguably longer. She says that if you think of a clock face and consider human habitation on this continent as being represented by an hour, then the European presence in Australia is merely the last half-minute of the hour.

All of which made the cave at Raft Point a very special place. Greg Mortimer, delighting in our enthusiasm, reminded us this was only the first of many fabulous rock painting sites we would visit. Some of the images were difficult to make out. Fellow journalist Mike Richardson's speculation that one sequence of Bradshaw drawings represented a squid chasing a goanna received serious consideration for about half a nanosecond.

We would have been back on board in time for lunch had not a couple of humpback whales appeared just off the point, breaching, blowing and diving as *Explorer* circled them, to our collective joy. The excellence of chef Adam's spaghetti bolognaise was almost compromised by the thoughtlessness of these humpbacks turning up when they did. Our theme of Wandjina dreaming continued in the afternoon when we landed on another beach nearby where there were rows of incredible stone pillars from two to four metres high, sculptured by wind and tide into all manner of fantastic and undeniably phallic shapes. The Aborigines believed they were formed by the Wandjina spirits who created stone representations of themselves.

Ros and I were talking to Mike Cusack about the year he spent in the wilderness with his wife, Susan, near the deserted Kunmunya Mission in 1987–88. We were getting closer to that part of the coast, and when we got to the feature named 'The Gutter' (where Mike and Susan moored their aluminium dinghy and outboard) some of the more intrepid walkers on board were to walk into Kunmunya where the Cusacks built their house. Mike described the round trip of eight kilometres and the very difficult terrain. Susan later called it more like 'a military obstacle course' in the book *Our Year in the Wilderness* they wrote together. Sadly, the dwelling they so painstakingly built was no longer there, burned out by one of the Kimberley dry season fires, started either by a lightning strike, Aborigines burning off, or pastoralists.

The idea of finding a couple to spend a year in the wilderness, existing on their own with no outside help or resources, living off the land as best they could, was the brainchild of the Australian adventurer and businessman Dick Smith. The peripatetic multi-millionaire devised his 'Couple in the Wilderness Scheme' influenced by a similar undertaking in Alaska and by his boyhood fascination with the story of Robinson Crusoe.

In a *Sydney Morning Herald* article in June 1987, Smith said of the Kimberley: 'Aboriginal man lived there in total harmony for 20 000 years. My quest is to see whether a white, modern Australian couple can live there for one year.

'I will be interested to see if they make it—if they don't that is a story in itself.' (Quite so, Dick!)

At the time Mike was the Ranger-in-Charge of Ferntree Gully National Park in Victoria, and Susan a naturopath. They had been married for thirteen years, but what they didn't tell Dick Smith or the Australian Geographic selection committee was that their relationship was a bit rocky at the time—in fact, they had been separated for four years! They reasoned that a year living in isolation would sort them out one way or another! (It did. They are still together and now have two children.)

Most of their one-and-a-half tonnes of camping gear, general supplies and dried food were transported by the barge *White Shadow* from Derby (a good deal of which was later painfully carted on their backs up the 'military obstacle course') while they cursed the heat and the flies and, on regular occasions through their survival year, Dick Smith, for choosing their camp site from his helicopter so quickly.

Mike and Susan had travelled on the barge with their gear, and on one hectic June morning at breakfast time,

Smith and Howard Whelan (editor of *Australian Geographic*) descended on them and whisked them away to the ruins of the old Presbyterian mission at Kunmunya that was abandoned in 1951 after 35 years on that site. At its peak it supported 300 people, and cultivated three hectares of vegetable gardens. The country was open with some light scrub, the grass burnt brown by the dry season. A watercourse and billabong surrounded by paperbarks seemed to indicate a suitable camp site, although Mike noticed that a rocky bar over the creek had barely a trickle of water running over it even though the wet season had not long ended. There wasn't much opportunity to look elsewhere because Dick Smith had to fly back to Sydney that afternoon to catch an overseas flight to Nairobi the following day. More attractive camp sites right on the coast could not be considered because isolation was an essential ingredient to the survival exercise, and visitors would inevitably drop in by boat.

What Smith and the Cusacks had no way of knowing was that an unusual failure of the wet season would quickly dry out the billabong (and the creek) and leave them in grave danger of serious dehydration as they fought with the local fauna over the soaks they dug in the creek bed to get any water at all for the first six months.

In the little time available, Smith did manage to fly most (but not all) of their heavy gear over the range from 'The Gutter', where Mike and Susan planned to moor their aluminium boat, and where someone on *White Shadow* had already spotted a salt water crocodile lurking—at four metres it was as long as their dinghy.

Mike told me (when we visited 'The Gutter' in *Explorer*) that he had to keep that resident croc in mind every time he went to use the boat. He went at different times of the day, and approached from different angles. Salties are very cunning, and study patterns of behaviour of a potential dinner. Mike and Susan carried firearms with them whenever they were away from camp, and had a stainless steel Winchester five-shot pump action shotgun for boat work. They had to use it once, 'in anger' when they were stalked by a big croc in the Lushington Valley, a watercourse running in from St George Basin. 'We had to shoot it near its tail to scare it off.'

On one memorable occasion, when he and Susan were down at 'The Gutter' taking the outboard off the dinghy for servicing, Mike was surprised, to say the least, by being attacked on dry land by a big bronze whaler shark.

'I was cross about that. The boat was just sitting on the waterline and I was carrying the 25 horsepower Evinrude engine when there was this great green swirl in the water. Susan was standing by with the shotgun and thought it was a croc, dropped the gun and ran and left me just holding the outboard. This bronze whaler came up out of the water to the gills, lunged and then spun around and took off. Had I been in the water I would have expected to be fair game, but on land! I was very indignant about the whole thing.'

'Apart from crocodiles and sharks, were there any other life-threatening nasties to look out for?' I asked.

'Ticks can actually kill you. There have been reported cases in the Kimberley of people dying because ticks have got themselves into some extremely difficult places, I suppose, and people have got toxemia or septicemia and died.

'There are centipedes around twelve centimetres long. The male has got little poison spines on its hind legs and can give a very nasty nip. We had scorpions as well, and particularly nasty looking hairy black spiders that seemed to like Susan and that are quite poisonous I believe.'

'You haven't mentioned snakes.'

'There are snakes in most places. But we had, amongst the repertoire, the Red-Bellied Black, the King Brown, the Taipan—which had finally made its way from Queensland—and the Death Adder. So there are at least four of the most deadly terrestrial snakes around Kunmunya.'

'Was either of you ever bitten by a snake?'

'Fortunately no. I think the record from strike-to-death for a King Brown is ten minutes. The woman who suffered that fate was actually bitten on the neck and it was almost a straight line to the heart, so she had very little chance. For us, realistically, help was a lot further away than it would take the venom to do its mortal thing.'

And the Kimberley looks so benign at this time of the year! Ros and I determined to keep a more wary eye out for snakes during our on-shore walks.

It was late in the afternoon when our excursion boat *Explorer* nosed its blunt bow gently onto the yellow sands of Careening Bay, where the explorer and maritime surveyor Phillip Parker King called by in 1820 to clean the hull of his badly leaking cutter *Mermaid*. A fascinating living relic of that visit is a big, double trunked boab tree behind the beach. King's party cut an inscription into this boab tree, and left an engraved plate nailed to another tree. The botanist on board, Allan Cunningham, thought at the time that the engraved plate would last a lot longer than the inscription on the 'Capparis' (boab) tree, but he was wrong. When they returned to the same spot a year later the plate had been rejected by the tree and covered in gum, while the inscription was as clear as when they left it—and still is. If anything, it is bigger, as the slow growth of the tree has enlarged the original letters. 'HBMC (His Brittanic Majesty's Cutter) MERMAID 1820' was clearly seen, highlighted by the late afternoon sun as the rattle and crash of expensive camera shutters—reminiscent of distant gunfire on the Western Front—captured images of this living historical treasure.

Walking along the beach to its western end I saw a young boab tree with fresh graffiti slashed into its bulbous trunk. Expecting to find the usual mindless name and date of some forgettable passing yachty or tourist, I was shocked and then angered to see that some mentally challenged crew members of an Australian navy ship had found it necessary to carve 'HMAS CESSNOCK 1992' into the tree. Perhaps when this is published a full naval inquiry and courts martial can be instigated. Bloody idiots!

The British settlement at Port Jackson was in its third decade before the powers that be got around to charting and surveying the north-western coast of the continent in any detail. Baudin, as we know, swept around the coast in 1801 scattering French names for posterity but not landing anywhere. Matthew Flinders also passed by during his circumnavigation of the Australian continent in 1802–03. But he had a better reason than Baudin for not coming close to the coast.

The British Admiralty had given Flinders a dud ship. The timbers of *Investigator* were rotten under its copper sheathing. Flinders realised this when he began to chart the southern coast of Australia. That is why he made such a thorough job of the southern part of the coastline, because he knew he'd be lucky to get his ship around the continent in one piece, let alone do much useful work the longer the voyage went on. (Flinders had a party trick of demonstrating the decay in his ship's timbers by poking his walking stick right through rotten patches in the hull.) He was forced by circumstance to give the treacherous Kimberley coastline a wider berth than his map-making skills deserved.

The man who got the job of first surveying the difficult northern and north-western coastlines of Australia was Phillip Parker King, the Australian-born, 26-year-old son of the Governor of New South Wales. The Lords of the Admiralty, in official instructions, were particularly anxious that he investigate 'any river on that part of the coast likely to lead to an interior navigation into this great continent'. The search for the inland sea was to remain a priority well into the nineteenth century. King was also given an exhaustive list of other things to report on ranging from climate, geology, fauna and flora to native tribes. It was a daunting task, and it took him four voyages to do it from 1817 to 1821. Strangely, history has not rewarded King with just dues. Marsden Hordern, who has written the definitive account of his voyages charting the northern and north-western coastlines of Australia, *King of the Australian Coast*, puts King's navigation, ship management and mapping skills up there with James Cook and Matthew Flinders.

He did . . . share with Cook and Flinders the quality of exactitude, and could equally have been the subject of Professor Ernest Scott's tribute to Flinders: '. . . it is his special virtue to have set down his facts with such exactitude . . . he never succumbs to the common sin of travellers—writing to excite astonishment in the reader, rather than to tell the exact truth as he found it. He was by nature and training an exact man.'

Yet Phillip Parker King, the modest, efficient achiever, has not received the accolades his work merited. Perhaps if he had been a flogger, or a drunk, or been the architect of a spectacular maritime disaster, he might have been better known!

His first ship was the 84-tonne cutter, *Mermaid*, which had to be obtained from the slender shipping resources of Port Jackson in those early days. *Mermaid* first surveyed around North-West Cape and Bathurst and Melville Islands—north of the present Darwin. The following year King went back up the east coast and around to Bathurst Island, and then south-east into the Joseph Bonaparte Gulf and Cambridge Gulf, noting that 'the character of the country here is entirely changed'. They went up the west arm of Cambridge Gulf as far as The Gut, and saw much evidence of Aboriginal occupation, but not the much needed fresh water. King went on to the 'labyrinth of islands and shoals' between Cape Londonderry and Cape Voltaire. In Admiralty Gulf provisions were short, his crew was sick, and as he still hadn't managed to find any water, he made for Timor.

During the third voyage, again in *Mermaid*, he reached the sector of the Kimberley coastline we were visiting in *Coral Princess*. King returned to Cape Voltaire from Timor to pick up his survey, and moved on to explore Prince Frederick Harbour where the 'indefatigable' botanist on board, Allan Cunningham, had a field day—or many of them. A worsening leak forced King to career his ship where we had seen his inscribed boab tree. To his horror, he discovered that not only was there massive damage to the keel and planking near the rudder, but that the whole ship was 'nail sick' under its copper sheathing. The original builders had used iron nails instead of copper, which had now rusted through. There was no option but to begin the long return journey to Port Jackson in New South Wales—if the rotting *Mermaid* did not sink underneath them. Even after careening and repairs, the cutter was still taking six inches (15 centimetres) of water an hour, and the pumps had to be manned continually.

On their way back, King diverted briefly to explore the mangrove-bordered Prince Regent River and rowed 32 kilometres up river in a whale boat, passing the spectacular waterfalls later named King's Cascades.

The Prince Regent River is one of the most spectacular geographical features of the Kimberley where a huge sandstone fissure is slashed into the hinterland in a straight line for 100 kilometres of navigable water. We would see that in three days' time. In the meantime we would split into two groups. 'The Intrepids' would walk with Mike Cusack from 'The Gutter' over the sandstone ranges to the deserted Kunmunya Mission and the remains of his and Susan's camp, and back. Those not seeking feats of strength and endurance had the alternative of visiting the remains of the failed settlement at Camden Harbour, first (and briefly) occupied by Europeans in 1864.

I don't mind a good walk, but there was no way I was going to miss out on seeing Camden Harbour, where we would see physical evidence of the most tragic, disastrous and ill-planned farming settlement project of the last two hundred years of Australian settlement.

It was all the fault of Lieutenant George Grey really, who wrote up Camden Harbour and its environs in terms that signalled a fertile land flowing with milk and honey. Hot rocks and spinifex would have been a more accurate assessment. Grey's enthusiasm and hyperbole about Camden

Harbour initiated the next phase of the exploration of the Kimberley coast.

Phillip Parker King had made a major breakthrough in advancing European knowledge of the coastline of north-western Australia, but had not located any major rivers. The dream of finding great rivers sourced by an inland sea persisted and, sixteen years later in 1837, the sloop *Beagle* (which Charles Darwin had used in his famous voyages) was sent to the north-west under the command of Captain John Wickham. On board were Lieutenants Stokes, Grey and Lushington. At Cape Town, Grey and Lushington chartered another vessel, *Lynher*, and made directly for Hanover Bay at the entrance of the Prince Regent River.

Lord Glenelg, the Colonial Secretary—was he the only colonial secretary to have his name as a palindrome?—had instructed the 26-year-old George Grey to explore the country south from the Prince Regent River. Grey, young and enthusiastic, nearly killed himself and his companions several times through over-eagerness. On his first effort he tried to walk overland to Hanover Bay with Lushington and four others and they were immediately overwhelmed by the rugged country, heat, and lack of water, almost failing to make it back to their ship. They had been away only 24 hours.

However, it wasn't long before Grey was off again, trying to move heavily laden ponies through the narrow gorges in the wet season. It was February. Progress was slow, and they were being shadowed by the Worora people, a large number of whom on 11 February ambushed and attacked Grey and his two companions. It was a very serious affair, and the Europeans were greatly outnumbered.

Grey was struck simultaneously by three spears; one wounded him deeply in the thigh and knocked him to the ground. But he was a cool customer, George Grey. In his journal this is is how he described what happened:

> I had not made two steps in advance when three spears struck me nearly at the same moment . . . I felt severely wounded in the hip, but knew not exactly where the others had struck me. The force of all knocked me down, and made me very giddy and faint, but as I fell, I heard the savage yells of the natives' delight and triumph; these recalled me to myself, and roused by momentary rage and indignation, I made a strong effort, rallied, and in a moment was on my legs; the spear was wrenched from my wound and my haversack drawn closely over it, that neither my own party nor the natives might see it and I advanced again . . .

Certain that they would all be killed, Grey shot dead one of the leaders of the ambush who had speared him, and was threatening him with a club. The battle stopped and the Aborigines carried away their mortally wounded companion, wailing with distress. Grey, in agony himself, allowed them to carry away his assailant without firing again. Under the circumstances, his humanity was remarkable. He wrote in his journal:

> To have fired upon the other natives, when they returned for the wounded man, would, in my belief have been an unnecessary piece of barbarity. I always felt deeply the death of him I had been compelled to shoot: and I believe that when a fellow creature falls by one's hand, even in a single combat rendered unavoidable in self defence, it is impossible not sincerely to regret the force of so cruel a necessity.

Returning gravely ill and in great pain to his camp, he sent a party back to *Lynher* for provisions. In a bad way, he had an abscess in his spear wound and felt he was dying. Two weeks later, he was still upset at having had to shoot one of his attackers. Aware of his distress, one of the sailors from his ship, Ruston by name, sat beside his wounded leader to cheer him up. He said to Grey: 'Well Sir, I'm sure if I were you, I shouldn't think nothing at all of having shot that there black fellow; why, Sir, they're very thick and plentiful up the country.' Grey wrote in his journal that he did not exactly see the consolation to be derived from this argument, but could not forbear smiling at its quaintness, and feeling grateful for the kindness with which it was intended.

A lesser man would have returned to his ship, but while Grey was recovering from his wounds, his companion Lushington explored further afield and discovered 'a tract of country of great fertility'. Only fourteen of their ponies were left from the original 26, but Grey pressed on for two more months with his explorations. Puzzled about why his horses were dying, he cut open the stomach of one to find it full of sand, and conjectured that they had eaten it while feeding on the scant vegetation. It was at this time that he made his famous Aboriginal rock art discoveries. Grey also discovered the headwaters of the Glenelg River, and by climbing to the tops of hills caught glimpses of what might be fine farming country, navigable rivers and fine harbours. But his health was bad, his party running out of food, and he got back to Hanover Bay to find both *Beagle* and *Lynher* waiting at anchor.

Still suffering from his wounds and half starved, Grey learned that Lieutenant Stokes had gone off on explorations of his own with two open boats. He had not found the entrance to the Glenelg River, but got very close. One of his assistants reported that he had not been able to sail completely around an island in a bay which may have concealed the entrance to a river. The cautious Stokes named the area Doubtful Bay, which was just as well, because the island did in fact conceal the mouth of the Glenelg.

Stokes had some terrifying experiences in King Sound with the tidal rushes and one of his crew described voyaging there as 'mangroves mud and misery'. Point Torment is named after varied horrendous experiences with mosquitoes, although the voracious pests actually did one of his officers a service. Lost without water in the mud of the mangroves near Point Torment, slipping about and exhausted, he fell down in a faint. He was instantly attacked by hordes of mozzies and their vicious stings goaded him back on to his feet. The exhausted man was forced to continue beyond normal endurance, and was eventually seen by those on the ship. So the mosquitoes saved his life!

At Point Escape—some of the names for Kimberley features were provided ready made—Stokes, then exploring the mouth of the Fitzroy River with two small boats, had a frightening night battle with the tidal surge roaring out to sea. Having survived that, he seemed to be a slow learner because he went on a shooting expedition with two companions on the tidal flats away from the boats. The incoming tide was remorseless. One of the party, a sailor named Ask, couldn't swim. They were up to their chests in rising water when Stokes attracted the attention of the yawl by firing his gun. But the longboats couldn't get to them

against the tide. The third man, Helpman, was able to swim
to the boat. Stokes stayed with Ask, whispering encour-
agement to him as the waters rose to his neck. Ask didn't
panic, which was just as well, because the water had risen
as far as his nose when the whaler reached them.

Captain John Wickham, in *Beagle*, had been more
successful than Stokes in discovering rivers. *Beagle* reached
Roebuck Bay in mid-January and surveyed the coast from
there to Point George IV before meeting up with Grey in
April. Putting up with swarms of attacking mosquitoes (he
was the one who named Point Torment in King Sound) his
sailors braved the tidal rips of the Sound to discover the
Fitzroy River—managing, despite the tides and rips, to
push a gig and a whaleboat 36 kilometres inland. Although
delighted with their find the sailors noted debris in trees
seven metres above the water and surmised correctly that
heavy floods sometimes swept the countryside.

Stokes, from his open boat, also explored Camden
Sound and reported very favourably on the area—too
favourably as it happened: enthusiastically endorsed by
Grey at the time, the reports influenced a disastrous
attempt to settle the area a quarter of a century later.

The last thing Grey did before leaving the Camden
Sound area was to plant coconut palms, bread fruit, pump-
kins and other exotic plants. He wrote in his journal that he
would 'very gladly have passed a year or two of his life in
watching over them'. But his seeds of empire at Camden
Sound were destined not to bear fruit. With the coastal
exploration largely completed, the next challenge was to
explore and develop the inland riches—pastoral and
mineral—thought to be waiting in the Kimberley.

It's worth noting that the Kimberley was the last place

in Australia to be colonised by Europeans. The earliest continuous white settlement did not take place until the late nineteenth century, and in some pastoral areas, not till the 1920s.

The disastrous, ill-planned and ill-researched effort to settle the country around Camden Harbour is a telling example of the difficulties of coming to terms with the complications of farming the far north, and particularly the Kimberley. In 1864—more than a decade before the surveyor Alexander Forrest led his expedition inland to discover the useful grazing country in the Fitzroy River Basin and across to the upper reaches of the Ord River— settlers were attracted to unknown territory because of liberal new land laws that came into effect in Western Australia early in 1863. This allowed anyone taking stock north of the Murchison River to occupy land there rent free for the first four years. Those who decided to take up this offer in the Kimberley looked towards the areas and harbours explored by George Grey in 1838—and Camden Harbour was where he had planted his pumpkin vines and other seeds and written lyrically about its potential for European settlement.

The land offer looked too good to be true. It was. The Camden Harbour Pastoral Association Ltd was formed in Melbourne with capital of £20000 and with the object of 'settling the very superior well-watered pastoral and agri- cultural country round Camden Harbour by placing one head of cattle on every 1000 acres'. Think about that for a moment—with that £20000 the promoters expected to secure 4 million acres of land and 4000 breeding cattle to stock it. Each share entitled the holder to a passage to Camden Harbour, rations for twelve months, a lease of

20 000 acres for twelve years—the first four rent free—and twenty head of cattle.

The first shareholders left Melbourne in November 1864 and arrived at Camden Harbour in December—the hottest time of the year with temperatures over 50°C. And remember, they'd just come from cool temperate Victoria. *Stag* was the first ship to arrive, twelve days before Christmas. Those on board expecting to see rolling acres of verdant pasture did not. They saw a muddy, mangrove lined coast which provided the only green. The grass was parched and dry, thinly disguising the rocky ground. And there was no water. Three horses were drowned getting ashore. The second of the three ships, *Helvetia*, arrived the next day. She had lost 60 sheep out of the 1600 carried. One man, an Italian, had been lost overboard in a gale, the first of a growing list of casualties.

The third ship, *Calliance*, struck a reef on the way, and to get off had to jettison large quantities of stores and hay for the animals. She arrived at Camden Harbour on Christmas Day. A settler noted briefly in his diary: 'Landing very bad.' Relatives back in Victoria could have no idea of the efforts of getting sheep and horses out of stinking holds and across mud flats where you could sink up to your waist, and a horse could get stuck and die—as happened to some.

Not long after *Calliance* arrived she was blown on to another reef and became a total wreck. Her captain was killed trying to get help.

Some of the settlers got stuck into shifting supplies, pitching camp and pushing inland to find some useful country among the hot stones. Others just wandered around in a bewildered state. Not understanding the big tides, the sailors had left unloaded supplies on what they thought was the high tide mark. The Government Resident, Robert Sholl, later reported: 'Hay, bran, biscuits and bacon were carried away by the high tides and left rotting on the sea shore. Necessity eventually taught them to make other arrangements but not until they had sustained heavy losses and received much discouragement.'

The sheep began to die by the hundreds. Weakened by the voyage, they came out of the holds into high temperatures and tried to graze on hot rocks which burned their feet. Most of the edible grass was on steep rocky slopes which they could not reach. Some kind of poisonous weed killed many of them, and dingos slaughtered other weakened sheep indiscriminately. Fresh water for settlers and stock was found after three days, but five kilometres away, approachable through a mangrove creek and then only at high tide. Boats were sent to Augustus Island for water but Aborigines there drove them off.

It's interesting that the presence of the Aborigines is hardly mentioned in contemporary accounts. They were thought of as part of the fauna, and there appears to have been little if any awareness that the settlers were usurping their land. No attempts were made to contact them and ask about basics like fresh water. Considering the scale of the European intrusion into their tribal territory, there was remarkably little conflict. Within two weeks of arrival, four settlers were attacked by a group of Aborigines who speared one settler—fortunately only through his trousers—and were scared off by gunfire. Later clashes were more serious.

The climate was a greater threat than the blacks. Two days after arrival, Vernon, a passenger on *Helvetia*, died of sunstroke and was buried quietly on a spinifex-covered island in the harbour the settlers named Sheep Island. His was the first grave to be dug under the shade of a clump of boabs there, and he was not the only one to die of sunstroke. The temperature in full sun on hot rocks was an incredible 57°C (136°F) for anyone foolish enough to be out in it. Clearly some were. Daily temperatures in the shade often got up to 52°C. Fever and blistering heat killed three settlers in the first three days.

As the weeks went on, more horses and sheep died. Those who struggled inland did find patches of promising country of 1000 to 3000 acres, but with no realistic way of reaching them over rocky country. The heat was unbearable. Sadly there are few contemporary descriptions of how these gentrified farmers from Victoria toiled in this tropical wilderness. The government were represented by R. J. Sholl, his son was a clerk, and there was a surveyor, a surgeon, a customs officer and three policemen. Sholl's reports were anything but complimentary about the way the Camden Harbour Pastoral Association was handling things on the spot. There was no leader and stock were dying partly through ignorance and neglect. As to the country, Sholl noted, it consisted 'mostly of grass covered stones'.

Settlers continued to die and the whole disaster was over within nine months. By January and February 1865, 72 settlers had left, and the Governor of Western Australia, Governor Hampton, instructed the Government Resident Sholl to assist the rest to get away if they could not finance their own passages. Some, though, struggled on until midyear. Mary Jane Pascoe died in childbirth, followed quickly by her newly born daughter. Her grave, with an inscribed headstone organised by her husband, was the best the few remaining settlers could provide. It can still be seen on Sheep Island. The other graves are unmarked.

Some of the bolder spirits petitioned the Governor to exchange their Camden Harbour land for selections in the Nickol Bay district (near where the town of Dampier now is on the west coast) and as a result some 300 000 acres were added to land already selected in that area. You'd have to give them full marks for their pioneering spirit.

I was intrigued to find out what remained of the very short attempt to settle this unforgiving area. While the intrepids amongst us joined Mike Cusack (who was battling the flu as he led his flock to Kunmunya) the rest of us settled back in our seats in *Explorer* on a simply gorgeous morning. We roared over a calm sea at 25 knots on the high tide past Sheep Island and picked our way carefully across slippery stones among the mangroves fringing the Camden settlement site. At 25° Celsius our landing was a lot more comfortable than the 50° plus temperatures that the pioneer pastoralists endured in December 1864.

We fanned out across the rocky terrain which was covered with dried grass that stood head high in some places and made it difficult to find the remains of buildings. It seems almost incredible that buildings of any substance were built at all in such a short time, but we found the corners of several stone structures—probably Robert Sholl's house, or the bond store, or perhaps the surgeon's residence. The stonework was beautifully done, shaped carefully without any mortar, yet with straight vertical edges at the corners of the building. There were no more than a few metres of wall left at any one point, but we did find shards of pottery and glass on the ground which we left with other collections gleaned by previous visitors.

I photographed Amanda Richardson (who would have won the award for the most fashionably dressed expeditioner at all times had we thought to arrange one) standing beside the remains of one of the stone buildings. Her journalist husband Mike was as fascinated by it all as I was and we struggled through tall scratchy dry grass trying to imagine what it must have been like 135 years before. Perhaps the women, from genteel Victoria, had come ashore attired in long black dresses and toques, but neither Mike nor I could find any reference in the literature describing how the original settlers were dressed.

The most poignant reminder of the Camden Harbour fiasco was Mary Jane Pascoe's grave, on Sheep Island, several kilometres offshore from the settlement. We had to approach cautiously as our Voyage Leader No. 3 Mark Buckingham—a regular visitor—said there was a resident salt water crocodile in the area. Mark nobly volunteered to act as croc bait and strode up the short steep beach to see if the coast was clear. It was, and we gathered around the grave and headstone of Mary Jane and her newly born daughter behind the stark trunk and leafless branches of the big boab tree that marked the spot. Mike Richardson carefully noted down the weathered words on the headstone in his notebook: 'In memory of Mary Jane Pascoe who died June 4, 1865, aged thirty years.' On the boab tree itself was a metal plaque, inscribed: 'To the memory of P. C. Walter Gee, died September 1865, aged 29 years, speared by natives while on duty with Sholl Expedition.'

We motored around to 'The Gutter' to pick up the eleven intrepids and ailing Voyage Leader No. 2 Mike Cusack. His partner Susan had dubbed the worst sections of the route from the coast to Kunmunya up a rocky creek bed as 'Nightmare Alley', and many of the walkers found it tougher going than they had imagined, even though we were enjoying comparatively cool, dry season conditions. No. 2 Captain Jason and the ship's engineer Carl had joined No. 1 Voyage Leader Greg to tackle the walk, and we Camden Harbour visitors waited shamelessly in shade and comfort under *Explorer's* canopy while the walkers straggled in. Expeditioners Sharon Burke and her husband Doug were among the last to arrive, with Sharon quite distressed by the rigours of the walk, but gamely determined to finish unaided, which she did.

Alex Awramenko had chosen to lash the waters with his collection of rods rather than walk to Kunmunya. He had caught mainly sharks from the stern of *Coral Princess* which further cooled any desire we might have had to swim from the vessel in the deceptively innocent looking blue-green tropical water. At night, with the floodlights pointed at the water just near the stern, sharks large and small could be seen or, as Greg Mortimer said wonderingly later, 'layers of sharks', as far as the light penetrated into the depths.

After dinner over a beer I had a chance to chat to Mike Cusack about revisiting the site of his and Susan's survival adventure. Although he had heard that the substantial hut he had built had burned down, he said he was surprised how many memories flooded back and how emotional he felt when he saw the blackened remains. Although the fickleness of the failed wet season had caused them real survival problems with lack of water—and might have forced an end to the year in isolation—there were many moments of great beauty and satisfaction to remember— like the little lizards and tree frogs that shared the house which Mike built just in time for the mini December wet season they eventually had. They became part of the family. Three particular tree frogs were nicknamed 'The

Tree Musketeers'. And in the last few months of their stay, when the weather steadied down, they were able to make ambitious forays in the aluminium dinghy, despite the fact that the outboard had been dunked in salt water three times in 'The Gutter' when king tides overturned their moored craft.

These exploratory trips, ranging as far as 50 kilometres around the coast, were exhilarating as they were camping on deserted beaches, barbecuing superb fresh fish caught during the day. They even got right around to the St George Basin into which the Prince Regent River runs from its spectacular 100 kilometre-long sandstone cleft in the Kimberley plateau.

Mike was looking forward to voyaging up the Prince Regent River to King's Cascades, which he had visited twice before. Despite the width of the river in its lower reaches, shoals and snags made it too dangerous to take *Coral Princess* all the way. We had to wait for the incoming tide to ride up in *Explorer* and two of the inflatable Zodiacs.

Mark Buckingham seemed to know every rock and submerged tree trunk as we roared up the Prince Regent River in *Explorer*, swerving from one side of the river to the other for a clear run. A benefit of getting so close to the banks was to see ospreys' and egrets' nests and their graceful occupants flying nearby. One of the great bonuses of this kind of travel in the Kimberley is the knowledge that absolutely nothing has altered since Europeans first visited this area. The river, and indeed the cascades, are unchanged from when they were first sighted by Phillip Parker King and his party in 1820. At that time he viewed the cascades, but did not need the water they provided. In 1821, however, when he returned with a new ship, the

170-ton brig *Bathurst*, there was no water to be found anywhere else at the height of the dry season.

Bathurst was too big to take up the river so they rowed a ship's boat. On July 25 they heard the very welcome sound of cascading water. King and his party had arrived at the top of the tide, and he decided to climb up the cascades to see if there was a big lake feeding them. He thought them only 12 metres high, but when he climbed up, found they were some 45 metres above the river and was disappointed to find them fed only by a small creek.

They had to water *Bathurst* by sending ship's boats up river to the cascades, and while this was going on, King decided to do some more exploring. But near St George's Basin his boat got caught in a dangerous rapid, and was nearly wrecked on the rocks. Not long afterwards, what they thought was a big floating log turned out to be a very large crocodile floating along as they do with just their eyes and nostrils out of the water. 'Very deceptious' King thought it, and fired a musket ball at point blank range which didn't seem to deter the salty one bit.

Back at the cascades King was also fascinated to see 'a curious species of mud fish' running about on the mud flats with open mouths, and managed to shoot three to study them. But he couldn't take them back to the ship as they would have well and truly gone off by then.

While we floated just clear of the pristine moss-clad waterfalls which were as King saw them in 1821, Mark told us of the terrible events that took place in this idyllic spot on 29 March 1987 when Ginger Faye Meadows, an attractive young American holidaying on a yacht, was taken by a salt water crocodile. In a bizarre twist, Ginger Meadows had been motivated to come to Australia after seeing the

Paul Hogan movie *Crocodile Dundee*. The charter boat she was on, *Lady G*, was having problems with its desalination plant and, like Phillip Parker King's expedition, had come to the cascades to take on fresh water.

A group of four, including Ginger, went into the base of the falls in a Haines Hunter speedboat which was tied to a tree root on the right hand side. The plan was to climb the falls to a billabong on top, but the climb was unexpectedly slippery and difficult. One of the four, Jane Burchett, was nervous about the climb, and thought the best thing to do was to swim to the speedboat and wait there. She did this, and Ginger Meadows called out to her to take a photograph of her near the falls. But the camera was out of film, and Jane was unfamiliar with the model. Ginger swam back to the boat to change the film, then suggested they swim to shore to the left hand side of the falls where the going looked easier, and do some exploring.

As they started to swim, Jane felt a strong sense of foreboding and told Ginger she didn't want to go on. At that moment the skipper of *Lady G*, Bruce Fitzpatrick, who had climbed up beside the cascades, spotted a large salt water crocodile heading towards the girls. He shouted to them to get out of the water. They tried to climb the slippery rocks under the falls. Jane screamed and took off one of her running shoes and threw it at the crocodile, which stopped momentarily. For reasons known only to herself, Ginger Meadows made a fatal error of judgment in the panic of the moment. A strong swimmer, the former model tried to race the crocodile to the bank, about 25 metres away. She didn't make it. The crocodile took her after only a few metres and they both disappeared.

The world's press went mad with the story—an attractive young American tourist eaten by a crocodile, publicity fanned by the success of Hogan's *Crocodile Dundee*. The rarity of such attacks can be gauged by the fact that it was only the second crocodile fatality in Western Australia in 150 years.

We sat in silence in *Explorer* for a minute or two.

Phillip Parker King's second visit to the cascades was in the dry season, and the crew of *Bathurst* saw clouds of smoke and then a raging bushfire—as the Worora Aborigines continued their dry season burning.

In early August they had a narrow escape at the outer entrance of the Prince Regent's River, when *Bathurst* was picked up by the furious tide and just carried along helplessly over and around shoals and rocks until they were finally swept out into a deep channel near the junction of Munster and Rothsay Waters. Eventually King anchored half a mile from the beach in Hanover Bay and prepared to go ashore for water and to drag a seine net along the beach for fish. They were closely watched from the bush by the Worora people.

The fishing went well, but contact with the Worora did not. King had hoped for a friendly meeting and rowed into shore with some modest presents—a clasp knife, some fish, and some rat-eaten ship's biscuits. To make the Aborigines feel at ease, he stood Bundell, an East Coast Aborigine travelling with them, in the front of the boat, naked. Picture this bizarre spectacle from the Worora perspective. They would have seen a boat full of white men in uniform with a strange nude Aboriginal at the prow being rowed towards them like some kind of anthropological trophy!

The meeting on the beach at first seemed to go well, both parties making signs of friendship as presents were handed over. The Worora people gave King a club and Bundell a belt of possum fur. Maybe they thought he needed some clothes. But as time went on the atmosphere soured, King decided to call it a day, and turned with his companions to go back to the boat. As they did so one of the Worora warriors hurled a four-metre spear through the air and struck the ship's surgeon, Montgomery, in the back with such force that it hung there quivering. Montgomery staggered, crying out, not surprisingly, 'Good God, I'm speared!'

He wrenched the spear from his back, drew his pistol and fired at the Aboriginals before collapsing on the beach. The rest of the party carried him to the boat and rowed quickly back to the ship. Fortunately the spear had missed any vital organs, although Montgomery gave orders that he should be bled from both arms. Curious medical thinking in those days. He surely needed all the blood he had left.

The officers angrily discussed the situation that evening and decided on a punitive expedition. One of the officers, John Roe, wrote in a letter to his father: 'Such was the consummate treachery of these brutes that they scarcely deserved to be ranked among the human race.' The next morning a cutter was sent ashore pretending to be on a peaceful mission. To their surprise the same men who had attacked on the previous day were walking down to the beach and laid down their spears as the boat came in. The marines in the boat took aim and fired at them, and the man who had speared Montgomery was wounded in the shoulder, but managed to escape into the bush. Going ashore the party managed to capture a large quantity of Aboriginal artefacts—spears, wicked stone spear heads with razor sharp points and serrated cutting edges, pigments, ochre, large shells for carrying water, fish hooks, threads made from human hair and other articles. Partly to punish the Worora people, and partly for scientific collections, all these artefacts were taken back to the ship.

Despite the unfortunate clash, King realised that the belligerence was part of perpetual warfare that had existed not only between rival Aboriginal groups, but with Malays arriving on the coast. In 1837 Lieutenant George Grey, following up King's Kimberley discoveries, was also attacked by the Worora people.

After the spearing of Montgomery—who recovered— King continued on with more routine surveying, charting the coastline from Camden Sound to Collier Bay, but strong tides and the lack of a second anchor forced him to postpone any close examination of the Buccaneer Archipelago until after a resupply voyage to Mauritius. He came back and got into what is now King George Sound, had several narrow escapes from strong tides rushing through narrow inlets, and then returned down the east coast to Port Jackson. But the Kimberley coast did not let them go before another frightening experience. While anchored near Cape Leveque, they were suddenly surrounded by whales which began leaping out of the water near the ship and thrashing their huge tails. This went on right through the night with the ship's company waiting fearfully for one tail to fall on the brig— which they rightly felt would have been disastrous.

The behaviour of humpback whales in the late twentieth century was certainly more benign as they obligingly spouted and dived for us on their summer excursion from

Antarctica, not displaying the slightest interest or concern. Unlike the crew of *Bathurst*, the only problem we faced on our various encounters with them in *Explorer* was being late for lunch after enjoying their impromptu display.

five

Into the Bungle Bungles

On Saturday 10 July we awoke to find *Coral Princess* swinging gently at anchor near Naturaliste Island in Prince Frederick Harbour—a timely reminder of the French and English rivalry about naming the unexplored Kimberley coast in the early nineteenth century. Baudin, who skirted the coast in 1801, named the island after one of his ships, and John Roe, Phillip Parker King's able Lieutenant on *Mermaid* who was given the privilege of naming the harbour in 1820, chose to honour the then Duke of York. Early risers enjoyed a superb tropical sunrise and, for the first time in our ten-day coastal cruise, we weren't going anywhere.

Greg Mortimer had arranged for a helicopter charter company to whisk some passengers from a beach landing area up over the escarpment to the spectacular Mitchell Falls, while the rest of us poked about sheltered inlets in *Explorer* and voyaged up the Hunter River enjoying brilliant reflections of red rock escarpments, boab trees and mangroves in the still, translucent water. Some chose to laze about on board or fish from the ship. Fanatical fisherman Alex Awramenko and his family elected to fly to the falls and in his absence Monica Smith landed a very handsome edible fish from a handline, making a welcome change from unwanted sharks. Her husband Dick Smith—not the founder of *Australian Geographic*—made it a family double by landing another. A three-metre salt water crocodile spotted swimming boldly out towards *Coral Princess* from the shore banished any lingering thoughts of even a quick dip from the ship. A beach barbecue that night—preceded by yet another postcard tropical sunset—and crab races rounded off a relaxed Kimberley coastal day.

I was particularly looking forward to our visit to Bigge Island, one of the larger islands in the Bonaparte Archipelago—and incidentally the furthest point from Broome on our voyage. Some of these larger off-shore islands sustain unique plants and animals that have developed in isolation from the mainland. Bigge Island has broad valleys with open shrubland and freshwater creeks lined with pandanus palms—as well as the ubiquitous spinifex grass and trademark coastal mangroves. Phillip Parker King (who must have been getting desperate for names on his surveys of the fractured Kimberley coast) named it after the formidable Commissioner of Inquiry, John Thomas Bigge, who had been sent out from London to New South Wales in 1819 to effectively put the cleaners through Governor Macquarie's administration. You can imagine how popular he was in Port Jackson, and he even came on board *Mermaid* in 1820 just before she sailed, as Lieutenant Roe said in his journal, 'prying' into their affairs. From most accounts the investigating John Thomas made a right prick of himself as far as the fledgling colony was concerned.

Bigge Island is uninhabited and has been so in living memory. Yet Aboriginal people certainly lived there in ancient times as we were about to discover. It is a treasure house of Aboriginal rock art galleries. As we voyaged up the eastern shore in *Explorer* we saw how the wind and tides had sculptured rock formations that resembled ancient Mayan ruins or crumbling Khmer temples. For our first landing, Mark Buckingham and Greg Mortimer led us to a massive overhang and cave formation with the biggest Wandjina spirit figure we had yet seen. Arched across the roof of the cave, its elongated body was at least three metres long. About 800 metres away, across a small spinifex dotted valley, we were treated to a second gallery where there were older, deep-ochre-coloured Bradshaw figures, their slender bodies and distinctive top-knot head dresses contrasting with the halo-headed Wandjinas without mouths, regarding us solemnly with their white wide eyes and long noses and sometimes painted over the older Bradshaws. As it is generally believed that the first humans to reach Australia did so through the Kimberley region, surely a properly conducted archaeological dig down through those cave floors with their layers of human habitation would yield valuable clues to the first occupation of this enigmatic coast. So much Australian pre-history remains unexplained.

To reach the second gallery we had walked across the narrow top of the island to the west coast, and were picked up by Mark in *Explorer* for a run further south to the jewel in the crown of Bigge Island—the galleries at Wary Bay.

Most Aboriginal rock art galleries are under stone overhangs, with paintings either on the roof or on protected inner walls. At Wary Bay, the fissures in the rock are vertical, allowing the visitor to walk straight inside with plenty of head room. Landing on a small curved white beach, we were astounded to see a cliff face indented with dozens of these vertical 'walk in' clefts in the rock. It was unlike anything I have seen before or since in any part of Australia where there are Aboriginal paintings or rock carvings. If visiting ancient rock art galleries can be likened to entering a church, this was the St Paul's Cathedral of Aboriginal galleries. As I walked into the first rock cleft, I was confronted by a huge Wandjina head with the usual white face, but staring green eyes. It seemed to be guarding the whole cliff face.

But Wary Bay also had other unique surprises. This is where there are paintings of pipe-smoking figures in coats, pantaloons and sea boots and wearing hats. There is a distinctly Dutch look about them. To one side, three of these pipe-smoking men are depicted in a small boat, its sides too tall to be a canoe, but which could be a ship's whale boat.

To complicate speculation about the origins of these pipe-smoking men, at their feet is a dog-like animal which Fred Westwood, a fellow Tasmanian, immediately claimed as a *Thylacine*, the extinct Tasmanian tiger which once roamed over the entire Australian continent. Its long jaw, tail and the clearly delineated stripes across its back seemed to support Fred's theory. On the other hand, might it have been the 'Dutchmen's' dog?

Two of the 'Dutchmen' were carrying containers, sharing the weight of one between them. Early European visitors to this part of the Australian coast were always looking for water, and may well have consulted the Aboriginal people in order to find it—well, so it seemed to me. Or were these 'European' figures transformed by the artists into Wandjinas? The curved shape of the headdresses would certainly support this theory. To say it was utterly fascinating is an understatement. Seeing these galleries was a privilege none of us there would ever forget. And, as usual with Kimberley galleries, it left us with more questions than answers.

Coral Princess had sailed around the top of Bigge Island to meet us. Voyaging back to the ship through bright sunshine, turquoise water and almost no wind, we were entertained yet again by great humpback whales diving and breaching—throwing their vast bodies into the air to crash back into the water—in an excess of (one presumes) sexual enthusiasm. Or perhaps they were just happy to be on holiday too, specially after the freezing waters of Antarctica.

Back on board the conversation naturally centred on the remarkable Aboriginal art we had just seen. Mike Cusack, who with Susan had explored many galleries during his wilderness year, was very knowledgeable about local Aboriginal culture. The couple had to get permission from the tribal elders to stay at Kunmunya and, towards the end of their stay, joined with some of the locals in hunting and fishing expeditions. Sadly, today there are none of the original Worora Aboriginal people—who gave Phillip Parker King and the early English explorers such a hard time—left on the coast.

Over a drink I talked with Mike about the legacy such a powerful experience of bush living and raw survival for a year left on his and Susan's life. Mike is not a man who finds it easy to talk about himself but he drew my attention to their collective summary on the final page of their co-authored book *Our Year in the Wilderness*.

Certainly we can say that Michael's teeth deteriorated rapidly and one fell out, that he's got more freckles and wrinkles and a few sun spots on his hands from constant exposure to intense sunlight, and that Susan still carries the polka dots of the tropical fungal growth that spread across her shoulders and back. Being fair skinned, we are probably predisposed to skin cancer and melanomas or something will no doubt develop. These are tangible, physical reminders of the year.

Other less physically personal changes were evident when they returned to Melbourne. Mike said that Susan adopted a:

simpler, practically austere lifestyle. She prefers the uncluttered look in our house; the need to display little pieces of memorabilia on all available bench tops, mantelpieces and shelves is no longer there and her vast collection remains in storage . . .

Probably more than anything else, our year in the wilderness has shown us the need for quality of life with dignity. Australia is a country that offers not only the space that permits two people to do what we did, but the personal freedom that gives them the chance to do it.

I suggested to Mike that visiting the Kimberley—even briefly as we *Coral Princess* passengers had done—had a similar impact on me as had visiting Antarctica. The experience of confronting nature on such an enormous scale is daunting, yet inspirational. Dr Phillip Law, the Australian Antarctic Division's first Director who led and participated in the post-war exploration of Greater Antarctica from 1949 till 1966, once told me that no one went to Antarctica without being deeply influenced by the experience. 'I think most who go to Antarctica for any length of time do go through some sort of personal re-assessment. A sense of feeling infinitesimally small in the face of the magnitude of nature.'

There is a tendency—perhaps triggered by the pristine vastness of Antarctica—to reflect philosophically on the way we inhabit this planet. I certainly did down south and found myself having similar thoughts on *Coral Princess* and during *Explorer* excursions in and around the ancient red rock ramparts of the Kimberley. Judging by the reflective awe in the faces of my companions from time to time, I sensed I was not alone in having these thoughts. It was a collective, unspoken realisation that experiencing this unique coast from the sea was one of those special journeys in life that we would re-live and reflect upon in later years.

Every sea voyage, combining a group of people most of whom have never met before, has its own dynamic. Living at close quarters, socialising, sharing meals and daily excursions with 28 fellow expeditioners soon forges new friendships. With our average age of 64.4, we were unlikely to experience the blazing but temporary emotional linkages that characterise cruise ships crammed with our children's generation, but we rubbed along pretty well nonetheless. The youthful men and women who crewed *Coral Princess* seemed to get on very well too. It was definitely a happy ship. As our bows were now turned towards Broome, there was an undercurrent of regret that the end of the voyage was looming—but not before some further Greg Mortimer-planned surprise adventures.

An impromptu night expedition in *Explorer* revealed the twists and turns of an unknown creek (with saurian eyes glinting from dark recesses in the mangroves), and we visited Montgomery Reef. Sure, we always knew we were going to the reef but since two huge tides, as always, controlled where we could go and when, this would be a far different experience to the benign coral cays of, say, the Barrier Reef on the east coast.

Montgomery Reef was named by Phillip Parker King after the irascible ship's surgeon of *Mermaid* who, contemporary diaries reveal, was not only an indifferent practitioner even by the standards of the day but whose abrasive and argumentative personality drove everyone to distraction in the small officers' mess. Perhaps King kept in mind that Montgomery Reef was drowned twice a day and would be forever! But perhaps I should not wish such petty thoughts on a fine commander and equable leader—who, the record shows, somehow managed to maintain cordial relations with his difficult doctor.

The surprise, for us, was the spectacular experience of visiting Montgomery Reef at low tide. The whole reef covers an area of 270 square kilometres. As the coral becomes exposed and the 10-metre tide begins to fall, water trapped in the inner areas begins to pour down the flanks of the reef and through deep channels forged over the years by this twice daily exodus. But the huge surface area of the reef and the vast amount of water to be disgorged mean that the contained sea water can never fully run off before the rising tide again pushes it back to flood the entire reef complex.

To approach the outer reef at low tide, up one of the major drainage channels, is to be surrounded by a plethora of waterfalls, rippling and cascading down the exposed coral with incredible force, and on an unimaginable scale. The whole experience was stunning. It was about 4 pm when we voyaged up one of the bigger channels, and the low sunlight gave an even more surreal impression of the tumbling ridges of outpouring water foaming over the exposed coral.

At a less hectic spot we were able to walk up on to the reef itself in ankle deep water, and view huge clams with their partly open shells—exposing the vivid yellow and black flesh of their digestive systems waiting for passing morsels of nutrient—as well as colourful soft and hard corals with occasional small fish and crabs darting amongst our sandshoed feet. As usual our octogenarians were sprinting ahead of most of us. The less sure on their feet were offered steadying staffs to lean on by *Coral Princess* crew members.

I had been wondering what was in the stainless steel container with a curved lid, carried on and off *Explorer* with some care and ceremony each time we voyaged away from our mother ship. If it contained cold drinks, we hadn't been getting any. Ros found out. Oxygen and a defibrillator in case of heart attacks, that's what! The same device saved the life of the media mogul Kerry Packer after his heart stopped and he fell off his polo pony some years ago. They are now popularly referred to as 'Packer Whackers'. I am happy to report that the container remained unopened for our entire journey.

Because of the obvious hazards of sharks and crocodiles, swimming opportunities had been scarce, but on the last full day of our Kimberley cruise we were bound for the ominously named Crocodile Creek for a final (?!) swim. The partly tidal pool is a popular spot for passing yachts and a tradition has grown up that people leave behind a buoy, lifebelt, oar, or carved pieces of driftwood inscribed with the names of a visiting boat's crew. The artefacts are hung beneath a steel and mesh shade cover that, we were told, was put there by the mining management for the workers of Cockatoo Island when the iron ore mine was in full production. Poor Ginger Meadows signed her name on a wooden plaque with the other crewmembers of *Lady G* before going on to her last fatal swim at King's Cascades on the Prince Regent River. Mark Buckingham asked us not to touch the plaque, because the curious fingers of passing visitors have already nearly obliterated the young American woman's signature.

It was low tide when we arrived at Crocodile Creek and we had to climb up a vertical, permanently fixed metal ladder to gain access to the swimming spot. It was quite delightful, a rock pool continually renewed with fresh water from a modest waterfall, but also partly saline because of the twice daily infusion of tidal sea water. The salt water sinks to the bottom, and small fish have become adapted to this cocktail of fresh and sea water. So has the occasional visiting saltie and Mark was first up the ladder to check the deeper recesses of the pool for a lurking croc.

With the pool declared croc free, we were quickly in it, rejoicing in the cool of the water and the spectacular setting. The old and bold were soon leaping up the surrounding cliffs like rock wallabies with their video and still cameras. Yet there was a sense of regret, too, because this was our last complete adventuring day. By the time we were ready to leave, *Explorer* had risen up with the tide to the top of the ladder, and incoming sea water was starting to trickle into the swimming hole. We were able to step straight onto *Explorer* from the rocks that had been six metres above our heads when we arrived.

No. 1 Captain Greg turned on the Captain's Farewell Cocktail Party that night on the upper deck with champagne and top shelf gins and tonics as well as lashings of cold beer and excellent red and white wine. Canapes too! With the compulsory picture postcard tropical sunset thrown in for good measure, it all seemed too good to be true. (The most serious problem that occurred on the voyage was the ship running out of breakfast marmalade.) An address list was passed around the dining room that night, and vows of continuing friendship and promises to exchange photographs were made. After dinner we gathered in the lecture room for a 'recap' on the voyage, led by Greg Mortimer. Expeditioners were encouraged to comment on any aspect of the voyage and Alana Awramenko, our sole teenager, made a brief and moving speech about how much the experience had meant to her. Not surprisingly, she had been apprehensive about being locked away with a bunch of oldies for two weeks, and what she said engendered a moist eye or two.

Next morning for the first time in two weeks the bridge was a no-go zone as the pilot came on board to guide us in to the Broome Deep Water Port jetty. Road trains crammed with bellowing steers were again waiting to go on board ships that would take them on their one way voyage to Asia or the Middle East. Somewhere ashore the next band of intrepid *Coral Princess* adventurers was preparing to embark. As we milled about with our luggage on the rear deck, the valiant *Coral Princess* crew were cleaning cabins, taking on supplies and preparing to do it all again. Mary Prentice, an Englishwoman on her first visit to Australia, was so overwhelmed by the powerful impact of her Kimberley experiences that she had tears in her eyes as she prepared to leave the ship.

Unlike most of the other passengers, we were not yet returning to the harsh realities of normal life: more than two-thirds of our Kimberley and west coast ramblings were yet to come. We tried not to look too smug. Penelope and The Manor were waiting safely for us at the Tarangau Caravan Park, but looking a bit down at heel, spattered with bird droppings, twigs and leaves. Before we started living in The Manor again, Ros wanted to get the wheel bearings checked. She claimed to have been hearing grating noises. I was not against this—we were on the brink of some hard outback driving on dirt roads—but we couldn't raise Ron Harris, the local Jayco agent, on the phone. By 8.30 am we were hammering on the door of his combined home and workshop. He was sound asleep for a very good reason—his third daughter, Jade, had been born the night before and he had celebrated with a few drinks. Well maybe more than just a few, he said. He looked monumentally hungover, and suggested that we come back a bit later. Ron is one of the biggest and most powerful men I have ever seen. His tattooed upper arms are the size of most men's thighs. In the circumstances his suggestion seemed very reasonable! Fortunately he is an amiable soul.

It turned out, later that morning, that our wheel bearings were perfectly OK. Ron didn't use a jack, but lifted The Manor off the ground with his bare hands (just joking!). As there was nothing to be done, he refused to charge us— even though waking him up early on such a morning might have warranted a double fee. We called back later and gave the Harrises a copy of our first travel book, *Penelope Goes West—On the Road from Sydney to Margaret River and Back*, with a special dedication to their brand new daughter.

We did have another important bit of equipment that needed attention. Our three-way fridge in Penelope had not been working properly since its plug had been damaged on the Tanami Track. Before we left on *Coral Princess* we had taken it to 'Phil the Fridgie' in Broome, who said it was working just fine, but not when we put it back in Penelope. With only one day for re-stocking, and our vital piercingly chilled ales at the end of the day in jeopardy, we headed back to Phil. As it happened, he looked more crook than Ron, but not because of celebration. He had a bad dose of flu, but in spite of that cheerfully dropped what he was doing to help out.

Phil suspected that as the fridge worked on mains power, a bad earth connection to the metal body of Penelope was causing problems with the 12 volt system. We had to rip all the drawers and wooden panelling out of the back of the luggage area to see what was going on, but the earth connection looked properly bolted in place and there seemed no reason why it shouldn't be working. Phil muttered and mumbled and scratched his head. 'This is interesting,' he said. Interesting! This was just the kind of situation that convinced God not to make me a mechanic. It turned out that there was a flake of paint preventing the critical nut and bolt from creating a valid earth connection with Penelope's metal frame! It was not something I could ever have picked in a million years.

With both The Manor's and Penelope's fridges working, our food storage bins brimming with supplies and both main and reserve tanks full of fuel, we were excited about taking to the road again. The plan was to retrace our steps to Halls Creek, venture into the Bungle Bungles—whether with or without The Manor still had to be decided—and then on to Kununurra before looping around to tackle the Gibb River Road that would eventually lead us back to Broome for the third time this trip. (We, and our young sons, had travelled the Gibb River Road in 1982 with our venerable VW Kombi, at that time considered a risky venture without four-wheel-drive.) Then we would push down into the Pilbara and explore the west coast—all new country for us.

We had to keep reminding ourselves that it was winter down south. News reports on the radio told of terrible storms near Perth, with luxury yachts sinking in stormy cold seas, but our Kimberley dry season weather was addictive—sunny warm days with a light easterly breeze. Heading east, we pulled into the roadhouse near the Derby turn off for a sandwich and cool drink. Literally as we pulled up, an Oka four-wheel-drive bus headed in nose to nose with us. Out piled the passengers including two familiar faces, Bill Bunbury and his wife Jenny, who had just been on a Gibb River excursion themselves with a group of about 16 people. Bill is a former ABC colleague who still works with the Social History Unit of Radio National. Not only have we known each other for many years, but Bill is a 'national living treasure' in the West for his excellent oral history-based programs, tapes and books.

While we gnawed at our corned beef sandwiches, there was much excited talk. Bill, Jenny and their party were all still glowing from having seen wonderful Bradshaw paintings at locations off the Kalumburu Road—'the best I have ever seen', said one of their party whose work had taken him to rock art sites in various parts of Western Australia and other states.

High praise indeed. These sites are not signposted, of course, but Bill said he would tell me how to find them. Out came notebooks and maps as I took down details. We only had a few minutes but it was a fortunate meeting. The Oka took off for Broome, and we headed in the other direction. I rattled on to Ros about how we were going to visit these Bradshaw sites. She seemed preoccupied.

'I'm the one who has been doing the planning because you won't face up to it, and so I've been working on a route and a timetable and now you want to do something else.'

'What's the point of having a trip like this,' I said, 'if you can't change your mind about what you are going to do when you get good unexpected information?'

I was surprised how irritated Ros seemed.

She said: 'If we spend too much time on the Gibb River Road—which we've seen before anyway—we won't have enough time to explore the Pilbara, the west coast, the wild flower country and goldfields which we haven't ever seen.'

'We've got three months, goddammit. Some people do trips as long as ours in six weeks.'

Ros was just warming up. 'The first month is almost all used up. If we don't plan some kind of a schedule and places to see we won't be able to visit all the gorges I've marked out on the Gibb River Road. If you are suddenly going to go dashing off looking for Bradshaws, how can we be back in Broome by the end of July and have a reasonable amount of time for the bits of Western Australia we haven't seen yet?'

'Stuff the gorges. We don't have to see them all. I'll trade half of them for Bradshaws.'

'You don't know what you're talking about. You haven't even looked at a map properly to see how long these side treks are going to take.'

By now I had a full head of steam. 'Of course I've looked at a map. I've just been looking at a very good one with Bill Bunbury. YOU don't even know where these Bradshaw sites are until I show you.'

We agreed to postpone debate until we could look at a map together, and drove on in silence.

It was late in grey nomad terms, 4 pm, when we joined the queue of caravans and campers waiting to get into the only decent caravan and camping park at Fitzroy Crossing. I was even reprimanded by the management for expecting to camp so late and directed to park in a bus zone. We didn't mind. There was unfinished business to attend to.

With a good map finally in front of us, we sat under the shade of a large river gum, listening to larrikin galahs screeching to each other as is their wont, while the blood-red sun slipped behind the eucalypts fringing the Fitzroy River. We had stopped screeching at each other and sat companionably sipping a cold beer—after offering a toast to Phil the Fridgie—while we sorted out our travel plans. Part of the problem was the necessity to retrace our steps after having had to hurry to Broome to catch *Coral Princess*. We traded a gorge or two, decided to give the country around Wyndham scant attention—in 1982 we had visited the famous hollow boab tree used as a prison—and factored in the Bradshaws which were only a day's run to the north of Drysdale Station which we had planned to visit anyway. And I agreed to take more interest in forward planning.

Next morning we were away early, bound for Halls Creek. We had decided to take a plane flight over the Bungle Bungle Range before driving in. Visitors are not permitted to go into the rugged western side of the park and it can only be seen from the air. The countryside is fairly dull between Broome and Fitzroy Crossing, either burnt scrub or spindly acacias struggling in poor soil, but about 100 kilometres east of Fitzroy Crossing it becomes what we think of as typically Kimberley, with occasional blood red, rocky hills studded with deceptively soft looking pincushions of spinifex on their slopes. There are plenty of small eucalypts scattered about nearing Halls Creek, and the country changes again from red sand to red gibber—those distinctive small smooth stones which look as though they have been polished. There are no large trees at all here as they all have their feet in stones. Ros remarked that the spinifex made the countryside look uncannily like an Aboriginal dot painting.

We covered the 290 kilometres to Halls Creek before lunch, and in the afternoon had time to run down the Duncan Highway to Old Halls Creek where Western Australia's first gold rush began in 1885.

On the way we planned to have lunch at Palm Springs which, according to the tourist literature, was a good stopping place. It should have been charming but an old tyre floating in stagnant water in the creek was not pretty and some idiot had left a camp fire smouldering which had already set fire to the dry grass around it. We scooped up some of the creek water to put it out and moved on through the low hills to where the brown adobe ruins of the Old Halls Creek post office still stand (the walls are made of an enduring mix of ant bed and spinifex), although the roof is long gone. Inside, some of the original fireplaces can still be seen, with stone decoration above slate mantelpieces.

At the turn of the twentieth century after the gold rush was over, the Western Australian government was forced to do something about the infrastructure of Halls Creek for the farmers. A splendid information board told us that the original Post Office was managed by one F. W. Tucket, known locally as 'WBL', an acronym for 'the whole bloody lot'. Tucket was a veritable Poo Bah—telegraphist, resident magistrate, registrar of births, deaths and marriages, commissioner of roads, warden and protector of Aborigines. There being no doctor, Tucket took that job on too. Apparently he had some rudimentary medical knowledge and when a stockman was brought in with a ruptured urethra, this enterprising public servant operated on him (directed by Morse Code telegraphed instructions) using razor blades and other improvised instruments. The stockman died—but not from Tucket's operation which was reputedly successful. The ringer was unluckily felled by a sudden bout of malaria.

Old Halls Creek, built in hilly but undoubtedly mineral rich country, was abandoned in 1955 and the present Halls Creek established 15 kilometres to the east on less interesting but more conveniently flat land. There is still activity in the original Halls Creek area and mining leases are still being worked. In a caravan next door to us in the new Halls Creek caravan park we met a Frenchman and his wife who were permanent residents and who won enough gold from their lease with a metal detector to sustain a jewellery business. He used a second caravan as a workshop. They even stayed right through the wet, which must have delighted the caravan park proprietors. They were an affable lot. When I asked if we needed a toilet key, the woman behind the counter said with a straight face, 'No, we issue you with a shovel'.

There was a debate going on between Ros and me whether we should tow The Manor into the Bungle Bungles. The National Park literature said definitely no caravans but did not rule out off-road trailers. In truth, although The Manor is high off the ground and has an off-road capacity, she is not strictly speaking what is called an 'all-terrain' model. Talks in the shower block (always a good spot for local information) with people who had been in and out of the Bungle Bungles were encouraging me to have a go. First, though, we were to see it from the air.

The flight left at 7 am, and there was a choice of two aircraft, a Cessna and a larger twin-engined Piper Navajo. Unfortunately we scored the Navajo, which has its cabin positioned with the windows above the wing. Having been promised unrivalled photographic opportunities by Oasis Air, I looked wistfully at the smaller aircraft with its windows below the wing. We managed to get rear seats, which gave a slightly better view, but most of the passengers saw more wing than Bungles. Having said that, we did manage to get some quite good shots, even through the scratched perspex windows. Given my time over again, I would have waited until we had driven into the Bungle Bungles and taken a helicopter flight on the spot with the door off to ensure unrestricted vision, but at that stage we did not know about the possibility of these flights.

With aircraft honing in on the Bungle Bungles from Kununurra as well as Halls Creek, pilots have to fly a designated flight path for safety reasons. At least from the air you could get an impression of the whole remarkable massif, sculptured by wind and water into extraordinary shapes.

While the distinctive beehive-like domes could be seen clearly from the eastern side, it was good to be able to view the great red rock buttresses to the west, which cannot be visited from the ground, and see the raised plateau of the Bungle Bungle Range with patches of vegetation and some permanent water. Perhaps I shouldn't have been so grumpy about the limited photographic opportunities. Sometimes it's a relief not to have to squint at a great spectacle through a viewfinder.

No climbing is permitted in the Purnululu National Park (for very good reasons we would discover later), the naming of which has faint Gilbertian overtones and echoes of calling Melbourne's annual street festival 'Moomba', when Moomba was reputed to be an Aboriginal word meaning something like 'where people gather together and have fun'. Others, however, say 'Moomba' is a Koori word meaning 'bum'. An Aboriginal joke? Ava Gardner did famously remark, during the filming of *On the Beach* in 1959, that Melbourne was a great place to make a film about the end of the world. The first use of the name Bungle Bungles is believed to have been by a pastoralist, Arthur Muggleton, in 1930. A common native grass found in the region is called 'bundle bundle' by the Aborigines. Perhaps Muggleton perpetrated an Irish joke. A more formal Aboriginal description of the area is Purnululu, which has been adopted for the national park. Bungle Bungles remains the popular name.

The turn-off to the Bungle Bungles is about 100 kilometres north-east of Halls Creek and we made good time despite quite a stiff head wind. Yet another glorious dry season day lifted our spirits as we drove through fairly typical Kimberley country, alternating spinifex with rough pasture on which Brahman cattle—highly sought after by the live meat market in Asia and the Middle East—were stolidly chewing. It was basically savanna, with no trees of any size, just a scattering of white-barked gums with their limbs twisted into contorted but pleasing shapes. Ros noticed a *Hakea* she had not seen before, quite bushy and tall with a distinctive purple flower. But rocks and ants' nests were the dominant features of this Kimberley land-scape, with occasional glimpses of mountain ranges ahead.

The track into the Bungle Bungles from the highway was a bit over 50 kilometres but likely to take us at least three hours over terrain definitely for four-wheel-drives only. We decided to risk taking The Manor in, partly because we were confident of getting her in safely, and because the business of camping without her was daunting. We have a small tent and a second fridge in Penelope, but as Ros pointed out, separating the supplies and equipment we would need for three or four days would be a pain. And we would surely forget something vital! Like a corkscrew.

Just inside the gate to Purnululu National Park we saw a cluster of caravans awaiting their owners' return. I caught a passing glimpse of one which had 'Infirmity' written on its side. On second thoughts it might have been 'Infinity'. After about 20 kilometres of mildly rough going the track became quite dramatic, winding in and around small rocky hills and then unexpectedly plunging down into wet, steep creek crossings. It would have been exceedingly embarrassing to be stranded in one of these so I engaged low ratio and first gear and was delighted how well Penelope pulled The Manor through the creek and up the very steep bank on the other side. There were seven wet crossings, and on the sixth I saw a four-wheel-drive coming the other way parked on top of a knoll until we could both pass.

'You're game bringing that thing in here mate,' the bearded driver said through his open window. It was code-speak for 'dinkum' four-wheel-drive enthusiasts resenting The Manor encroaching on their hairy-chested domain.

'No problems at all,' I said cheerily, hoping I was right.

His vehicle had its bull bar festooned with rusty wire cable, and a very professional stump jack on the rear bumper. Clearly we were amateurs of the first rank. I was getting the strong impression that not only do the heavy-metal off-road-ers resent the presence of poofy campers like The Manor coming into places like the Bungles but feel even more disgruntled when we get there and they see us living more comfortably than they do. Ros says I'm fantasising about this, but that's my theory and I'm stuck with it.

We reached the park rangers' settlement in two-and-a-half hours, which wasn't bad going. As we went to book in, we saw Colin and Marilyn—who had delivered the execrable bottle of muscat to us in Broome on behalf of our friends Greg and Heather—now camped at Kununurra. They had left their camper and come in with their four-wheel-drive, on Greg's insistence, with camping gear lent to them. They seemed a bit ill at ease about it all. Greg and Heather had also urged them to do the Gibb River Road, but they had only done half before two punctures and no spare forced them to return.

I was feeling very smug about the way the The Manor had performed as we headed towards the camping grounds. We were delighted to find that there were two zones—one for people with generators, and the second designated a 'quiet' area. I find this wholly admirable. There is absolutely no need to make isolated bush camps hideous with infernal machines. Technology is now available, with

(Left) The deceptive tranquillity of King's Cascades, on the Prince Regent River, where swimming is not recommended. (Right) Our intrepid Voyage leader Greg Mortimer makes the point that geologists have rocks on, as well as in, their heads.

The remarkable rock art galleries of Wary Bay, Bigge Island.

The mysterious pipe-smoking 'Dutchmen' of Wary Bay.

Thylacine (extinct Tasmanian tiger), or dingo?

(Left) I didn't expect to meet Malcolm Fraser in the Kimberley. (Right) Floodwaters over the millennia have sculptured the Bungle Bungles and carved out these spectacular gorges.

Penelope and The Manor bungling happily into the Bungle Bungles in red-blooded four-wheel-drive territory.

Not a pretty sight—but a delightful solar-powered shower in our Bungle Bungle camp washes off the day's dust.

These were the best Bradshaw figures we saw near the King Edward River—complete with distinctive top-knots and trademark dangling ornaments.

Unexpected visual surprises lurk in the Aboriginal rock art galleries of the Kimberley.

A fusion of Wandjina spirits and earlier Bradshaws. The dark brown Bradshaws seen lower down were originally painted over by later Aboriginal artists, but have re-emerged over time.

Dickie Tatya mourning the demise of the trusty—now rusty—Chev ute he used to drive on Mt Elizabeth Station.

Joyous reunion with the Williams. From left on the Wyndham Wharf: Tim and Ros Bowden, Heather Messer and Greg Williams. In front: Ryan and Todd Williams.

A spectacular Sticky Kurrajong flower—or Kimberley rose—at Bell Gorge.

The mendicant 'ninja' turtles at our Bell Gorge riverside camp smiling in anticipation of more tucker.

'We are only mildly amused.' Note the unmistakable profile of Queen Victoria on the right as the Gibb River road cuts through the limestone escarpment of the Napier Range.

Penelope is dwarfed by a 2.7 kilometre-long empty ore-carrying train returning 430 kilometres from Port Hedland to BHP's Pilbara iron ore operation at Newman.

solar cells, auxiliary batteries or bottled gas, to run fridges, cook and have lights without these anti-social excrescences. Fancy wanting to watch the telly in the Bungle Bungles for God's sake! I can't recall how many times I have been camped in a nice quiet spot, by a river or billabong, and seen a caravan and utility approaching with one of these cursed generators on the back. The owners then start up the genny, hop into their van (where they can't hear it) to watch telly, leaving their roaring, horrible, selfish power plant to ruin the ambience of what had been a nice place. So the thought of those technologically crass campers all banged up in the one place breathing in each other's two-stroke fumes seemed to me utterly appropriate.

To further improve our sense of well-being we found a terrific camping spot near a dry creek bed, under some big broad-leafed trees for shade and with a view of the escarpment which was just beginning to turn crimson in the rays of the late afternoon sun. We immediately decided to stay for at least three nights to enjoy this exclusive creek-frontage. In the distance we could see queues of late-arriving desperates with no alternative but to head for the generator area.

There was a pit toilet within reasonable distance, and a watering point to and from which we could see other campers carrying buckets and containers reminiscent of a scene from an African village. The Department of Conservation and Land Management (CALM) also supply barbecues and, for fuel, mill ends from the more commercially pragmatic side of their operations.

We realised next morning that we had been away exactly one month! We woke after a surprisingly cold night, down to 7°C—not so unusual when we considered that it was winter, we were inland, and Penelope's altimeter showed that we were camped at 400 metres. The days were warm enough though, at around 30–33°.

It was time to explore, and we drove 30 kilometres around the south-west corner of the Bungle Bungles massif where the famous striped beehive domes can be seen, and where we planned to walk to a feature called Cathedral Gorge. Photographs do not prepare you for the bizarre reality of the Bungle Bungles. Awesome, unique, weird and improbable are the adjectives that spring to mind. It seems incredible that nature has layered the rocks so elegantly with red, grey-green and black bands.

Climbing on any of the Bungles rocks is forbidden as the famous red, black and grey stripes are actually a thin crust on top of soft white sandstone that quickly erodes if disturbed by climbers' boots. Occasionally you see areas of white, where the protective crust has broken down for some other reason, and the soft sandstone underneath erodes out quickly to form caves and overhangs like cavities in old teeth.

The whole massif is what is left of an extensive blanket of sand and gravel that filled the Ord Basin about 360 million years ago in the Devonian period. About 300 million years ago this region was involved in extensive geological activity during which the underlying rocks were moved and tilted. Erosion by wind and water began then, and was dramatically increased about 20 million years ago, when there was a sudden lowering of the sea level causing rivers like the Ord to cut down into the old land surface and, in so doing, carve out the sensational sculptured terrain of the Bungle Bungles.

There would be very little left at all now if it were not for the remarkable protective coatings that have stopped the soft sandstone from being completely eroded down to the plain. The coatings are a curious mix of mineral and biological activities. The orange bands are thin coatings of iron-oxide cemented sandstone. The dark grey stripes are a protective coating identified by Dr Patrick McCarthy of the Australian Biological Resource Study, Canberra, as cynobacteria (also known as blue-green algae) and not lichen. These single-celled organisms can survive quite extended dry periods. The algae are dull grey during the dry season, but become from shiny dark green to almost black after rain. Surprisingly, both coatings are only a few millimetres thick but have managed to prevent the final erosion and destruction of the ancient Devonian sand and gravel deposits.

The two kilometres to Cathedral Gorge were quite easy walking, with great red sandstone walls rearing up on either side, and occasional stands of *Livistonia* palms—relics of a wetter era—surprising and delighting the eye. At the head of the gorge was an unexpected bonus, a great rock cavern gouged out from the Bungles sandstone at the bottom of a wet season (now dry) waterfall. It was also a natural sound shell in the centre of which was a circular area covered with soft white sand and a billabong of permanent water. The early afternoon sun shafted down the red rock shelf on the eastern side from a small patch of blue sky framed by the great rock faults that had created the gorge. It was an area that demanded respect, and Cathedral Gorge was appropriately named. Chattering walkers who came in lowered their voices quickly, not only because of the acoustics amplifying their cheerful talk, but as tourists do when entering the great cathedral spaces of St Paul's or Chartres. They just stood and stared in awe, as we had when first entering the chamber.

On the way back down the gorge Ros stopped to take a photograph on her prized new Minolta 600si camera. It made an odd noise, causing her to glance down at its read-out screen. There was one word displayed: HELP. From whom, we wondered? As it happened, we were in one of those areas of Australia most remote from technical assistance. Ros looked and felt distinctly peeved. She was very fond of her camera with its new and technically sophisticated digital features—all now as useless as the proverbial bull's tit.

I still had my little happy-snap instant camera but that was hardly the point. Ros fell silent and seemed to brood as we continued the walk, breaking off to follow a short diversion, Piccaninny Gorge, which is flanked by superb beehive formations and other striped rocky curiosities. I noticed a three-metre termites nest which looked uncannily like a statue of the pregnant Virgin Mary. Ros had not noticed this, because she had sat down in the shade of a rock doubtless reflecting on her recent unscheduled and regrettable camera accident. In an effort to cheer her up, I found a long dead stick, managed to hoist my bush hat up on top of the Virgin Mary's head, then suggested Ros photograph us both with my Mickey Mouse camera. Not only did she seem reluctant to do this—and was essentially unamused—but when I managed to recover my hat and put it on, I found it covered with angry red ants which bit me.

We returned to the car park and drove to the public phone. 'Help' was not forthcoming. The expert in Sydney said a camera chip had gone down, and it could only be fixed in Melbourne or Sydney. Bloody computers. Fortunately Ros had brought her older Minolta camera body as a back up, and at least all her lenses could be pressed into service. So she was still in business, but the light in her photographic eye dimmed a bit from that moment on. She said it was rather like me having to move from an iMac computer to a clunky old 1987 Macintosh Plus.

After lunch at camp, we indulged in the luxury of an afternoon nap before enjoying a solar bush shower. Ros was intrigued by the large-leafed trees we were camping under and took a leaf to the ranger station for identification. It had rough bark and was clearly not a eucalypt. It turned out to be a most interesting tree—*Terminalia ferdinandia*—commonly described as a billy goat plum. The local Bardia people called it a Gubinge tree, so the rangers said. It has a pistachio nut-sized fruit recently identified as the most concentrated source of vitamin C on the entire planet! It is currently being investigated as part of a project which aims to identify useful native Australian flora with medicinal or food value. It was good to know that we weren't just camped under any old tree.

We were up by 5.30 next morning to retrace our tracks to the beehive formations. Ros wanted to photograph them again in case the film inside her carked camera had been compromised. I took this as an encouraging sign that her photographic enthusiasm was making a comeback. As one of the young women rangers was knowledgeable about the local flora, we stopped in at the ranger station again to ask about a *Grevillea* with flowers like pale yellow spikes. It turned out to be *Grevillea pyramidalis*, or caustic bush, which has quite poisonous and nasty qualities. The Aboriginal people used it to make sure the wounds from their ceremonial cicatrices didn't heal too quickly, thus ensuring nice big permanent scars.

I also asked about quite a common big-leafed plant with a spiky purple flower which looked a bit like a Royal Hakea. It wasn't. It was the appalling *Calatropis procera*, another very nasty number. The seeds of this charmer are believed to have been imported by Afghan cameleers as padding in camel saddles. *Calatropis procera* took off like wildfire in Australia and is found just about everywhere in northern Australia from Queensland to Western Australia. It is highly toxic to humans, although cattle can eat it without ill effects. It can be sourced to Asia and Africa originally, although the CALM plant book said that people 'in Arabia and Africa used its latex for arrow poison'. So that was quite a nice little toxic horticultural double we came up with to begin the day.

We planned to walk to Mini Palms Gorge, accessed from the north-western side of the Bungle Bungles massif, where the tiger striped formations give way to red conglomerate cliffs which also conceal spectacular gorges. Our walk took us up a creek bed, and it was quite hot and difficult walking over smooth stones and gravel in the dry watercourse. Sometimes we had to squeeze through narrow clefts between the rocks where boulders had fallen down into the gorge from the high cliffs on either side.

A group of returning walkers, about our vintage, had to wait while we eased ourselves through a tight pinch. We passed the time of day and one of the women said: 'This is Frank's favourite place.' I gathered from her description of Frank (who had surged ahead) that he was her energetic and peripatetic life partner. 'Whenever he's stressed in the city, he just thinks of Mini Palms Gorge and feels better.'

At the head of the valley (after negotiating another tricky rock fall) walkers could see the mini palms, which were ordinary *Livistonia* palms stunted through lack of light. The poor little things were also bent sideways from the force of the water which battered them during the wet season. In the dry season Ros thought they were increasingly at risk from the dust, stirred up by literally hundreds of visitors walking through, because a coating of dust stopped them from photosynthesising properly. CALM has built a viewing platform on top of the rock fall to look down at the bedraggled little palms at the head of the gorge but Ros felt it might be better if CALM forbade walkers to climb down to them in the interests of the struggling plants' survival. If they don't, Frank might have to find another symbolic place to make him feel better.

Wherever you go in Western Australia, you can't help being aware of the omnipresent CALM, nor can you escape polarised opinions about its operations. There seemed to me to be a basic difficulty for them in being responsible for conservation and also the exploitation of natural resources—cutting down old growth and regenerated forests for timber. However, they weren't cutting down trees in the Bungle Bungles, and their control and management of national parks and nature reserves in the Kimberley were generally good. The men and women staffing the Bungle Bungles rangers station were well informed and helpful and normally the printed signs giving information about animals, plants and even history were well done. The Mini Palms Walk was an exception—pitched to a mid-primary school level. Believe it or not, one expensive metal plaque on a stand had the image of a tree etched into it. 'Like all living things, this tree is sustained by sunlight', the caption began cheerfully,

while a little further on a notice gave the surprising information that trees have roots to 'take from the soil the
essential nutrients for plant growth'. (Funny that. Perhaps
some people think they have them simply to stop the tree
falling down.)

'So the cycle of life continues' burbled the blurb. I
wondered who CALM thinks comes to these places, if not
some of the most ecologically aware travellers in Australia.
One notice ended with, 'Enjoy the journey'. Dangerously
close to 'Have a nice day' I felt.

I would like to read more specialised information about
the vegetation and geology.

Ros thought I was a bit hard on CALM. She thinks of
tourists and national parks as representing a kind of war—
with CALM rangers being a kind of officer corps in this
struggle between the ecologically sensitive environment
and the assaults of four-wheel-drive vehicles and an expo-
nential surge of tourists.

'Rangers stop people destroying things by making rules
about where vehicles can and can't go,' Ros said. 'They
provide camping grounds to contain the human impact on
the park to specific areas, provide water and pit toilets,
arrange not only fixed barbecues but wood to burn in them
so people don't get it from the natural bush. In a sense they
are here to stop people loving the Bungle Bungles to
death.'

Her analogy of war was enhanced by the constant buzz
of light aircraft and helicopters in the mornings and after-
noons as wave after wave of aircraft flew over the red
bulwarks of the Bungles. Perhaps the bull bar encrusted
four-wheel-drives were the armoured personnel carriers or
light tanks of the invading forces. The 16-seat OKA

four-wheel-drive buses represented the heavy tanks of the tourist assault forces.

In a later conversation with Kimberley CALM supremo, Al Grosse, the metaphor of environmental war between visitors and the parks they were loving to death was carried even further. The importation of seeds in campers' socks and swags is a major concern.

'They sweep dust out of their cars and seeds as well,' he said. 'Paradoxically, it is the most popular parks that take the brunt of this unwanted invasion.'

It was our last night in this ecological war zone, but the surroundings were too peaceful and beautiful to sustain the metaphor. We enjoyed a mid-afternoon cuppa under the billy goat plum trees, gazing out at the Osmond Range as its steep cliffs gradually reddened in the low afternoon sun. I said to Ros that after I had organised our solar bush showers, it would be time for a nice cold beer or glass of red wine. She said a very worrying thing.

'Don't you ever consider how much more we could do if we didn't drink?'

I sat in stunned silence for a while. Could she be serious about this? We didn't consider ourselves heavy drinkers, although nary a day went by without an evening libation or two—and it must be admitted, on certain occasions three or four. It was such a congenial part of our lives both at home and on the road that the thought of suddenly going cold turkey was a rude shock.

Fortunately she was not being serious. But I was so shaken by her remark that I found it necessary to regain my composure by extracting a splendidly cold can of beer from The Manor's valiant little fridge a tad earlier than usual. Ros did join me, I was relieved to note.

six

The Bradshaws

After all the angst of deciding whether or not to take The Manor into the Bungle Bungles we tootled out triumphantly in two hours instead of the two-and-a-half it had taken us to get in. We needed to refuel and stopped at Turkey Creek, the last roadhouse before Kununurra.

There is a large area of Aboriginal land between the Bungle Bungles and Kununurra. The Turkey Creek roadhouse services these scattered communities, as well as catering for passing truckies, other locals and tourists like us. The place was in a certain amount of chaos when we pulled in because buses, four-wheel-drive tours and tourists all were wanting fuel and fast food. The fuel price was high (for those times), 98 cents a litre, and it seemed the managers must have had a few 'fill up and run' experiences. Signs on the pumps instructed us to pay first, then fill up, which made it difficult to guesstimate how much fuel was needed. The pump was supposed to stop automatically when the requisite amount was achieved, but the system didn't work, and I unwittingly clocked up a few litres extra. Sorting that out administratively took about half an hour. Getting hamburgers as well would have taken even longer. Apart from the usual take-away cholesterol time bombs of deep fried chips, battered savs and Chicko rolls, 'Gameburgers' were advertised on a dilapidated blackboard:

Croc burgers
Camel burgers
Buffalo burgers
Barra burgers
Roo burgers

A chalky flourish at the bottom of the board asked: 'Are you game?'

The croc burgers were $11 each. We weren't game.

The country changed again as we got closer to Kununurra and the highway snaked through hilly terrain with boulders bigger than the trees. The distant hills were not red any more but brown and wreathed in great plumes of smoke signalling dry season grass fires. We made it to Kununurra by lunchtime, and found Greg Williams and Heather Messer had organised us a space only one away from their much-travelled caravan. We had a joyous reunion. The little boys hadn't grown as much as I expected in almost two years, although Ryan (8) was sporting two big front teeth and Todd (10) was reputedly becoming interested in girls.

After nearly five years on the road, Greg and Heather had decided to head back to the east coast and Coffs Harbour, a decision driven largely by the boys' future schooling—and advice from Todd's new remote area teacher who recommended that after six years on the road it was time the boys attended a conventional school.

We talked all through the afternoon, catching up on what had happened since we first met them at Cape Arid National Park on the south coast of Western Australia and they had invited us to 'Cocktails at Six' at their caravan, overlooking the Southern Ocean.

Kununurra is the service town not only for the pastoral industries sustained by the Ord River dam, but for the rich Argyle diamond mining operation 200 kilometres to the south. Greg, an electrical engineer, was hoping to get work there to augment the fading family fortunes and was waiting on a clearance from the Australian Federal Police.

It was agreed that we would stop giving each other bottles of crook port or muscat which was a great relief to all. We did give them a good bottle to break the pattern, as the $2 gargle I gave Greg the summer before last finished up augmenting the brake fluid for his Toyota. Or so he said!

We joined Greg and Heather the next day on their early morning walk at six around the canals and sluices of the Kununurra Diversion Dam for the Ord irrigation scheme. The Ord was dammed in 1971 and Lake Argyle was formed by a huge earth and rock fill dam wall which created Australia's largest artificial reservoir—5.7 million mega litres. Situated 48 kilometres from Kununurra, the dam drowned the original Patsy Durack homestead, now reconstructed as a museum. Intended to transform the region into a powerhouse of sustained agricultural development, the Ord development at first suffered from the tyranny of distance as well as various voracious pests and bugs which attacked the early irrigation crops of sorghum, oilseeds, vegetables and fruit. In the unprofitable times Kununurra used to be called 'a frontier toy town fastened to a white elephant'. Its fortunes were tied to the success of the irrigation area and now, after some difficult years, a combination of tourism and expanded development is underpinning the future of the thriving town of some 6000 people.

At the dawn of the twenty-first century, Kununurra is straining at the leash. There are plans for a second irrigation area north of the town on the lower Ord, if negotiations with the local Aboriginal Miriuwung people over native title and land can be successfully completed. Ord Stage II, which may eventually triple the 14 000 hectare size of the irrigation area, is expected to support a large-scale export sugar industry. Tourism in the area already earns as much money in a year—$60 million—as fruit growing and crop farming.

And of course the Argyle diamond operations are huge, with further prospecting being actively pursued. Greg was marking time—until his escutcheon was proved stainless by the Federal Police and he could work at the Argyle mine. (He passed the probity test and got the job not long after we left.) Meanwhile, he very kindly attended to some of our minor electrical problems. Apart from fixing my parking and brake lights which had suddenly ceased to function, he fitted Penelope's little fridge with a new power plug that, he assured me, could never go wrong. He had fitted a similar plug in Colin and Marilyn's natty and solidly built camper—which looks like a small A-frame house when in camping mode. (It looked to me quite rugged enough to have gone into the Bungle Bungles, but that was their decision.)

Colin and Marilyn joined us for 'Cocktails at Five'. Six o'clock seemed very late in this part of the world, on the fringes of Northern Territory time but one-and-a-half hours the wrong way. During a fairly lively session the conversation turned to dreams. Colin—who was about to turn 60—said that the older he got, the more intense his dreams were becoming. I said that my father, who lived till 91, experienced the same phenomenon. According to Colin, the dreams encompassed the most extraordinarily detailed flashbacks of his early boyhood.

'The other night I dreamed I was lying in lush grass in my cricket flannels waiting to bat, and actually smelling the fragrance of that slightly crushed green grass. It was incredibly vivid.'

I asked him impertinently if he had been fortunate enough to relive some of his early sexual experiences so acutely in his dreams. His answer was discursive, but an elegant put-down.

He asked whether I had seen the television series *Seven Up* where a television producer had interviewed a number of British seven-year-olds and followed up with the same individuals at the ages of 14, 21, 28 and on into adulthood. It was still being filmed.

I said I had.

'You may remember a little Yorkshire farm boy who was asked a very personal question by the interviewer about his attitude to girls. The lad paused, kicked a gumboot into the turf and replied slowly and deliberately: "Aye doon't aanswer questions lyke thaat".'

I conceded game set and match to Colin.

We also talked of the Aboriginal rock paintings we had seen and my fascination with the Bradshaws. Greg offered to introduce me to a fellow resident at the caravan park, George Kulek, who is a freelance photographer with a particular interest in Aboriginal rock paintings. George spends six months of each year in the bush tracking down rock art galleries, some of which are unknown even to the present generation of Aboriginal people and anthropological archaeologists.

We met at his caravan the next day as he was preparing his four-wheel-drive for another expedition. His partner, Sue, obligingly produced mugs of tea while we talked about his Bradshaw project.

His interest was sparked by coming across a field report of Fred S. Brockman, Chief Inspecting Surveyor of Western Australia at the turn of the twentieth century. The report was written in 1902 and titled 'Exploration of North-West Kimberley'. Brockman ranged widely through the Kimberley, following up on the original exploratory journeys in 1838 by Lieutenant George Grey—who was the first European to see and describe the fabulous rock art galleries in the area. Brockman was fascinated by them too and, using his surveying skills, tried to relocate the sites Grey had seen. At the end of his report, George Kulek was delighted to discover, was an appendix containing a collection of wonderful black and white photographs of these and other sites he found, taken with a big glass plate camera.

George determined to find the galleries featured in Brockman's photographs and journals, and photograph them again to discover how much they had faded or deteriorated a century on. He said he was sometimes out for six weeks at a time in extremely rugged country. Clearly not a project for the faint-hearted. *Australian Geographic* was a part sponsor of George's attempts to trace the journeys of Brockman, and he hoped eventually to publish a book about his research if he could interest a publisher. I mentioned the Bradshaws that had been described to me by my chance meeting with Bill and Jenny Bunbury. George knew the sites, of course, and confirmed our mud map of how to find them.

The whole question of access to Aboriginal art sites in various parts of Australia is complicated and continually under review. While it has been argued by some that there is no cultural continuity between the older Bradshaw art and the continuing tradition of Wandjina and other Aboriginal art styles and practices, the question of ownership remains. Clearly, any visitor must respect the wishes of the people on whose traditional lands the art sites were located.

It is an issue addressed by the respected prehistory scholar and archaeologist Dr Josephine Flood.

> In view of the Aboriginal cultural revival of the last few years and the increasing demand for cultural tourism, most site managers now consider that at least a small selection of sites should be open to visitors, so the present generation may have the pleasurable, educational and uplifting experience of seeing some of the material evidence of this complex, age-old culture.

Flood described three categories of sites. Those which were open to the public, those that could be visited only by special arrangement, where permission for access must be obtained from Aboriginal custodians, private landowners or state authorities, and sites which could not be visited at all because of their importance in the story of Australian prehistory.

Fortunately for us, the King Edward River sites first mentioned to us by Bill Bunbury were in the first category and included in reputable travel books like Ron and Viv Moon's *The Kimberley: An Adventurer's Guide* (also mentioned by Josephine Flood in her landmark book *The Riches of Ancient Australia: An Indispensable Guide For Exploring Pre-historic Australia*).

When I told George Kulek where we were going after the Kimberley, he kindly alerted me to the petroglyphs—not paintings, but Aboriginal rock engravings—that could be seen near Marble Bar, Newman, and on the Burrup Peninsula near Karratha.

Before tackling the Gibb River Road, we had a day out with Greg and Heather and the two boys, an excursion to Parry's Lagoon, an area of wetlands and a bird sanctuary near Wyndham. The site was well managed with roofed viewing platforms built out over the water on stilts and connected to the land by metal walkways. The huts had adjustable blinds on the windows and even a little shelf at elbow height for steadying binoculars. A wild duck obligingly swam past with a line of fluffy little ducklings paddling furiously behind, much to the delight of Todd and Ryan.

We were not far from Wyndham and drove in to try to find the caravan park where Ros and I and our two boys had stayed in 1982. The park had been beside tidal flats which seemed to stretch to infinity. We woke up one morning to see in the distance a solitary and completely naked man solemnly doing tai chi exercises. But this time the park had gone so we drove to the Wyndham wharf which is a semi-circle, allowing the road trains full of sad-eyed, floppy-eared

Brahman cattle bound for slaughter to load their cargo on to the waiting transports at high tide and drive off again without turning, as they had to in Broome. The tide was rising, and little mud skippers were hopping in and out of their burrows as the brown waters crept up to the base of the mangroves.

We drove up to the Five Rivers Lookout, under the frowning brow of the Bastion Range. From this almost 360° vantage point there is a splendid view of the chocolate brown waters of the King, Pentecost, Durack, Forrest and Ord rivers which all flow into Cambridge Gulf. Escaping from the fast food trucks and tourist buses we drove down into Three Mile Valley where we found a secluded picnic spot for lunch. Small boys delight in vulgarity and I amused myself by teaching Todd and Ryan a disreputable little ditty:

> Ask your mother for sixpence,
> To see the big giraffe;
> With horns on its head
> And hairs on its . . .
> [Pause for effect]
> Aaask your mother for sixpence (etc.)

I hoped Heather would forgive me.

We would not see Greg and Heather again 'on the road', but probably at Coffs Harbour after they faced up to 'normal' life. Or as normal as it could be for such a lively and innovative family. Heather was doing well at local markets with her landscape photographs, framed, and with little panels of shells, seeds or dried flowers to match the image. (As it happened, they managed to stay away almost another whole year.)

As we headed, fully charged with fuel and supplies, towards the turn-off to the Gibb River Road, Ros was reading the *Kununurra Echo*. She found a most peculiar item in the Public Notices section. Under the image of a multi-tiered wedding cake was the following:

THE ORD RIVER MAGPIES—are proud to announce the uniting of two aspiring club members Thomasina Portia Delecta (alias Tommy) and Brantley Hilton-Sheraton (alias Bronwyn). A mock wedding service and buffet meal will be held at the Mercure Inn large conference room on Sunday 1st August 1999 at 12 noon to commemorate the joining. For bookings and any enquiries contact . . .

What did it all mean? The union of a 'same sex' couple—in Kununurra? If not, why a mock wedding service? And we will never know . . .

We planned to spend a few nights at the El Questro cattle station, which has been developed as a 'top of the range' tourist stay at $1000 or so a night in a purpose-built lodge high on cliffs overlooking the Chamberlain River. Fortunately for the budget traveller, excellent camping for a far more modest fee could be enjoyed near the old homestead. We did not have a long day's run, and felt we got off to a splendid start by finding an Aboriginal rock art site—described in Ron and Viv Moon's excellent four-wheel-drive book *Discover Australia*—nine kilometres along the Gibb River Road. After checking in at El Questro we were lucky to get a splendid, secluded water-front camp site on the Pentecost River. No sooner had we pitched camp than a group of black cockatoos flew into a dead tree and chattered away while grooming each other amiably. A good omen we felt. They were charming to look at through binoculars.

El Questro was another of those mysterious names without an obvious source. The original land-holding, taken up in 1909 as a horse depot by one Jack Spurling, was called Ascot and the present El Questro is on what was known as Spurling Paddock. After several more owners came and went, a tough ex-drover, Charles MacMiking, took it over in 1958 and registered the name El Questro. Local speculation is that it was meant to be the Spanish for 'land of great beauty and great mountains'—but that ain't so. The only literal translation to get anywhere near it is 'El Castro' which, in northern Spain, means 'dwelling with much land'. It was said the ex-drover often 'borrowed' cattle from his wealthier neighbour on Doon Doon Station and that the butcher in Wyndham turned a blind eye to the varying brands on the beasts supplied to him by MacMiking.

By 1984 El Questro took in one million acres, supporting some 5000 cattle. The Salerno brothers, James and Ben, were the first to realise the potential of the station for tourism and encouraged endurance horse rides and 30-kilometre marathon foot races. Matteo Springs, Amalia and Emma Gorges were named after the Salerno children. The present tourist operation was developed from 1991 when William Burrell bought the property from the Salerno syndicate. It is still run as a working station, with Brahman cattle gradually taking over from the original, now inbred, red Kimberley Shorthorns first introduced to the region by pioneering families like the Duracks. The combination of cattle station, wilderness park and tourist attraction has been incredibly successful and has an inter-national as well as Australia-wide profile. Open for seven months a year, it caters for 35 000 visitors annually and has a staff of 46 during the season. What is remarkable is how uncrowded it seems, with river-side camp sites like ours well screened from our neighbours.

At 3 pm we knew we had left it a bit late for a walk to the El Questro Gorge, and had to turn back when the shadows under the tall palms and smaller screw pandanus palms made it hard to see the track. As we had booked on a river excursion to the gorge the next day we weren't too fussed. Besides, the camp site was so pleasant, it was hard to find reasons to go on excursions. The El Questro management put out some interesting information about litter, and how long it hangs about in the bush before it decomposes. I had no idea rubbish was so enduring.

Orange peel or banana skin—two years
Cigarette butt—five years
Wool sock—five years
Plastic bag—30 years
Nylon fabric—40 years
Tin can—50 years
Aluminium can—100 years
Glass bottle—1 million years
Plastic bottle—indefinitely

I was not aware that the ubiquitous plastic bottle could outlast glass.

We had time before the river trip next afternoon to walk to the thermal pools at Zebedee Springs. Believed to have medicinal properties, they did not help to save the life of Michael Marshall, the young son of Morris Marshall who went into partnership on El Questro with the formidable Charles MacMiking in 1964. With no other medical treatment available the little boy was taken to the springs regularly but died of leukemia in 1963. He was nine years old.

The spring gushes from the base of a rock face, and flows down into pools trapped between rocks and tree roots. Pleasantly warm, they are irresistible to most visitors. We had taken our swimmers, and lazed about in them for some time.

We try to avoid organised tours, but the advertised boat trip was the only way to experience the Chamberlain Gorge. As the price included a short walk to view some Aboriginal rock art galleries it sounded pleasant enough. We drove ourselves to the starting point, and hopped on board the excursion boat which was moored near the car park. It was peaceful looking at small fish nibbling at a fringe of weed on the punt's side, watching reflections in the still water and listening to the birds calling. The arrival of the station bus with thirty people broke the spell. It also brought us—I'll call her Sophie—our guide for the trip.

Sophie was an attractive young woman in her early twenties wearing a park ranger-style uniform, broad-brimmed hat and a name badge. Grabbing the on-board microphone she started to warm us up as if we were a live television audience waiting for the big moment at Channel Nine's now departed 'Midday Show'.

'Are we all happy to be here?' she bellowed cheerfully. There was a subdued response from the passengers on board and a low moan from me.

'Oh that's not good enough. I need a much more lively response than that because we're going to have such a WONDERFUL time.'

I whispered in Ros's ear that I was going to kill Sophie and no jury would convict. But on she went relentlessly, amplified by the excursion boat's crackling sound system.

'Let's really hear it this time. Are we going to enjoy ourselves?'

Somehow she got a loud enough yelp from the mob to satisfy her. But it didn't stop there. 'Where were we all from?' I suppose I should have tried to stop her, but we were numb with shock. It was as though she was addressing fourth grade primary school children. Or should I say second? Most of us were old enough to be her parents or, in some cases, grandparents.

In Sophie's defence she was a bit steamed up because she had left two passengers (and a small child) behind at the main camp and they were being brought down by another staff vehicle. And in fairness I should concede that once we were underway her commentary was quite well informed about the flora along the gorge and later, when we sedately cruised the four kilometres to where river rocks stopped further navigation, about Aboriginal art. On a one-to-one basis she was also quite sensible. But she must have been through a tourist guide school somewhere that recommended anyone over the age of fifty be treated as though they were intellectually challenged.

At the head of the gorge we stepped on to the river rocks from a small gangway and walked to the main art site which I found most interesting—a mix of Bradshaws and later Wandjinas.

On the second site we came to the smashed floor of a previous cave that had broken away from the cliff. One Bradshaw—they are certainly resilient—was lying exposed to the elements and nearly unwittingly touched by me, while seeking a handhold.

Seeing the paintings alone made the excursion fee worthwhile and the gorge, with its high rocky walls and fringe paperbarks and eucalypts on the banks, was really delightful. Sophie seemed talked out and mercifully shut up completely after a rock wallaby was spotted on one of the ledges. I had a chat with Albert, our skipper, a laconic Oz with a dry sense of humour. As we passed the spot he told me about a crocodile attack on the Chamberlain River in 1991—it was January and the wet season—on El Questro's neighbours, the Heneggers, who was crossing the river in a canoe. A big saltie sensed dinner. According to Albert, the person paddling happened to look behind and saw a great croc approaching with its mouth open. He thrust his paddle into its mouth, which put it off a bit. However, it attacked again and bit the canoe, which rolled over. At that stage they were in the middle of the gorge which is at least 100 metres wide.

The croc, fortunately for the passengers, savaged a backpack in the confusion of it all, and the stranded canoeists made it to shore—probably walking on water by that stage.

(The attack made the national news, of course, and the Crocodile Farm at Wyndham sent down a team to trap it. Named Doc, it is now an attraction at the farm's central lagoon. Doc reputedly shows little interest in backpackers.)

Ros had heard scare talk about the appalling condition of the Gibb River Road from some women using the public telephone near the main office. Corrugations, red dust, sharp tyre-piercing rocks and patches of bulldust seemed to be the main concerns. We headed out of El Questro at 6.30 the next morning to tackle it. The Gibb River Road passes through quite dramatic country just beyond the El Questro turn-off, running along a valley bordered by mountain ranges with rakish cliff-top escarpments all sloping to the east, tilted that way when the Kimberley region went through its geological upheavals 300 million years ago. We started to see some of the trademark Kimberley boab trees, but no big ones. (The so-called 'Prison Tree' near Wyndham with a hollow trunk is thought to be 4000 years old.) The road wasn't too bad, and we stopped to photograph Penelope and The Manor crossing the causeway over the Pentecost River, on which we had similarly photographed our VW Kombi 'Gertie' in 1982. Ron and Viv Moon's book warned about crocodiles in the Pentecost River so I thought it best that I drove and Ros walked across the knee-deep water with the camera. I had a far better appreciation about how to drive across creek crossings and it was important our skills be properly shared.

A little further on we saw a 44-gallon drum on top of an overturned trailer marking, we thought, a side road or access to a property. As we got closer we read the white painted letters on the drum. It said simply and enigmatically: CHUNKY BOYS. A gay stockmen's support group? A meeting place for overweight station owners' sons? Ros thought it might be a famous outback rock group of whom we knew nothing because we are old and out of touch.

For a while there were two huge graders ahead of us on the road doing a stately tandem. When we passed them we hit the vintage Gibb River Road corrugations complained of by the tourists at El Questro. I was in four-wheel-drive anyway at that stage, and decided to try to get up to 60 kph, or even 70, to see if I could ride over the top of them. This was successful and as we hurtled over those bone-crunchers I marvelled at the power and comfort of the Landcruiser, hoping the tyres would stand the strain and that The Manor would too.

We stopped to talk to a family with a Nissan and camper trailer who were mending a second puncture. They had big wide radials, and swore that the right thing to do was to run on them at high pressures. I'd been down that road— so to speak—on the Tanami. Still, he was entitled to his opinion and as many punctures as he could cope with.

We pulled off to what we knew as Joe's Waterhole in 1982, now 'Jack's Waterhole'. There were a gate, office and toilet block now where before there had been nothing. It cost us $1 each to go in which we did for old time's sake. The story of Ros's bush shower has gone down in family history. There she was, stark naked in a completely deserted wilderness, washing the Gibb River Road dust off when our two boys Barnaby and Guy ran up shouting, 'Mummy, mummy, there's a tourist bus coming'. There was too, full of adventurous seniors on a camping tour. But it was an unexpected sight in this isolated area. The lake is an oasis of bird life and greenery in this parched and stony region.

After Jack's Waterhole the corrugations simply got worse. A lot worse. I hammered on, getting up to 60 kph and over when I could. It wasn't always possible. Still, we were making surprisingly good time and could have done our 300 kilometres and got to Drysdale River Station for lunch. Ros wisely suggested otherwise, and we pulled in— appropriately enough—to the Gibb River itself just after noon and set our table up beside the water and some bushes with startlingly red flowers.

The 60 kilometres up to Drysdale River Station was a super-highway by comparison. It had been recently graded we learned when we reached the station. I drove straight to the diesel pump and noted that the price per litre was an agreeable 00.00. When the bloke—who introduced himself as 'Echo'—came to serve me, I said it was refreshing to find people giving the stuff away so far from major towns.

'Hardly,' he said, explaining that the old pump couldn't cope with prices over a dollar a litre. The going rate was 116 cents a litre. But it did have to come a long way and we were pleased to see it.

'Echo' also knew about the Aboriginal rock art at the King Edward River. He gave me added clues how to find it and suggested we camp nearby at Miners Pool (only $2.50 per person per night) and do a day trip the following day without The Manor. He also passed on the welcome news that the grader had been up almost as far as we wanted to go—the turn-off at the King Edward River.

Miners Pool turned out to be another top camping spot as is so often the case in the incomparable Kimberley. The camping ground was mercifully divided into generator and non-generator areas along the high ground beside the river bank. Flotsam and jetsam caught in the branches of trees (and we were high on the bank) several metres above our heads gave a timely reminder of what happens in these parts in the wet season.

We swam in the Drysdale River—this is not croc country—entering the clear water across a small sandy beach where some children were making castles, moats and canals the way kids do. Each of our camping spots seemed to top the other—although our exclusive nook at El Questro with river frontage was hard to beat.

Ros whipped up a delectable vegetable curry and rice and we sat outside The Manor as an almost full moon rose in front of us through the river gums. We watched as we sipped our tumblers of red wine and listened to Joan Sutherland and Luciano Pavarotti sing operatic highlights on our little portable CD player and speakers.

Camping, we believe, is not about donning hair shirts and eating hard tack. But maintaining a varied menu for eight days with a tiny fridge and minuscule freezer compartment took careful planning. In case other travellers are interested, this is how Ros did it.

FOOD FOR EIGHT DAYS' TRAVELLING

Essentially this is about main meals only—lunches for us are tomatoes, fresh or canned meat, tinned beetroot, mayonnaise, bean mixes, cheese, biscuits, and fresh or dried fruit depending on how long we've been on the road. And breakfasts are just cereals, a cuppa and sometimes toast and marmalade if we are not rushing off. We use powdered skim milk on the road, which seems so close to the real thing that we don't bother to get fresh even when we can on our longer trips.

A defrosting chook or chunk of beef (which doesn't have to fit in our small fridge) is cooked on day one in the camp oven. If beef, this is used cold for lunches as well. Vegies are roasted with the meat.

Then things have to be juggled more carefully. The Manor's tiny freezer space can freeze a packet of bacon plus two packets of chicken thigh fillets—enough for three meals. In the non-freezing part of the fridge, Ros keeps a couple of portion-sized pieces of porterhouse (or even fillet with luck) and some lamb fillets. These last us for three to four days, and can either be cooked on a barbecue or used as stir fry in a wok, if it is not possible to have a fire in the open—which happens quite a lot in national parks in the dry season. Ros sometimes makes a marinade of Tikka sauce and yoghurt for the chicken, or some oil, soy and garlic for meat if it is done on a hotplate—sometimes the only option if a camping ground has a gas barbecue.

Vegetable curries made with potatoes, onions, chick peas, coconut milk, canned bamboo shoots and various other trimmings are popular with both of us and the ingredients don't take up space in the fridge. Ros will make enough for two meals—also a way of stretching ingredients which might otherwise get too elderly. Wasn't that why spicy curries were invented in the first place?

We also carry pasta in various forms, tomato paste, bottled pesto and tinned tomatoes which can be used as the basis for pasta sauces which don't need refrigeration. When bread runs out we cook a damper in the camp oven. This is never eaten hot, but is toasted for breakfast and cut in thin slices at lunchtimes.

Bacon and eggs—a kind of pub breakfast eaten at night—is also a longish term option as the bacon is frozen in the little fridge freezer and the eggs keep well in the outer fridge.

We carried things like cans of stew on our last major trip but never got around to eating them. They were much travelled tins when we brought them back to Sydney across the Nullarbor in our emergency deep storage bin.

Penelope does have a modest wine 'cellar' with bottles for special occasions (and for our hosts if we are visiting) and there is some hard liquor too—Jameson's Irish Whisky, cognac and Bundaberg rum. The whisky and cognac generally come home with us too, but the rum works well in the bush. Our friend Ted Egan introduced us to a great outback drink on the banks of the Diamantina River in 1976 when we joined him at the Birdsville Races. Rum, lime juice and water in an enamel mug (oh well, a tumbler will do) doesn't need to be chilled and seems to slip down terribly well in the bush. We manage to find space for a few cans of beer in limited fridge space. A cold can at the end of a hot day's travelling is always welcome. We follow that with a libation or two of cask red—white is too difficult to chill. And it has to be admitted there is the tradition of liqueur muscat to be kept up—but not every night.

Thus do the gastronomic pleasures of life accompany the Bowdens when they get away from it all in Penelope and The Manor.

FINAL THOUGHT: Meat has to be boneless or it takes up too much space in the fridge and might reduce the area needed for beer. 'Beer for bones' so to speak. A good trade.

And Ros says that badly corrugated roads blunt cooking knives.

The temperature dropped to a chilly 5°C overnight, but rose quickly with the sun.

Our run to the King Edward River was a 200-kilometre round trip. It turned out to be an unexpectedly smooth ride as the graders had just been through—in fact we caught up with them just as we got to the turn-off from the

Kalumburu road. It was like an outback expressway. I had to reign myself back from doing 110 kph which would not have been sensible on loose gravel. As it was, we varied between 80 and 90 kph through mostly flat country with waist high dry grass or, if it had been recently burnt, green sprouts that were being enjoyed by sleek-looking cattle. The country was lightly wooded, sometimes more heavily so in the wetter valleys where melaleuca paperbarks and white gums stood tall. There were also stands of tall *Livistonia* palms, and some pandanus. The early Kimberley explorers must have been delighted to discover this country which is clearly able to support stock.

We crossed the King Edward River, glad that we did not have The Manor since it was deep, stony and awkward. We located a side track described by Bill Bunbury, and drove through light bush towards sandstone rocky outcrops. A set of Wandjinas almost waved to us from a large overhang. Some lunatics had actually camped nearby and a later visitor had up-ended a rock in their fireplace and suggested in blunt language that *no camping* at such a significant site was a better option. Someone had lit a green-leafed smoke fire quite close to the paintings. I hoped this was evidence of Aboriginal people visiting. We found no Bradshaws of any note other than faded images painted over by later artists.

We returned to the road—if the rutted track could be so dignified—to try another location, and almost caused a traffic jam. Five four-wheel-drives screeched to a halt in the dust and inched past us. They were the vanguard of a 'tag-along' group, driving down from the Mitchell Plateau. (Tag-along tours churn through the countryside swallowing each others' dust. Only the leader knows where to go, and the others follow—literally blindly.) One of the drivers told me there were six more vehicles to come. They represented a four-wheel-drive club besotted with Land Rovers and Range Rovers. Fortunately we managed to turn off down our side track before the rest came through, but we had not seen the last of them, alas.

What happened then was pure magic. After the first site my hopes of finding the superb Bradshaws we'd had described to us were fading. Fortunately we kept exploring around likely rock formations, and were rewarded. The best Bradshaws were in a tiny little 'window' in the rock, like icons displayed in a church, all on their own, and quite exposed, but beautifully detailed and formed—topknots, arm tassels, the lot!

We also found a gallery wall that had Wandjinas painted over Bradshaws, but with enough remaining to photograph and see well. We had stumbled on a rich display of ancient art. An orgy of photography took place—Ros mourning the absence of her computerised Minolta. The rocks, and the general area of the paintings were simply superb. It was easy to visualise tribal people living there close to good water. In one gallery the lower rocks were polished as smooth as glass, doubtless from the rubbing of many bare bums over thousands of years. Ros nearly joined the bare bum club herself at that point as the button securing the waistband of her shorts burst off in this intriguing location while she was slithering along under a low overhang as countless indigenes must have done before her.

These singular paintings were named after the explorer Joseph Bradshaw, who was looking for new grazing land near the Prince Regent River. On 16 April 1891, he recorded in his diary his amazement at what he found:

I rode out and found that the river at this place emerges through a gorge in the sandstone range, and from a large rocky pool . . . On the west side of the river in the secluded chasms of these rocks were numerous aboriginal paintings which appeared to be of great antiquity, and I do not attribute them to the presentations of the Black race.

The English explorer George Grey, who half a century earlier was the first European to see 'Bradshaws', described them beautifully:

Some of the human figures were life-size, the bodies and limbs very attenuated, and represented as having numerous tassel-shaped adornments appended to the hair, neck, waist, arms and legs; but the most remarkable fact in connection with these drawings is that whenever a profile face is shown the features are of a most pronounced aquiline type, quite different from those of any natives we encountered. Indeed, looking at some of the groups, one might think himself viewing the painted walls of an ancient Egyptian temple. These sketches seemed to be of great age, but over the surface of some of them were drawn in fresher colours smaller and more recent scenes, and rude forms of animals, such as the kangaroo, wallaby, porcupine, crocodile &c.

The origins of the people who painted the Bradshaws are unknown. Did they come in and then leave? Or perhaps they died out, or were killed by the ancestors of today's Aboriginal people. There has been informed scholarly speculation about the tasselled and amulet wearing immigrants. And why were their dark, slender paintings so much more enduring than later Aboriginal work?

Traditional Aboriginal elders of the west Kimberley, now dead, told anthropologists that the Bradshaw figures were the work of 'a little bird called *Kuyon*, who lives in the rocks'. *Kuyon* was not considered a Dreamtime being but was a medium-sized grey mottled bird that can still be seen in the area. The birds were said to peck their beaks on the rock until they bled from the tip. They then created the Bradshaw drawings by applying their own blood—which also conveniently explained why so many painted panels were painted high up on cliffs, inaccessible to visitors today.

Bemused by the richness of it all we drove back to the King Edward River for lunch. Backing out into the 'road' to turn I nearly had a heart attack. A red 4WD with Tasmanian number plates had sneaked up right behind me, and I nearly collected it. Why was he so close, and why didn't he sound his horn when he saw my reverse lights come on? It would have been a bizarre place to have had an accident. I was not able to discuss the matter as he headed off across the river. Perhaps it was just as well.

Back at Miners Pool camp the dreaded tag-along party with eleven vehicles had invaded our sanctuary. Well, they had every right to be there too. They were cheerful and loud and into the tinnies by mid-afternoon. We were camped under a rough-barked tree with a small leaf (not a eucalypt) which had a small, yellow berry-like fruit. Doubtless the ABC's Bush Tucker Man could live on it for days, but we didn't like to try it in case it was poisonous. Perhaps we should have harvested some because Ros realised we were away from supplies for nine days not eight and might be reduced to sardines on damper for dinner on day nine. In the meantime we made do with grilled chicken thighs in a marinade of Tikka and yoghurt.

Not even the roars and cheers of the rowdy Victorian tag-alongs could mar our second evening at Miners Pool. As the moon rose behind the screen of trees to the east we saw a curious phenomenon. Something seemed to have taken a bite out of its side. It gradually dawned—perhaps 'eveninged' would be more appropriate—on us that we were seeing a partial eclipse of the moon. The reflected light dimmed and the stars made a temporary comeback as the sun's shadow invaded almost half the moon's visible surface.

A special day.

seven

You Can't Drink Tea
Through a Fly Veil

One of our changes of plan, after we'd met Bill Bunbury on our way to the Bungle Bungles, was to visit Mt Elizabeth Station run by Peter and Pat Lacy. It wasn't far inland, as we noticed on the map, from Walcott Inlet and Raft Point where we had not long before voyaged on *Coral Princess*. Like Drysdale River Station, to eke out their dwindling pastoral dollar the Lacys encouraged tourists and Bill told us about their station tour which also included some rock art sites. Peter's father, Frank Lacy, had settled on the property, then virgin country, in 1946. He arrived in the Kimberley from New Zealand in 1923, aged 25, and tackled about every job a young adventurer could do—drover, mailman, administrator on an Aboriginal mission, mechanic and cattleman.

Bill Bunbury, whose wide knowledge of the pastoral history of Western Australia is manifested in his many books and radio broadcasts, said he thought we would be interested in meeting the Lacys. Frank Lacy first saw the country during World War II when he drove bullocks from Katherine along the Fitzroy River to Broome to provide essential meat for the war effort. He was fascinated by the lush and fertile high rainfall country of the inland plateau and was granted a pastoral lease in 1944. Bill said that the present owner, Peter Lacy, was part Aboriginal. His father Frank was engaged to the matron of the Wyndham hospital during the later years of the war, but she was posted south and refused point blank to isolate herself at Mt Elizabeth. Frank tried a spell south too, living at Nannup where his fiancee was working, but was unable to leave his beloved Kimberley. He then courted Peter's mother, Teresa Bardwell, in Derby and they were married in 1944. The adventurous couple raised their children and developed Mt Elizabeth Station from 1946 on. Bill said the station was run in a distinctive way and thought we would find a visit there extremely interesting.

The Gibb River Road improved dramatically west from the Kalumburu turn-off. The 25 kilometres of private road into Mt Elizabeth Station were fair to middling, with occasional patches of bulldust and a couple of wet creek crossings, but presented no problems for us. Driving past the station airstrip on our right we reached the homestead by lunchtime. A young woman at the office (who, like Sophie, had also attended the school of tourist management that dictated all travellers should be addressed in the sing-song tones adopted by some kindergarten or primary school teachers) told us that Peter Lacy was away mustering for a week and that Pat Lacy was out leading a station tour. She could not tell us if we could go on a station tour the next day but did direct us to the camping ground about two hundred metres away.

We chose a shady corner under a large white-barked gum, screened by pandanus palms from the few campers already in residence. When we went to wind the roof of The Manor up into camping mode, one of the side canvas strips (which wrap around the telescopic supports to shield them from dust) fell to the ground. The eyelet in the top had not torn, so Ros quickly deduced that an important nut had fallen off a critical bolt. She was quite right. The telescopic supports, absolutely vital to getting our happy home up and livable, were connected to the four corners of our roof by quarter-inch bolts and nuts. One nut had fallen off, thanks to the corrugations on the Gibb River Road, and the bolt was in danger of slipping out. This could have been quite serious and we were lucky to be at a station with a big workshop where there were glass jars full of bits and pieces that mechanics and handypersons like to have about. I found a nut which fitted and screwed it on. It seemed a good idea then and there to tighten up the other three vulnerable nuts holding the roof to the lifting system. When the roof was finally raised, Ros found the errant nut on the floor. But there was another puzzle. The water in The Manor's 60-litre tank was brown with dust after only a day's run. We wondered if there was a crack in the top of the tank. This was a repair I couldn't attempt so we had to wait until we got back to Broome and our friendly Jayco agent Ron Harris. Fortunately we carry two extra 20-litre jerry cans of water for drinking, and the dirty brown water could do for washing up and selves.

No sooner had we topped up our water supplies when a cloud of dust and roar of motors announced the arrival of the Victorian Land Rover tag-along mob heading relentlessly for the camping ground. Were they stalking us? None of them spoke in a normal voice. They shouted at each other, even around a camp fire. They were cheerful and harmless enough but camping with them every night was wearing thin. I was desperate to find out where they were going next so we could break the nexus and ambled over to the small ablution block where a couple of them were waiting for a shower.

'Gudday.'

'Gudday.'

'Good day's run?'

'I dunno, mate. All I could see was the dust of the bloke in front of me.'

That seemed to be the downside of tag-along travel—not seeing anything of the countryside. 'Where will you be tomorrow night?'

'Buggered if I know mate. We just tag along. We'll finish up in Broome eventually though, I do know that.'

They didn't know where they were going and weren't quite sure where they'd come from. But their leader did know and that was all they needed to know. A strange business. Every day the same, a blur of dust, bone-jarring roads and boozy camps with nary a moment for solitary contemplation of the unique Kimberley environment. There was no guarantee we wouldn't have them for the rest of the week!

At 4 pm we went over to the homestead to meet Pat Lacy, who had returned with her tour. She hadn't intended to lead it, but the Aboriginal stockman who was supposed to had been delayed. Pat was a tall, fit, no-nonsense countrywoman who managed to spare a few minutes to have a cup of tea with us despite having been away from the station all day. First the bad news—she was fully booked for the station tour the next day as a 16-seat Oka four-wheel-drive bus was coming in and there were no spare seats. The good news—we could 'tag-along' in Penelope if we wanted to, which we thought would suit us just fine. She thought the tour would be led by Dickie, the stockman who hadn't turned up that morning. If he didn't show, she would do it herself.

Pat explained that Mt Elizabeth was one of the few stations still using Aboriginal workers since the decision to give award wages to black stockmen had ended the long association of Aboriginal people with the pastoral industry. Some years ago the Lacys hived off a section of the property and gave it to the local Aboriginal people who had worked on the station since Peter's father Frank started it. This was partly because the Aboriginal community there could not get government assistance while they lived on station land. She said it was a sheer delight to see the enthusiasm and pride that the Aboriginal stockmen displayed in the lead-up to the muster, the actual muster and their superb bushcraft while working the cattle on Mt Elizabeth. 'It seems to be in the blood.'

The closing of the meatworks in Derby, Broome and Wyndham, Pat said, meant that the closest abattoir for Mt Elizabeth Station beasts was either Katherine or Perth! This meant a prohibitive cost of $140 a head to get their cattle to slaughter.

'The Kimberley really lost out, and I don't know why. It simply isn't worthwhile to get our meat to market, so tourism helps fill the gap.'

Pat said that things had been particularly bad since the American meat export trade collapsed. Mt Elizabeth Station was not yet ready to enter the live cattle industry because they needed to change to Brahman cross cattle, and were doing so.

I asked why Peter was out mustering if there was no market?

'You have to muster each year to protect the quality of the herd, weed out the scrub bulls and try to get the Brahman cross stock up and running.'

Pat Lacy was running the station and the tourist operation in the meantime, and Peter would be out mustering for another week. I felt like asking her what she did with her spare time . . .

The Oka, with sixteen people on board, rumbled in at this point like a Sherman tank. The camping ground was bursting at the seams and a whiff of sewage percolating across to our camp from the small ablution block suggested the overloaded septic tank system had similar problems.

Not far from us an older couple were camped beside their flat-bed utility in a traditional canvas A-frame tent that looked like a relic of the 1950s. It was. Pam and Pat Miller, whom we had spoken to briefly before the invasion, were in a state of deep shock, sandwiched between the tag-alongs and the Oka group who seemed, if anything, louder than the Victorians and were putting up a small village of sleeping tents.

Pam and Pat came across to The Manor for 'Cocktails at Five'. Pam brought with her an intriguing plate of nibbles—some home-made salami, a kind of flat crisp bread and Dutch rusks. They don't have refrigeration and rather gloried in doing things the old-fashioned way. 'After all,' she said, 'refrigeration in cars and campers has only been available for the last 25 years.' They ate rice, lentils, station meat when they could get it (it is illegal to sell it these days) and whatever else didn't need a fridge.

Their great joy was to get away from it all and camp alone in wild places. They had just spent a week completely on their own at Walcott Inlet, which can be reached from Mt Elizabeth Station down private tracks and is considered a tough call even with a four-wheel-drive. That was why they were spooked by being surrounded by crowds of shouting people.

We judged Pat was in his early seventies and Pam her sixties. They were adventurous travellers. Last year they went on a driving tour (not driving themselves) in Mongolia! Going across one river, the vehicle following with all their luggage was swept away by the water, and had to be rescued using a horse and a borrowed Russian tractor.

Ex-colonials from Kenya, when they chose to get out before independence they looked at a map of the world for countries with the right climate and empty space. Western Australia fitted the bill. Now their farm inland from Geraldton was run by their children and they were free to travel. Their four-wheel-drive Mitsubishi utility had a cabin on the back, not for sleeping but for stores and spares. It looked like a mechanic's workshop, which is what it was, because Pat was working as a mechanic when he went to Kenya and met Pam, a farmer's daughter. His own background was a bit difficult to work out. He seemed very British but grew up in Argentina and so spoke fluent Spanish—with an Argentinian accent as he realised when he went travelling to Chile in recent years and wasn't popular! He had to modify his accent.

Despite their pride in not having a fridge, Pat seemed to relish a couple of cold cans of beer. It was well and truly dark when he and Pam headed back to their camp, now subsumed by other campers. At about 11 pm we were all wakened by a blood-curdling scream from the Oka camp. We found out later that a pet joey from the homestead had tried to climb into the nice warm pouch of a sleeping bag which already had someone in it. The young kangaroo would not take no for an answer and had about three attempts. There were lots of pets wandering about near the homestead and camping ground, including a big domestic turkey (destined for Christmas?) and the odd peacock. We heard Pat and Pam leave about 6.30 am—seeking their bush solitude that had been so noisily interrupted.

It was tag-along time for us, but only for a day. Pat Lacy drove down to the settlement to pick up our guide, Dickie Tatya, an elderly Aboriginal smartly turned out in a white Stetson, long-sleeved shirt and blue jeans. Mt Elizabeth is one of only several stations accessible from the Gibb River that arrange visitor tours led by members of the local Aboriginal community to sites where the stories associated with the rock art are shared. The Oka was full of amiable Victorians on a 'design your own tour' arrangement with a driver and cook. They had flown to Darwin and boarded the Oka and then headed off to the Kimberley. They would fly home from Broome after three weeks away.

Mt Elizabeth Station was 263 000 hectares—a modest holding by Kimberley standards. We followed station fences along flat grassy plains for about 30 kilometres and then turned left into more interesting undulating, lightly timbered rocky country. The first stop was for a rock art gallery site and, as the Victorians piled out of the Oka, Dickie asked them to stay back until he announced our arrival to the Wandjina spirits and requested permission to visit. Walking ahead, the old man called out in Aboriginal language, his voice echoing around the rock walls while our spines tingled. Then, and only then, were we allowed to walk to the gallery.

On one of the stops I saw the same yellow fruit that I'd seen on a small tree by our camp at Miners Pool. But it would not have sustained Les Hiddons, the ABC's Bush Tucker Man, for very long at all. Dickie identified it as the quinine bush. It is very bitter and not used by the Aborigines for anything—not even medicine. It was, said Dickie, only eaten by emus!

The lunch stop was splendid. We walked to a picturesque pool set among white-barked river gums and pandanus palms. Across the water we saw a big cave with more rock paintings which some of the better swimmers swam over to see.

On our way back—we had come out about 45 kilometres on a Walcott Inlet Road—there was an unscheduled stop at the old homestead where Frank Lacy had begun the property and where the young Peter Lacy grew up. Dickie Tatya wanted to go there because he had worked there as a young stockman. The original homestead was still brightly whitewashed but as we walked closer we could see that twenty years of neglect and the unforgiving Kimberley climate had taken its toll. The earth and stone walls had started to bulge out away from the wooden corner supports. Inside white ants had built their red mud tunnels up the stone walls to invade the timber frames, joists and ceiling. (Pat Lacy told me later that the termite trails needed to be knocked down regularly but the people who lived there for several years after the Lacys left had not bothered and, with the white ants now well entrenched, the old homestead could not be saved.)

We wandered through some of the corrugated iron outbuildings which were in better shape. We found out later that Peter and Pat Lacy lived in one of them as a young married couple. In one shed there were the remains of an old pedal radio—the pedalling mechanism only—and an ancient Singer sewing machine.

Dickie was quite emotional about going back and told me he remembered many good times. I asked him to pose beside the rusting bonnet and body of an old Chev utility he once used to drive.

'Sometimes at night I see lights here,' he said. 'Then I blink and the lights have gone.'

Pat Lacy told us that the family had to move because of lack of water. The river nearby, which used to be deep enough to fish and boat on, gradually dried up—perhaps as a result of sand bars further up. 'Peter's mother remembers fishing with Aboriginal women on its banks as a young married woman and catching lots of fish.'

Back at the camp ground Ros was cross with herself for miscounting the number of days we would have on the Gibb River Road before getting back to Broome. I felt mildly culpable, having mucked around with her carefully worked out schedule in my relentless quest for Bradshaws. We had to disgorge ourselves of another gorge. Manning Gorge got the chop. Perhaps next time. We planned to spend several nights at Bell Gorge National Park which was well recommended by Greg and Heather in Kununurra—and with luck we'd be without the dust-swallowing Land Rover tag-alongs. We had become quite fond of the Oka Victorians after our station tour, during which we had tagged along ourselves! That evening I glanced up to see what looked like a blue and yellow rocket arch slowly across the horizon to the west. It must have been a meteorite, and quite close.

The further west we travelled, the better the Gibb River Road surface became. We refuelled at Mt Barnett Station at 106 cents a litre. It was always disquieting when the dollar total exceeded the number of litres. Stopping to gather some firewood by the roadside to load on our roof rack in case we were permitted to have a camp fire at Bell Gorge, we were overtaken by the Oka lot who waved and tooted as they left us choking in their dust. They were parked at the Ininti Aboriginal Settlement Store when we pulled in for a cold drink, and yelled out that we should give them our firewood. I told them to get stuffed. That seemed to surprise them. I said that kind of language represented the charm and grace of my middle-class upbringing. They said it was coming down to their level. I said I couldn't remember leaving their level. And on we went.

At Bell Gorge the best camp sites were arranged along the river El Questro style and even had flushing pump-out toilets! This was to protect the environment, not to pamper visitors. The National Park rangers looking after Bell Gorge were Jan and Trevor, known in CALM jargon as 'mobiles'— meaning they lived in a caravan and moved around Western Australia to different areas where they were needed. Jan told us to look out for the little turtles in the creek which were being scientifically investigated.

We arrived at our creek-front camp site at midday, and it was hotter than we had been used to in the Kimberley until then. The dreaded Western Australian bush flies were out in force. The Manor is well flyscreened, but you had to be careful not to carry platoons of them inside on your back. If they got into Penelope they did not fly about distractedly as bush flies generally do, but concentrated on faces and relentlessly headed for eyes, ears and nostrils. Occasional spluttering signalled breathing one of the little beasties down your throat. Sitting outside in the shade to write my diary, I achieved great comfort by wearing a close-meshed fly veil. It was gratifying to watch the bush flies marching up and down the mesh in fury and frustration. Ros handed me a cup of tea, and I had a false start.

'You can't drink tea through a fly veil,' said I profoundly, and Ros said, 'That could make a chapter heading!'

We decided not to tackle the gorge until the cool of the early morning. The weather seemed much hotter and more humid. We thought perhaps it was some kind of front coming through, or the dry season just getting hotter.

The turtles were intriguing. We climbed down the bank and clusters of the little creatures rose to the surface expectantly. Above their eyes they had cute little orange flashes which gave them a jaunty air, rather like Macaroni penguins much further south. Ranger Jan said the kids called them Ninja turtles. We succumbed to blackmail and fed them some small pieces of bread. This attracted the attention of some black fish called sooty grunters—they reputedly grunt disgustedly when caught—and there was unseemly jostling. The Ninja turtles cleverly formed a scrum with their carapaces edge to edge and kept the grunters out while they scoffed the bread. Their DNA is being tested to possibly identify them as a unique subspecies.

Jan's partner, Ranger Trevor, arrived to collect our modest camping fees and warned us not to leave buckets of water outside the Manor (which we would have done) as little marsupials can come along in the night, climb in and drown. It was not something that would have occurred to us. We were allowed to light a fire in the regulation CALM barbecue and had the luxury of a camp oven baked chicken dinner later while little bandicoots scuffled through the undergrowth as we ate.

After dinner we sat back with a glass of one of Greg Williams' less poisonous muscats, watching as the stars blazed overhead.

Ros had been musing about the increasing pressure of tourism on the Kimberley country and made the point that the onslaught was at least only seasonal. The country got a compulsory rest for about half the year because of the wet season which washed and cleaned it ready for the next dry season visitor invasion.

We set off for Bell Gorge about 7.30 am. There were already a cluster of vehicles at the car park. Ros had been wanting to photograph the lustrously red Kimberley Kurra-jong flowers, but the trees we had seen until then were bare. Up the hill from the car park she saw two photo-graphers with tripods photographing a large bloom that was conveniently low on a Kurrajong, but Ros felt it inappro-priate to go near them while they were working. She made a mental note to go and photograph it later.

When we did come back and struggled up to the tree, we found that the photographers had nicked the bloom! Even though it was a national park and all. There was another tree nearby, but the flowers were too high. Bastards! I wish we'd disturbed them after all. I told Ranger Trevor about it later and he was furious, but we had no reason to note the registration number of the car when we first saw them, and the pusillanimous pluckers had probably gone by then.

Unlike other gorges we had visited and accessed from

underneath, Bell Gorge is reached from above. There is a boab tree, with a bell carved into its bloated trunk, beside a steep stony path which leads down to the valley floor where a pristine stream tinkles musically along. It was a great luxury to be able to drink the water—sadly not possible almost anywhere in Australia these days due to agricultural or other human-caused pollution.

At the waterfall at the head of the gorge—it continues in true Kimberley style 100 kilometres down to the sea—we walked along a rocky ledge and were able to look back at the cascades. They were at least running, but would be at their most spectacular in the wet season. The less intrepid could swim in shallow pools at the head of the falls, but the best option was to do a rock scramble around a roughly marked trail down to the base of the falls where a great deep pool was joined in a chain with other ponds. It provided a magnificent swimming spot much appreciated by those energetic enough to climb down from the cliffs above.

The car park had filled up when we got back with several varieties of four-wheel-drive adventure tours, including one from Tasmania. 'Booking ahead essential' said their blurb on the side of the truck as they had a two-year waiting list. Once the red centre and Alice Springs teemed with coaches and camping tours. Now the action had moved to the Kimberley with Alice Springs on the outer. The Kimberley was booming.

Friends who do not go camping tend to be incredulous about our habit of pulling up and camping alone out in the bush or desert. 'But is it safe?' they ask.

'Probably safer than walking down your suburban

street,' we generally say. After all, Australia is not like Africa. There are no lions, tigers, elephants or hippos. Kangaroos and emus do not have a proven track record as killers, although snakes have despatched the odd unlucky soul.

But for those not used to outback driving and camping in Australia, the very thought of camping in isolation is one of utter vulnerability.

'But someone might come along and . . .'

'And what? Rob us, shoot us—is that what you mean?'

The cities are a less safe bet than the bush, it seems to me. A psychiatrically disturbed gunman randomly sprayed bullets around a shopping mall in Sydney a few years ago and killed innocent shoppers. The Hoddle Street massacre still haunts the minds of Melburnians who also recall how a demented man gunned down people in the street for no discernible reason. Bags can be snatched, or elderly people bashed for the few dollars in their purses or wallets, yet no one seriously avoids shopping malls—for safety reasons, anyway—or has a second thought about walking down the street.

The outback seems tranquil and innocent by comparison. In all our travels we can only remember one worrying incident when we camped off a back road too near Bourke on a Friday night and were harassed by a utility load of shickered shooters who shone their spotlights on our camp, jeered and shouted obscenities before driving further on. We had our two young children with us and did not relish the prospect of this rowdy mob returning in the early hours of the morning having seen us there earlier. More for peace of mind than anything else we moved camp to a roadside stop near the main highway. Perhaps nothing would have happened, but we felt uneasy. In retrospect it was not sensible to have stopped so close to a major town on such an obvious drinking night.

We believe that the further 'out' you are, the safer it is. The only problem for us in isolation is being seen by other campers who feel it necessary to join us for collective security.

Chatting with Ranger Trevor at Bell Gorge National Park, we were reminded of a dark period in the Kimberley's history in June 1997 when the innocence and joy of remote camping were savagely compromised. Trevor was caught up in two weeks of terror when a deranged 'Rambo'-style gunman murdered five campers in the Top End. On 10 July, Marcus Bullen (70), a former deputy mayor of Fremantle, and his son Lance (42) were fishing at Timber Creek, enjoying the superb dry season weather in company with thousands of other Australians in the region at that time of the year. A German tourist, Josef Schwab (26), stalked them and shot them both with a military assault rifle. Their naked bodies were buried in shallow graves near the river and their vehicle and clothes were torched, presumably to conceal evidence.

There was little for police to work on. They were keen to interview the driver of a white Toyota four-wheel-drive utility seen in the area—but in the Top End, such vehicles are as common as Volvos on Sydney's North Shore.

Five days later Schwab struck again, this time further west near Kununurra. Two air traffic controllers, Terry Kent (36) and Phillip Walkemeyer (26), and Phillip's fiancee Julie Anne Warren (25) were also on a fishing expedition. They were camped by the picturesque Pentecost River on the Gibb River Road, over which we had passed a few days before. The crazed Schwab stalked them as they sat around their camp fire and shot them all in the back. Again he stripped their bodies naked and burned their car with their belongings inside. This time he threw their bodies in the river, probably hoping crocodiles would dispose of the remains. Terry Kent was married with three small children. Julie Warren and Phillip Walkemeyer were to have been married a few weeks after the fishing expedition.

The Top End and Kimberley regions went into shock. The police organised a massive aerial grid search across three states from the Northern Territory to Western Australia and down to South Australia. Station guns were leant beside front doors and windows. The dust cloud of every approaching vehicle to remote settlements was subjected to anxious scrutiny. Clearly a deranged serial killer, whose vehicle had not even been properly identified, was on the loose. A white Toyota utility and a battered beige Ford Falcon were suspected, and it was clear that the murderous mystery maniac could strike again at any time.

Road blocks were set up, all camping banned, and tourists travelled in convoys for safety. At that stage our amiable Ranger Trevor was involved in getting campers out of the Bungle Bungle ranges. (Later on our journey we met a Western Australian couple in Karratha, Judy and Alan Wilkins, who were in the Bungle Bungles at the time and were approached by a very nervous Trevor. Alan said he calmed down a lot when it became clear he and Jude were not gun-toting killers, but genuine campers. Trevor suggested they get out of the area for their own safety and they did.)

The breakthrough happened when a pilot mustering

cattle on Jubilee Station near Fitzroy Crossing on 19 June
spotted a white Toyota utility out in the bush concealed
under a green tarpaulin. A team from the Western Australian
Tactical Response Group armed with rifles, hand guns,
tear gas and bulletproof vests was immediately flown to
the area. As police approached the vehicle, a man dressed
in jungle greens, with a bandanna tied around his fore-
head, sprang out from hiding and began firing at them
with a high powered rifle. In the jargon of such occasions,
police 'returned fire' and he was shot dead. No police were
injured.

Later investigations showed that Schwab (26), who had
been trained in the use of weapons during his military service in Germany, had come to Australia the previous April,
hired the Toyota utility from Brisbane Airport and disappeared. He told the car hire people that he would bring the
vehicle back in a week. Sources in Germany revealed that
Schwab was a loner with a mean streak who had a background of car stealing and violence. Despite that, he had
worked as an armed security guard in Germany, including
a year's stint in that capacity at the United States Embassy
in Bonn! Schwab had told friends he intended to emigrate
to Australia and make a new start. Ranger Trevor, who
called by to check when we were leaving, said it was a
bizarre episode he was glad to have seen resolved. Since
then people had been camping out with impunity, as they
should be able to do.

We said farewell to the mendicant Ninja turtles and tossed
them a last few scraps of bread. The sooty grunters had
given up trying to breach the carapace curtain.

On my birthday, 2 August (I missed the Horses' Birthday by only one day), our food supplies were running down a bit. It had been eight days since our last resupply at Kununurra but I was confident Ros would rustle up a reasonable feed at a yet to be selected bush camp to celebrate (or mourn) the beginning of my 63rd year. In fact she was muttering slightly about the number of gorges and interesting cattle stations we were not going to be able to visit because of my Bradshaw obsession and explorations.

The western end of the Gibb River Road passes through rich cattle country, which was not discovered until more than a decade after the Camden Harbour settlement disaster. In 1879 surveyor Alexander Forrest led an expedition from the De Grey River in Western Australia right through to the Overland Telegraph Line in the Northern Territory. This pioneering journey revealed useful grazing territory in the Fitzroy Basin and the headwaters of the Ord River.

Forrest's report whetted the appetites of budding pastoralists across the country. As well as noting the rivers he had seen, he estimated that the region boasted 'an area of 20 millions of acres of good, well-watered country, suitable for pastoral purposes, besides a large area suitable for the culture of sugar, rice or coffee'.

The story of the opening up of the Kimberley cattle country is a magnificent saga well documented in books like Mary Durack's classic *Kings in Grass Castles*. The cattle droving feats were staggering, and involved somehow getting cattle over dry stages as long as 80 kilometres in from the east. Nat Buchanan was the first to drove cattle from Queensland in 1884, bringing 4000 head to what would eventually be the Ord River Station. The Aborigines called Buchanan 'Old Paraway' because he was always coming from far away. (Our friend Ted Egan had written a song about him.) Buchanan cut a distinctive figure on his horse with his flaming red hair and green umbrella to protect him from the sun.

Then came the Duracks, a year later, who had driven cattle from Cooper's Creek in Queensland to the black soil plains further north of the Ord. That journey took two years! But surely the greatest epic cattle drive of all time was in 1886 when the MacDonald brothers arrived at Fossil Downs near Margaret River with their cattle which they drove for 5600 kilometres—from Goulburn in New South Wales. Just think about that for a moment...

The droving route from Thylungra in Queensland stretched north to the Gulf and swung west into no-man's-land. On the map it looked simple enough, and measured a fairly neat 2500 miles—4000 kilometres. In fact, it veered around the compass points from water to water, grass to grass, and no one knew how long the journey was in 'drover's miles'.

These droving feats were extraordinary. When calves were born along the way the drovers tried to save them. The newborns were slung in canvas hammocks under the wagons and then put back into the mob with their mothers in the evenings. But if there were too many, they had to be destroyed. Mary Durack writes in *Kings in Grass Castles* of one of these epic treks by her forbears:

It was one of the drovers' saddest reflections that they had been forced to dispose of no less than 1300 new-born calves during the trip. It was a complete waste, for stockmen were oddly squeamish about eating veal, or 'staggering Bob' as it was known in the cattle camps.

In 1882 prospectors Philip Saunders and Adam Johns retraced Alexander Forrest's exploratory journey along the Fitzroy and found small traces of gold near the upper tributaries of the Ord River. In 1885 gold was also found near Halls Creek and gold fever lured 2000 prospectors into the area. They had to make a difficult journey from the shanty towns of Derby and Wyndham and some died on the way. Typhoid, dysentery and scurvy killed many prospectors before they had a chance to dig a shovelful of dirt. There was the usual mix of hard drinkers, fortune seekers and the inevitable thieves and swindlers, but there wasn't much gold and by 1890 it was really all over.

However, the gold rush did help pastoral settlement because it had forced the state government to establish the infrastructure so badly needed—the port towns of Derby and Wyndham along with police stations, telegraph and mail services.

The Aborigines, already being displaced by the squatters, could not be expected to be enthused by the arrival of the diggers. When they defended their territory by spearing gold miners, retribution was swift and horrible. One miner, George Hales, described an ambush:

> Having bailed up a large number of blacks in a gully who showed fight, they proceeded to slaughter them with repeating rifles. It is certain a great many of them were killed, some say at least a hundred. The blacks could not understand why their comrades dropped one after another, although they could see nothing coming towards them.

It did not take them long to understand about guns. There was resistance to white incursions with some impressive guerilla warfare. The most notorious and effective was the case of Pigeon, a black police tracker, whose tribal name was Jandamarra. In 1895 Pigeon was helping a Constable Richardson bring into Derby a group of Aborigines wanted for murder, cattle spearing or absconding from gaol. One of the most wanted was an Aboriginal warrior called Ellemara. Pigeon and another Aboriginal tracker known as Captain captured Ellemara. But on their way back to Richardson's police outpost to chain Ellemara to the other group of outlaws waiting there, Ellemara successfully appealed to their black patriotism to stop being tools of the white man's oppression and switch sides so that they could fight, with their own people, to wipe out all whites.

Pigeon and Captain were not only trained to use guns, but also knew about police strategic techniques. When Pigeon got back to camp he shot Constable Richardson and freed the chained blacks. Led by Pigeon the group took off to ambush a white party on its way to set up a cattle station. They shot and killed two Europeans and then had plenty of guns and a store of food. Pigeon's Mob, as they were called, held out for two years, carrying out raids on settlers, and systematically trained a large group of Aborigines to fight the settlers and police. Their women were used as lookouts on the hill tops. Their bushcraft, guns and awareness of white tactics made them formidable guerillas.

Pigeon was mortally wounded and died in a gun battle with police near Tunnel Creek (which he used as a hideout) in 1897. The Australian author Ion Idriess wrote a book about the affair called *Outlaws of the Leopolds*. There is a strong element of admiration at the exploits of these fighters for Aboriginal independence in Idriess's account, which was a brave position to take in 1952 when his book was first published.

We called in to Windjana Gorge (not far from Tunnel Creek where Jandamarra made his last stand) to marvel as travellers do at the huge limestone cliffs pierced by the 3.5 kilometre gorge through coral reefs on a long gone Devonian sea coastline before sea levels fell. Johnston freshwater crocodiles were sunbaking sleepily beside the still waters of the gorge. As they are fish eaters and reputedly not interested in eating people, visitors sometimes pose beside them. OK, so I did too . . .

We paused at the remains of the police post at Lillamaloora where Pigeon shot Constable Richardson 125 years ago. Almost in the shadow of the sinister Napier Range, its limestone walls were still well preserved. Richardson was shot, it is said, as he was resting while reading a copy of the *Police Gazette*. There is a memorial for him near the remains of the station.

> Dedicated to the memory of constable William Richardson who was killed in the line of duty on October 31, 1894, at Lillamaloora Police Outpost whilst on patrol from Derby Police Station.

Aboriginal resistance is also commemorated elsewhere. Ranger Trevor had told me only that morning that Jandamarra was shot by one of his own people, another police tracker—a sad commentary on divided loyalties and confirmed by the information board at Lillamaloora.

> On April 1, 1897 [Jandamarra] was shot near the entrance to his hideout at Tunnel Creek by an Aboriginal tracker Mongo Mick who was reputed to have the same magic powers as Jandamarra.

Trevor was interested in Jandamarra because his sister-
in-law had married into an Aboriginal family connected
with Jandamarra. He said he had been given new information on the affair and hoped to write about it one day. It was
a remarkable coincidence, I felt, to visit the historic police
post on the same day I had spoken to Trevor about
Jandamarra. 'Six degrees of separation' . . .

It was getting late and we still had to choose a birthday
bush camp. With the sun low and red on the horizon we
turned right off the Gibb River Road towards the May
River and drove along some rough tracks through river
gums and dry grass searching for solitude. I found a place
where we could turn in a small clearing and switched off
Penelope's engine.

It was not safe to have a fire with all the dry grass
around us. Besides, we had nothing left to barbecue. I set
up a folding table beside Penelope to plug my computer
into the Landcruiser's battery system and opened my diary:

As I write these few lines Ros is in The Manor preparing pasta
with tomato and pesto sauce. We have been away from Kununurra
now for eight nights, and our fresh supplies are running low. But we
will eat well nevertheless, and wash it down with a bottle of
Tasmanian pinot noir a friend gave me from his own small vineyard
for a special occasion. That has arrived. The sun is setting through the
river gums behind me, and there is stillness and peace enhanced only
by the occasional bird call.

I cannot think of a better location to notch up 62 years. With luck
I hope we'll still be camping in wild and remote places—and
many do—in our eighties.

eight

Engorged

For the third time in a month—twice by road and once from the sea—we were headed for Broome. This historic settlement had become our service point and springboard for north-western adventure.

We farewelled the Gibb River Road a few kilometres south of Derby and detoured to drive through the town we first visited in 1982. The boab-lined main street led straight to the wharf which, like Wyndham, was semi-circular so the road trains crammed with cattle could drive on and off without turning. As in 1982, it was low tide when we arrived, and the mud and mangroves seemed so far below the concrete pylons of the wharf that looking down induced vertigo. Ros remembered that on our first visit we had been engulfed by a cloud of what we thought were midges, but turned out to be sandflies. There was an emergency dash for the sanctuary of our Kombi van but the damage had been done and our two little boys scratched and itched horrendously for the next week.

Arriving at the tree-shaded Tarangau Caravan Park at Cable Beach was like coming home. We even had the

luxury of an on-site visit from Ron Harris (the genial giant
of the Jayco agency) to drop out The Manor's water tank
and find out why our water kept getting muddy. Ron just
managed to squeeze his big frame under the camper and
quickly sourced the problem. All water tanks need a
breather hole and the manufacturers had recessed one in
the top of the tank. This was fine for sealed roads and urban
situations but hopeless in outback conditions. As we drove
along the tank flexed, water bubbled out, mixed with dust
to become mud and was sucked in and out continuously. No
wonder our tank water was brown. Ron just fitted a breather
pipe with an elbow joint exiting to the rear, and end of
problem. To be fair to Jayco, they had fixed this glitch in
later models. We had to find out the hard way.

After Broome we were heading into new territory, away
from our 1982 Kimberley explorations and south on a fairly
vague itinerary that would take us to the Pilbara and the
Dampier peninsula, alternating coastal travel with excursions into the Mid West and old gold mining towns,
hopefully including some of Western Australia's legendary
wildflower territory. We had planned to include Perth
before heading home across the Nullarbor. But we were
keen to remain flexible and take advantage of good advice
along the way—one of the great joys of nomadic travel.

We stocked up in Chinatown where modern super-
markets are cheek by jowl with Yuen Wing's wonderful
old-fashioned store crammed with tinned lychees, curry
powders, chillies, bamboo shoots, coconut milk and everything from shiny metal woks to electric rice cookers.
An elderly Chinese woman sat by an equally venerable
cash register. I half expected to see an abacus. When I
exchanged pleasantries her beaming smile and an accent as

Australian as billy tea demonstrated both classic Broome friendliness and its legendary multiculturalism.

It is quite extraordinary how some people in camping grounds will live near you for days but wait until you are hitching up your camper or caravan before coming over to have matey conversations. 'Hans' had recognised me from ABC TV and mooched over to chat.

'Vat a nice camper you haf—can you take it anyvere?'

I muttered at him while wrestling with lowering The Manor's coupling onto the tow ball. On a previous expedition I was distracted at a similar critical moment, did not lock it on properly and we were saved from disaster only by an afterthought when we had actually started off. Ros was aware of this at such times and was not welcoming. She said it might be necessary to have a sign printed to display while I was linking up: 'MY HUSBAND IS ABSENT-MINDED. DO NOT TALK TO HIM WHILE HE IS CONNECTING CAMPER TO CAR.'

We topped up with fuel at a BP service station we had not used before. I asked to use their toilet and was given a key. In this part of the world that was usually how they went about keeping the blacks out but they'd gone to extreme measures here. After circling the complex twice I still couldn't locate the dunny until a staff member indicated an unmarked door.

We retraced our route west again for about 40 kilometres to the intersection with Highway One and headed south towards Port Hedland, 610 kilometres away. The country was fairly bleak as the highway skirted the edge of the Great Sandy Desert on our left, and was too far inland to see the Indian Ocean on our right. The sparse scrub and expanse of flat country reminded us of the Tanami Desert. There were some occasional cattle to be seen grazing on marginal pasture. We planned to turn due south down to the Pilbara before reaching Port Hedland and before that we would stop overnight at the 80 Mile Beach caravan and camping ground about halfway between Broome and Port Hedland.

Turning into a roadside stop for a cuppa, we discovered a collection of grey nomads enjoying an al fresco camp. There were basic facilities there—a shaded area with picnic tables, a water tank and a long-drop dunny that Ros reported had no seat, no paper and was exceedingly unsanitary in every way. Camping was, however, free. One of the caravans overnighting there had a large sign painted on its side in black letters: 'WE ARE SPENDING OUR KIDS' INHERITANCE.' I had a brief chat with the unrepentant owners, Ruth and John Hogg from Gulgong. They were doing just that.

At the turn-off to our evening stop a sign said: 'There are no strangers at 80 Mile Beach Caravan Park—only friends you haven't met.' Was that compulsory? All 160 powered sites were occupied, which didn't bother us. The camping areas were nearer to the beach and less crowded. Fishing was supposed to be good there. Walking up and over the sand bank revealed a truly amazing spectacle. As far as the eye could see in both directions, beach fishermen and women stood shoulder to shoulder, no less than ten metres apart, their lines cast into milky coloured shallow water. We watched, fascinated, for twenty minutes and not a single fish was caught by the thirty or so anglers we could keep tabs on, thus bearing out my late father's contention that people go beach fishing for reasons other than catching fish.

It was difficult to find a space to swim between the anglers, lines and baited hooks. We did not intend to do more than go in waist deep and submerge ourselves briefly as the rather laconic woman at the park shop had said we should take care because of sharks. She failed to mention other hazards like sea snakes which we noticed swimming gaily along, their sinuous necks held high out of the water. Lots of them! Next morning Ros bought some local maps which had more specific information:

> MARINE DANGERS. Care should be taken when entering these waters. Sharp coral, sea snakes, stone fish, sting rays, cone shells and sharks may be encountered.

The barefoot Bowdens considered themselves fortunate to have survived their impromptu dip. It was safer marvelling at the spectacular sunset as the sun dipped into a bright pink sea and streaky scattered clouds on the horizon turned blood red, then crimson.

Large, remote caravan parks are like small towns with a population—not all transients—of 500 or more people. Here the office shop had local craft work for sale, crocheted moccasins, scenic paintings on wood saws and high kitsch maps of Australia with gorges, waterfalls and bright red rocks. Entrepreneurial activity was everywhere. A sign outside the women's toilet block advertised haircuts for $6. Ros could not resist buying the 80 Mile Beach Travellers Cook Book prepared by locals to raise money for the all-important Flying Doctor Service—of particular concern to the older age group well represented at

Ancient carvings on sunbaked rocks at Punda, near Newman, Pilbara.

(Left) Colourful layers of sedimentary rock make useful handholds as we explore the deep
gorges of Karijini National Park. (Right) Ros is actually able to touch each side of the
bottom of Weano Gorge as she climbs down to Handrail Pool in the Karijini National Park.

Water splashed on the rocks brings out the brilliance of jasper gemstone at Marble Bar.

Flame Grevillea, near Newman, Pilbara.

We bought 'French' marmalade from Italian Vera Yugolinda's roadside stall, dangerously close the the infamous, now closed, blue asbestos mine in the Wittenoom Gorge.

The mysterious 'climbing men' petroglyphs of the Burrup Peninsula. Nothing remotely like them has been found among the 10 000 other rock carvings on the peninsula.

Petroglyphs of two bush turkeys on the Dampier Peninsula.

(Left) Vain search for 'rough' water under a dry waterfall at Kennedy Range National Park. Two days later a sudden storm turned it into a wet one! (Right) 'Flintstone rock', at Mt Augustus straddles a small creek, creating a natural cave that is decorated with ancient rock carvings.

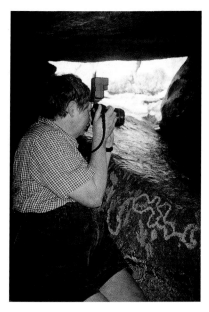

(Left) Ros under 'Flintstone Rock', photographing the curious wavy lines etched into the granitic stone—a style reminiscent of John Olsen. (Right) The rare Mt Augustus foxglove which grows along creek lines on and near the world's biggest rock.

The unexplained European ship at Walga Rock.
Who drew it and why?

The natural rock gallery at Walga Rock, where the ochre drawing of a European ship shares space with traditional Aboriginal rock paintings.

Grinding stone and natural rock bowl at Erong Springs Station—a poignant reminder of ancient community life.

Camping at Erong Springs Station. Ros is always saying I travel with everything including . . .

Fancy doing that just for us . . . a carpet of everlasting daisies at White Wells Station, Mid West, Western Australia.

The wonderfully macabre wreath flowers we found in a gravel pit near Pindar, east of Geraldton.

Morning coffee on the road from Paynes Find to Sandstone—there wasn't a lot of traffic about.

80 Mile Beach. Over the previous four years a core group of park winter residents had raised funds for signal flares for the airstrip, a two-way radio and first aid equipment. The 1997 first edition of the cook book sold out in an hour! It specialised in quickie recipes for campers:

Lazy French Onion Dip

sour cream—300 ml
French onion soup—1 pkt

Mix together and chill. Serve with biscuits.

Others were more elaborate, like 'Cheesy Vegetable Curry' and 'Heather's Special Occasion Apple Pie'. Home-spun hints were included: 'Chopping the ingredients lets the calories leak out.' Ros found the ladies' loo doubled as an information kiosk. One woman, who made hats out of plastic bags, had run out of raw materials and put out an SOS for used shopping bags.

A bronze plaque near the office commemorated lives lost on the unprotected shore between Broome and Port Hedland. In the 1897 cyclone, 24 luggers were wrecked on this coast and the bodies of 136 sailors washed ashore. Many of the destroyed vessels were named—*Cocoa Nut, Edith le Grand, Maggie, Mary Ann, Pearl, Ranger* . . . The plaque was commissioned in memory of one of the pearling captains, John Alexander Graves, by his descendants. Captain Graves and his son John were lost in the wreck of *Osprey* in 1897. Their bodies were never recovered. The Museum of Western Australia information board nearby told us: 'Wrecks sometimes emerge from shifting sand and one is only 500 metres away from this spot.'

The winter dry season tranquillity we were enjoying gave no inkling of the violence that cyclones could and do inflict on this coastline in summer. In the days before the weather satellites and weather forecasts we now take for granted, cyclones hit without warning and took a terrible toll.

Ever since I was a boy growing up in Tasmania I have been fascinated by Marble Bar. Long famous for being the hottest place in Australia—between 31 October and 17 April 1924 it racked up 170 days in a row when the daily temperature exceeded 100°F (37.8°C)—it often got honourable mention from the one-time radio quiz king Jack Davey. He generously bestowed prizes on lucky contestants for holidays in unlikely places like Innamincka and Marble Bar. Whether any of the winners ever went there I do not know. Ros did not share my fascination for Marble Bar. She had not included it in our schedule and we had a slight travel tiff about going there. However, we were driving 500 kilometres inland to Newman, home of a mammoth BHP iron ore operation and site of the biggest open cut mine in the world, and it was sort of on the way. Refuelling at the Pardoo Roadhouse, we turned off Highway One down a surprisingly good dirt road past an abandoned mining town at Shay Gap, and a dead camel—which made a change from the usual kangaroo carcasses. We did not linger to take a photograph as its aroma invaded Penelope's air-conditioning at 100 metres.

We were making good time so we decided to detour to a spectacular break in the distant hills called Coppin Gap. It took a few false turns to locate it, but it was worth the effort. It has a spring of permanent water—polluted with cattle poop—and extraordinary mineralised striated rock, whorled and twisted by ancient volcanic upheavals in an exotic melange of black, red and brown.

Later we wished we had taken better note of the twists and turns of our route in, because we made the classic mistake of turning left instead of right at a key intersection and set off confidently to the west—instead of north-east—towards the 'closed' community of Bamboo Creek instead of south to Marble Bar. Blissfully unaware of our mistake, we admired the countryside looking washed and serene in the low afternoon light. At a distance the young green but very prickly spinifex clumps gave the impression of soft English pasture—broken only by large red rocks, looking uncannily like statues of cattle. We came to a halt beside a rather unwelcoming sign announcing that the closed mining community of Bamboo Creek was imminent and did we have permission to enter? Not only did we feel unwelcome, but we didn't want to go there anyway. We turned around smartly and headed back the way we'd come, arguing over our imprecise map and muttering occasional oaths.

It was getting late and we were lost. We were not in a serious predicament by any means as we had plenty of food, water and indeed shelter. If we had to camp out until the next day it would be no great drama. However, we preferred to get to Marble Bar that evening as planned. No traffic came along and the sun was sinking slowly in the west—as it tends to do quite regularly and dependably in the late afternoon. At least it showed us where west was. After an hour Ros spotted a Toyota utility parked on a dirt airstrip with the driver mercifully in sight. He was surprised we were looking for Marble Bar, as it was 75 kilometres away. He sorted out our navigation problems, and we cruised into the Marble Bar Caravan Park at dusk and fell heavily down the inside of several cans of wonderfully cold beer.

The discovery of gold in the area in 1891 sparked a rush to Marble Bar, which by 1893 supported a population of 5000 people. So confident was the state government's belief in the area's future that a row of handsome public buildings was built in stone—Post and Telegraph Offices and quarters, the Mining Registrar's office, Warden's Court, Police Station and Sergeant's Quarters. They were so solidly built (for 7949 pounds 11 shillings and twopence in 1896) that they still stand and have been beautifully restored.

The town was incorrectly named. What was thought to be a deposit of marble which crossed the Coongan River eight kilometres from the town was in fact jasper, a highly coloured quartz, which in this area is banded with vivid dark red and purple stripes that shine and glow photogenically when water is thrown on them. Harvesting jasper from Coongan River is now banned for aesthetic reasons but there is an abandoned quarry on a hillside thoughtfully set aside for tourists to fossick for chunks of the brightly layered gemstone.

Sizeable nuggets of gold were found in the Marble Bar district. The biggest ever nugget, 413 ounces, was located in 1899 and named 'Bobby Dazzler'. Nuggets are still turning up. 'George's Nugget', some 200 ounces, was located by lucky old George as recently as 1995.

In 1911 a railway was built connecting Marble Bar with Port Hedland, 200 kilometres away, and it ran until 1951. It was to be replaced by a sealed road but the townsfolk are still waiting. Marble Bar is a service town for the pastoral industry and a little mining and fossicking still go on. The Ironclad Hotel, the town's first watering hole, offers colder beer today than before refrigeration when beer was stacked on wire frames and covered with damp hessian to keep as cool as could be managed in the 100°F plus summer heat.

I was pleased to have visited Marble Bar but Ros kept her counsel about it. Newman was 300 kilometres further inland over a fairly basic dirt road with wet creek crossings from time to time. Huge road trains, crammed with mournfully bellowing cattle, also used the road and we were pleased to be waved past by an obliging driver emerging slowly from a river crossing. Passing these behemoths and their attendant dust cloud on the open road was not an option. One of the few service points on our route was Nullagine which, like Marble Bar, had its genesis in the gold rush days. On the outskirts of the settlement I was intrigued to see a sign requesting trucks to 'drop their dust' before entering the town. What could this mean and how could trucks drop their dust anyway? Penelope's was sticking to her like the traditional excrement to a blanket.

I asked the cheerful woman at the service station about it. 'Trucks,' she said, 'pick up a lot of very fine dust not only from the mines, but the roads. By simply stopping and starting off again before coming into town a lot of this drops off the wheels. There are people with asthma in the town who really appreciate it. But if you are interested in signs, turn left after you cross the river into Skull Springs Road and you'll see a beauty.'

The ominously named Skull Springs Road headed north-east towards the Great Sandy Desert. The sign we had been told about did not mince words:

WARNING

<u>NO</u>—FOOD, WATER OR FUEL AVAILABLE BEYOND THIS POINT

BEFORE YOU PROCEED—

1   Have you checked road conditions?
2   Is your vehicle suitably equipped?
3   Do you have sufficient food, water and fuel?
4   Do you know the area you are entering?
5   Have you notified Nullagine police of your intended movements?

IF IN DOUBT DO NOT PROCEED BEYOND THIS POINT!

<u>DO NOT</u> BE NUMBERED AMONGST THOSE WHO HAVE PERISHED IN THIS AREA DUE TO THE LACK OF PREPAREDNESS

That seemed clear enough. We retreated and continued south towards the safety and security of Newman. Just outside Nullagine, the country changed dramatically from rocky outcrops and innumerable creek crossings to a flat plain with grass and tall trees—obviously good cattle country. The road was better too, and we made excellent time to Newman, an archetypal Pilbara company town with parks, green lawns, modern housing and a smart shopping centre. Interestingly enough, its population of 5000 people was the same as Marble Bar boasted at the turn of the twentieth century.

We were back in grey nomad territory because of the black top road connecting Newman with Port Hedland. We had chosen to come the hard—but more interesting—

way via Marble Bar. Most caravan travellers, however, seem to be obsessive about dust and unsealed roads, and now we were surrounded by gleaming, freshly-washed vans and sparkling chrome radiator grilles. Penelope had a rather perky look, with a clutch of dusty firewood sticking up from her roof rack while The Manor wore her red dust like a coat of honour.

'How did you get on with all the dust?' I heard a passing nomad ask Ros.

'Fine thank you,' she replied briskly. 'No trouble at all.'

It seemed strange to us that people worried so much about red dust. There is a lot of it in outback Australia. Provided it doesn't rain and turn into sticky glue, it is part of the whole experience.

We donned hard hats and did BHP's bus tour to be able to see the largest open cut mine in the world. The tour was well done and our tour leader had once worked for the company. It is amazing what a hard hat and safety glasses do for personal image. One fairly ordinary looking white-haired bloke on our bus was instantly transformed into someone who could have been the managing director of BHP. Ros said I looked like an ageing, out of work security guard.

Everything about the Pilbara is huge. The iron ore operation is demolishing an entire mountain, Mt Whaleback, which is a gigantic deposit of extremely high grade iron ore—most of it around 68 per cent. The ore was discovered by a lone prospector, Stan Hilditch, in 1957. He was looking for manganese, but noted the mountain of iron ore and, as prospectors do, kept quiet about it for some time. In the 1950s the prospects of developing an iron ore operation 430 kilometres from the coast seemed remote.

Stan kept mum until 1960 when Australia lifted its war-time induced ban on the export of iron ore to Japan. He told his business partner in Sydney, Charles Warman, of his secret. Warman famously told him: 'Forget it . . . iron ore is a cheap commodity . . . and it's too far from the coast.' But Stan convinced Warman to persevere, and the initial developers were an American company, AMAX, and Australia's own CSR. In 1967 BHP took over the project and still runs it today. The Mt Whaleback deposit is said to have at least another 45 or 50 years of reserves.

The scale of it all is larger than life. Not only did a railway have to be built covering the 430 kilometres to Port Hedland but a deep water port had to be dredged and constructed there to accommodate the great ore-carrying ships. Huge trains of ore trucks, hauled by four diesel locomotives, transfer 25 000 tonnes of iron ore at a time on the purpose-built line. These trains are 2.7 kilometres long! The sleepers are concrete because termites would have quickly chewed out wooden ones. The Australianness of the operation was confirmed to me by the interesting statistic that for every mile of track laid, 400 gallons of beer were consumed by the workers.

Water to sustain the town and the mining operations is drawn from the quaintly named Ophthalmia Dam 16 kilometres north-east of Newman. We drove out to have a look at it and found that so great an expanse of fresh water in such arid land was indeed a sight for sore eyes. It takes its name from the Ophthalmia Range, a chain of hills first seen (with difficulty) by the explorer Ernest Giles in 1876. Mt Whaleback, now rapidly becoming a hole in the ground, is part of the Ophthalmia Range, itself connected to the Hamersley Range further to the east, where other large deposits of iron ore are also being mined. Needless to say, Giles was suffering from an attack of ophthalmia when he named the range. Ophthalmia Dam is a popular camping spot visited by Mt Newman residents for fishing and water sports. It took us longer than it should to locate it as again we took a wrong turn. Blind stupidity, really.

Ros and I were yet to see any of the Aboriginal rock art of the Pilbara which we had been told was totally different from anything we had encountered in the Kimberley. We got directions to a site named Punda, about 50 kilometres from Newman. It was a delightful drive, part of it on a company access road which ran beside the ore-carrying railway line. We then turned down a track so narrow that I had to fold back Penelope's side mirrors as we squeezed through a long corridor of acacias, kept trimmed only by occasional passing four-wheel-drives. The desert was blooming and vivid blood-red infusions of Sturt's Desert Pea were growing in the centre of the track—thus being difficult to avoid. (This distinctive flower is named after the explorer Captain Charles Sturt who saw and gathered it near Cooper's Creek in 1844. Perhaps it should have been named after William Dampier who first collected and described it much earlier during his visit to the north-west coast of Australia in 1699!)

There were low rocky hills in the distance and we needed to engage four-wheel-drive to negotiate the last few kilometres through rocky creek beds and over large boulders. The reward was an introduction to petroglyphs which were—for us—an entirely new form of Aboriginal rock art.

At Punda (and at other Pilbara sites we were to see later) the figures and designs are etched into exposed granite boulders. They are not under shaded overhangs like Wandjina or Bradshaw paintings, but are in full sun and they confront you with their presence rather than hide away. The art is divided into two styles—concentric circles deeply cut into the hard rock, and recognisable shapes like boomerangs, kangaroos, emus, snakes, human stick-like figures and other striped shapes which could have been fish or perhaps ceremonial shields. These had been 'pecked' into the rock by artists using a stone hammer and chisel.

In her book *The Riches of Ancient Australia*, Josephine Flood points out that these etchings would have been far more spectacular when they were first done, as the granite and dolerite rocks have a very dark brown surface, or patina, due to concentrations of iron oxide in their surface layer. The fresh etchings would have exposed the lighter rock beneath. Over time the indented engravings have been muted by the re-emerging iron oxide. It is almost impossible to estimate the age of this work. Flood writes that where deep grooves have been weathered back to the colour of the surrounding rock, the repatination would have taken thousands of years—probably a minimum of 10 000. Often these engravings are found near oval patches of rock worn smooth from women's grinding of grass seeds into flour. The engravings in these locations, she believes, were therefore likely to have been part of everyday life and not sacred. Good permanent water in the Punda area made it an obvious place for community life.

Present Aboriginal communities have no links or Dreamtime legends connected with this singular art. There is an enormous variety. Sometimes the figures of animals are life size. Flood writes:

> Some humans are realistic, others are anthropomorphous, involving supernatural features such as pincer-like hands and feet with only two digits, two-toed tracks, protruding muzzles resembling kangaroos or dogs, antennae-like projections waving from their heads, and great enlarged genitals. They are usually portrayed with legs pointing in random directions, as if floating rather than standing on the ground.

Although petroglyphs are no longer being created and their significance is lost, Flood points out that they are part of a living culture and some Aboriginal people are sensitive to visitors going to certain areas without permission. (We checked with the local tourist bureau before visiting Punda: that is recommended practice before planning to visit any Aboriginal art site.)

We had heard that the Burrup Peninsula, near Karratha, was a treasure trove of petroglyphs and we were looking forward to that. But first there was the much vaunted Karijini National Park, to which Greg Williams and Heather Messer, among others, had given their gold seal of approval. With more than 600 000 hectares, it is one of Western Australia's largest parks—a mix of massive mountains and escarpments which rise out of flat valleys. The main features for visitors are the great gorges which have eroded through the high plateaus and offer not only breathtaking views but great walking and swimming. To access the gorges you have to climb down from very well designed camp sites close to the edge of several. The main camp site is at Dales Gorge which has easy walks to a number of spectacular features. We quickly drove the 200 kilometres from Newman to enjoy one of the best national park camp sites we had yet encountered, and immediately decided to stay five days. An Irish couple we met on the rim of Dales Gorge on our first evening came for two days and stayed two weeks.

Full marks to CALM for the design of the camping area at Dales Gorge. The sites made you feel you were the only people at the park—perhaps that may be a slight exaggeration, but the Dales Gorge camp ground is designed very cleverly in a series of one-way loops. Strategically situated between camping bays, screened by trees and shrubs, are well-tended long-drop toilets and complementary CALM gas fired barbecues and hotplates. Each loop is named after a native animal. We settled down happily in Euro Loop, well away from coach tour groups and unspeakable users of noisy generators who were splendidly quarantined in Galah Loop. Unconscious or deliberate irony? With The Manor erected and awning, chairs and table in place, we sat and gazed out to distant red rock mountains peppered with the ubiquitous spinifex. We were barely conscious of another living soul and forgave a few gorge walkers who moved discreetly through our line of vision. Magnanimity springs from experiencing pristine landscape.

Almost at our feet (although we had to walk a few hundred metres to see it) the ground dropped away into the deep fissure that included Munjina Gorge, Gales Gorge, Fortescue Falls and Circular Pool. Our next five gorgeous days involved climbing down and walking beside lazily flowing dry season rivers, surrounded by vertical red rock walls and stunning scenery. Our first walk into Dales Gorge was a splendid introduction to the park. Circular

Pool is underneath a waterfall, slowed to a dry season trickle but shaded by curved towering rock walls. Someone had thrown an inflated truck tyre into the pool and we watched three small boys splashing happily, climbing on it and pushing each other off.

The sedimentary rocks at the bottom of the gorges are layered in a kaleidoscope of colours—brown, black, yellow and sometimes vivid blue and red as we found in later excursions. There was a lot of yellow ochre about, which previous walkers had used to scrawl happy faces on the smooth stone surface of the track. If only graffiti could always be so temporary and benign. Circular Pool was a dead end, so we turned around and walked upstream to Fortescue Falls which were blessed with a reasonable amount of water. Climbing above the falls we found a wonderful swimming hole, fed by a smaller cascade. CALM had thoughtfully provided a wooden platform and ladder for bathers. We swam among pretty little fresh water fish. As there is no water supply at the camp sites the opportunity to bathe was doubly appreciated. The climb back up the gorge at that point was easier than our descent and we were back at our superb camp site by mid-afternoon.

At 4.30 pm, after all our walking, I had a strong urge for a cold beer. We normally try to hold off until 5 pm, but rules are made to be broken. Anyway, as Ros sensibly put it, 'what would Ed say?' Ed and Joan are journalist friends who are great appreciators of food and drink. They do not manage to exercise very much, and Ed claims to drink at least a litre of red wine a day. When Joan felt that Ed (then in his mid-fifties) should have a medical check up the results revealed that he had the blood pressure of a baby, his arteries swept clean—as the French would concur—with his daily libations of red wine. I should also say that the report on his liver was faultless and he was generally in enviable shape.

The doctor he had visited was of conservative mien and clearly appalled by Ed, his overweight condition and unrepentant hedonism. The examination was at 11 am, and at one point the doctor got up abruptly from his desk and walked to a glass fronted cupboard to get something. As he pulled open the glass doors he turned to Ed and asked abruptly: 'Do you drink?'

Ed brightened visibly. 'Why yes, thank you very much.'

'No, no, no—I'm not *offering* you a drink, I want to know how *much* you drink!'

I felt that in the circumstances Ed would have approved, so we had a beer.

As it was forbidden to light fires, I headed for the CALM-supplied gas barbecue. 'When all else fails read the instructions', the old saw hath it, and I did read them conscientiously. In this case the instructions were standard, but the barbecue was not. The push button lighting procedure would not work for me and to compound the difficulties the gas taps were loose and worn. When, in desperation, I tried to use matches there was a loud explosion and I lost most of my eyebrows and a front fringe of hair—also seriously startling a young American couple seated at a nearby picnic table. I was not irreparably damaged but it would have been inconvenient, to say the least, to have come this far without injury only to be blinded by a CALM barbecue.

There is a second camping area 50 kilometres deeper into the park near Weano, Hancock, Knox and Red Gorges, but we doubted whether we could do better than where we were and therefore took a series of day trips in Penelope rather than shift The Manor. Each gorge we went to seemed more spectacular than the last. Visitors have the easy option of viewing the abyss from road level or climbing down for, as one signboard indicated, 'a journey to the centre of the earth'. The walls of Weano Gorge narrowed so dramatically that you had to squeeze through to get down to a swimming hole.

Totally engorged for one day, we returned to our top camping spot for the night and headed back to Kalamina Gorge, only 35 kilometres from Dales Gorge, the following day. At the car park we met a Victorian couple we had seen parked beside the road the day before. They were standing in the middle of nowhere gazing fixedly into the middle distance. We puzzled about this at the time, but when we met Ian and Coralie, all was revealed. They were keen bird watchers, and Ian had just spotted the lesser titted thripple banded finch he had been seeking for weeks. What were we going to look for in Kalamina Gorge?

We had to admit to nothing in particular other than being there. I sensed Ian and Coralie thought this behaviour frivolous and that we should have had a more serious purpose. They were completely besotted with bird watching. Ian showed me his little battery powered whistle which allegedly duplicated the calls of different birds to attract them within binocular range. He couldn't make it work, but he is a virtuoso whistler and warbled a range of calls so realistically I thought the whistle must have worked after all.

Our timing for Kalamina Gorge could have been better as we coincided with a bus tour. Our newly awakened sense of not having a dedicated purpose was reinforced by a stern looking woman in a bush hat who, professional water bottle slung from her waist and bird watching binoculars at the ready, walked towards us. We passed the time of day as one does.

'Not many birds about,' said Ros cheerily.

'That's because there are so many *people* down here,' she said testily—although she was part of the tour.

Our Karijini camp had been so enjoyable it was difficult to shift. Our five nights at Euro Loop were a record for us on this expedition and surprisingly cold until I worked out that Penelope's altimeter had us at 700 metres. As we were reluctantly packing we had a visit from a precocious six-year-old on his bicycle. His parents were camped nearby, and we felt we knew more than we needed to know about them after Jeremy had gone into intimate details of why his mother couldn't do long walks at the moment.

He asked where we were going next and we said we were going to call into Tom Price and Wittenoom before heading back to the coast. Jeremy was full of information about all this. He said Tom Price was as big as Hobart. He was wrong about that—Hobart's population hasn't dwindled to 5000 just yet—and that we could get a permit from a service station just outside Tom Price which meant we could use a company road that ran beside the railway line to get back to the coast. He was right about that. We read in one of our guide books that the average age in Tom Price is nine, so Jeremy would have had lots of playmates if he lived there. These Pilbara mining towns have good deals for families with young children.

Tom Price—which is, incidentally, Western Australia's highest town at 747 metres—is on the western edge of Karijini National Park, and we were heading into Lang Hancock territory. The feisty old mining tycoon first pegged out leases for blue asbestos in Wittenoom Gorge in 1934. He was one of the earliest pastoralists to get a private pilot's licence, and after having been being forced by bad weather into a bit of low flying through the headwaters of the Turner River in the Hamersley Range, he also made the first major discoveries of iron ore in the Pilbara and promptly pegged them out. The original development of these deposits was by the Rio Tinto Mining Company of Australia in 1959, with Hancock pocketing vast sums from the royalties over the years. In 1963 Hancock discovered further extensive iron ore deposits at Paraburdoo, also in the Hamersley Range. The Tom Price mining operation and Paraburdoo are now controlled by Hamersley Iron and both operations are connected with a purpose-built deep water port at Dampier.

A rugged individualist, Lang Hancock used his great personal wealth to push his many controversial barrows. These included the Westralian Secession Movement, tax concessions on all incomes earned in far northern Australia, forced sterilisation of all mixed-blood Aborigines and an Australian version of apartheid for full-blood Aborigines who Hancock thought should be corralled in the Ord River area. He lent his support and financial backing to Sir Joh Bjelke-Petersen's abortive bid to enter Federal politics in 1986. Controversy surrounding Hancock survived his death in 1992 with his Filipina wife Rose (whom he married in 1987) and the daughter from his first marriage, Gina, involved in continuing acrimonious and very public dispute over the terms of his will through numerous colourful and allegation-ridden court cases.

Meanwhile, the great trains full of iron ore continue to trundle through to the coast from the Hamersley Range and out to the industrialised world, following Hancock's original iron ore discoveries. But his first mining venture is as dead as many of the people who worked on it—the lethal blue asbestos mines at Wittenoom, a name now inevitably linked with ghastly and invariably fatal lung disease. Mining operations ceased in 1966 but by then some forty people had died and many residents and former residents were already ill with asbestos-related diseases.

We wanted to go to Wittenoom Gorge, not because of a death wish, but because the gorge is reputedly one of the most beautiful in the region and actually connects with the Karijini National Park. We were also curious to see what remained of Wittenoom town because people still lived there—indeed we had been told about a caravan park, a gem shop and other tourist attractions. But this was all by word-of-mouth from other travellers. When we asked at the Newman Tourist Bureau about Wittenoom, the woman behind the counter just clammed up, said she could not tell us anything, and had been told to tell people not to go there.

Our maps showed fuel available at the town so we did not bother to top up our reserve jerry cans at Tom Price. We figured it would be better to wait until Wittenoom so we could leave for the coast with full tanks—there being no fuel available on the company road until we reached Karratha. This was a mistake, as we were soon to find out.

No sooner had we turned east along the Wittenoom road, which runs along the plain with the Hamersley Range on the right-hand side, than a large sign informed us that there were no services or fuel to be had from that point. We stopped by the roadside and did some quick calculations to see if we had to return to Tom Price for extra fuel, but decided to give it a go. It would be tight, but probably OK.

It was becoming clear that tourists had to work hard to get to Wittenoom.

The drive skirting the Hamersley Range was so beautiful that we risked burning precious fuel to run into Hamersley Gorge, which is also part of the Karijini National Park and which we were effectively circumnavigating. I have probably bashed the adjective 'spectacular' to death when attempting to describe Pilbara gorges, but the Hamersley Gorge was a remarkable vista, with great twisted and gnarled fault lines in sheer cliffs of red rock dropping down to a series of picturesque rock pools with visitors swimming in them. It would have been good to join them, but we needed the rest of the day to make a brief excursion to Wittenoom (trying not to breathe too deeply while there) and then find a spot for a bush camp before heading back to the coast and the petroglyphs of the Burrup Peninsula.

After we left Hamersley Gorge, the Wittenoom road ran down through a gorge so narrow only single file traffic could get through and it became clear we were driving down a creek bed. What we would do if we met a road train coming the other way could only be conjectured. Good practice for backing a trailer for one of us—almost certainly me. This prospect overshadowed our appreciation of what was a dramatic part of the journey.

Wittenoom town is just outside the entrance to Wittenoom Gorge and, not surprisingly, it has a dejected and run-down atmosphere—crumbling bitumen streets dividing blocks of dry grass where formerly there were shops, hotels and miners' houses. Once a prosperous community of 1500 people, it declined inevitably after the mine closed in 1966. Every now and then in this grid of mostly empty streets there is a house, ranging from ramshackle humpies of scrap timber and rusting corrugated iron (one had a crudely lettered sign, KEEP OUT—TRESPASSERS SHOT) to better preserved and maintained dwellings. We located the caravan park which was doing a modest trade with a sprinkling of intrepid tourists and was managed by a cheerful Continental woman who had only been there six weeks, after having been asked to run it for two weeks.

The political hub of Wittenoom is the Gem Shop run by Lorraine Thomas, also a local councillor, who gave us chapter and verse on the conspiracy of bureaucratic forces outside the town to squeeze everyone out and close it down. Despite the awful legacy of the blue asbestos mine further up the gorge, many residents loved the area and wanted to stay. Tourism was seen as Wittenoom's only chance but, according to Lorraine Thomas, all that changed in 1979 when the Western Australian government, in cahoots with the agencies and departments under its control in the Shire of Ashburton, effectively tried to close Wittenoom down, discourage visitors and even take the name off the map. That at least, said Lorraine, had been successfully legally challenged.

(I put Lorraine's conspiracy theory to the test when I visited the Karratha Tourist Centre a few days later. The woman I spoke to there refused to give me any information on Wittenoom even when I told her I had heard that tourists went there. When I pressed her to explain why, she said it was on the direct orders of the head of the Tourist Commission.)

The thirty or so Wittenoomites were putting up a tough fight to survive. When the last service station closed, the sign we had seen was put up—saying no fuel was available in the town. But, Lorraine said, fuel was available and could be sold legally in jerry cans. (I pricked up my ears at that, but unfortunately she only had petrol, not diesel.)

The Progress Association argued that the risk of airborne asbestos fibres in the town was negligible—no more nor less than people who live in cities are exposed to in their daily lives.

There was a certain black humour about Wittenoom. Among the souvenirs to be had at Lorraine's excellent gem shop was a beer stubby holder with the slogan: I VISITED WITTENOOM AND LIVED!

The reality is that Wittenoom is situated at the entrance to one of the prettiest gorges in the region with lovely swimming holes along the creek leading up the valley. After listening to Lorraine Thomas—although Ros remained apprehensive—I decided to drive further up the valley past where the blue asbestos mine was, to a place on the map called Old Settlement.

Ignoring the turn-off to the mine, we drove up a charming valley to where we could see a small cluster of buildings—and an unexpected sight. Beside the road was a small stall, run on the honesty system, with fresh vegetables, pickles and jam. As it happened, the person responsible was there re-stocking. We were nearly out of Ros's legendary home-made grapefruit marmalade, and thought it wondrous we should find a substitute in Wittenoom of all places. Which is how we met Vera Yugolano, a dark-haired middle-aged woman wearing bright red woollen stockings under a full skirt. Vera did indeed have marmalade, several varieties as it happened. Her 'French' marmalade had carrots in it, she said, and there was strawberry and tomato jam as well.

We chatted for a while and I asked her the origins of her name. She said her parents were Italian and had come to Australia as migrants before World War II. There is no Italian word or name beginning with Y, and Vera said their name had been corrupted to Yugolano by an official writing out their birth certificates who found it easier than getting his head around their real name. Similarly, her Christian name, Verena, had been shortened to Vera. The only problem for Vera was that people often thought she was Yugoslavian—which she did not find a plus. She said her brother had changed his name back to the original Italian by deed poll but she hadn't bothered.

Vera had never married and was raising money for charity and 'causes' by selling her vegetables, jams and pickles to passing tourists. Behind her stall was a historic building—a 'spinifex house'. This was the Wittenoom version of the Coolgardie safe on a grand scale. It had clumps of spinifex hanging in its wire walls, over which water was originally dripped slowly to cool the contents.

Like everyone else in Wittenoom, she was passionate about living there and about its tourist potential. Ros and I both thought she seemed a bit challenged in the breathing department, but that may have been due to non-asbestos related causes. The name Wittenoom has an ominous ring to it—rhyming with doom. I wondered whether it might have had a better chance of survival if it had been called 'Happy Valley' or some such.

By this time we were feeling so relaxed about blue asbestos that—on Vera's directions—we actually drove to the mine site. It was only when I realised we were walking on little shredded bits of blue stuff—which of course were the lethal mine tailings—that we gingerly and carefully removed ourselves, trying not to raise any dust and breathing, it has to be admitted, as lightly as possible. It was extremely silly of us to have gone there—as Ros quite rightly made clear to me.

It was 4 pm by the time we left Wittenoom, with only an hour of daylight to find a bush camp. We ran up the Roebourne Road for about 40 kilometres and drove off on a side track on a whim, which led to a gravel pit but with some open space among the spinifex nearby. There is a family joke about me stopping for lunch in gravel pits, but this was a very superior location. A mulga tree shielded us from the road, and the quarry was useful as a safe fireplace. As the sun set, we saw the new moon for the first time in conjunction with the evening star against the red haze of the cloudless sunset. The distant acacia and mulga trees were etched in black and white against the dying light of the already set sun.

I barbecued chicken thighs in tikka sauce, with potatoes and mushrooms, and Ros cooked some of Vera's home-grown cauliflower (pressed into our hands as we left her). Life seemed very good indeed. I wrote in our diary:

> We are utterly alone. Absolutely no one on this earth knows we are here. No one is likely to disturb us. What a country Australia is to allow this to happen. We glory in being by ourselves and love the solitude. We have—in daylight—a wonderful view of the distant Hamersley Range across an ocean of spinifex and occasional scrub. As I write the Southern Cross is blazing down and the Milky Way is clearer than I have ever seen it. Almost certainly we will not have a bush camp as isolated for the rest of our journey. It is a moment worth treasuring, and we are doing just that.

nine

Blown Away

Driving in the Pilbara under cloudless skies raises the spirit. We were heading back to the coast at Karratha and, before we joined Hamersley Iron's access road beside the railway line, we gloried in the expanse of spinifex, red earth, mulga, occasional creek beds, floodways and dramatic scarlet bursts of Sturts Desert Pea seeking sunshine by creeping out from the roadside, almost under Penelope's wheels. A passing Oka tour bus labelled 'Snappy Gum Safaris' reminded us of these attractive eucalypts, common in the Pilbara. The gutsy little gums have a snow-white bark and love digging their toes into stones and perching on rock ledges where nothing else seems to grow.

After two hours, as per our regular routine, I handed over the wheel to Ros reluctantly—she is a very competent driver—because I just love outback driving in the ideal conditions we were experiencing. It was not possible to doze in the passenger seat because an unexpected dry creek crossing could cause neck dislocation. I found the best way to snatch a few moments' rest was to grasp the 'Jesus handle' above the passenger door with both hands and rest my head on my forearms. Jesus handle?

On one of our first central Australian excursions in the early 1980s, a friend lent us a venerable Landcruiser for a few days to drive down the bed of the Finke River, to the south-west of Alice Springs. This was a huge adventure and the first time we had experienced four-wheel-driving. Northern Territory historian and friend Peter Forrest came with us as driver and guide. The route down the river bed involved lowering tyre pressures drastically to negotiate stretches of soft sand, and Peter gave a flawless demonstration of handling a vehicle under those conditions. Sometimes we had to drive up on to the river bank and down again to avoid fallen trees. On one of these occasions Peter suggested we 'grab the Jesus handles'. Naively I asked him why he called them that, but before he could reply I looked ahead down a vertical drop into which we were just about to plunge, screeched 'Jeeeeezus!' and grabbed the handles with both hands. When Peter stopped laughing he said I'd answered the question myself.

We joined the railway line access road about halfway between Tom Price and the Dampier Peninsula, just below the recently established Millstream Chichester National Park, about 150 kilometres from Karratha. I was confident we would have enough fuel after the Wittenoom diesel drought, but that would depend on how rough the going was. Our permit stipulated that we had to drive with headlights on at all times, not exceed 90 kph (seldom possible in any case) and that we should avoid wearing red clothing because the drivers of the 2.7 kilometre-long ore trains were instructed to stop if they saw red. I hoped it would stay warm because my only windproof was bright red.

The road signs were forthright. 'GORGE.' By that stage we were heading down the steep bed of a creek which had briefly become the road. At least it saved Hamersley Iron from having to blast a new cutting for the access track. The train line arched grandly overhead on its concrete pylons as I negotiated Penelope and The Manor over large smooth stones. Other hairy sections were announced by notice-boards reading: 'DANGER—STEEP GRADES—40 KPH' and, a few hundred metres later, 'YOU HAVE BEEN WARNED'. But the road was mostly in good shape, and negotiable at a safe 80 kph. We saw only one ore train rumbling along steadily towards the Dampier Peninsula. Our fuel worries were unfounded. I was just about to switch on to the reserve tank when we came upon Highway One. It was curious to be so suddenly back in civilisation with sealed roads, service stations with flushing toilets and the ordered efficiency of a large caravan park.

Karratha is the dormitory town for the huge offshore North West Shelf Gas Project and the loading facility at the terminus of the railway lines over which the great trains of iron ore from the Tom Price and Paraburdoo mines are transported. It also supports the staff of Dampier Salt, one of the biggest salt evaporation operations in the world. There are no tall buildings in Karratha because cyclones are frequent. For sensible practical reasons even the big super-markets and shopping centres are single storey buildings with low profile steel roofs. On 7 March 2000, seven months after we left Karratha, Cyclone Steve roared in from the Indian Ocean and crossed the coast near the town caus-ing widespread damage but thankfully no loss of life. Such chaos was still far removed from our dry season serenity and we chose the Rosemary Caravan Park on the northern side of Karratha (closer to the Burrup Peninsula we planned to explore) for assignations with automatic washing machines, hot showers and other necessary servicing of much travelled persons. Happiness, in these circumstances, is a good toilet block or blocks, and the Rosemary's were spacious, efficient and clean. The park was well run. Notices requested campers not to drive across the lawns to park their caravans because of irrigation pipes. They also requested that visitors conserve precious drinking water by not washing cars or caravans. Ros noticed a bloke, two spaces up from us, breaking all those rules. Why do arrogant bastards have to spoil things for everyone else?

There were plenty of shade-giving trees, home to raucous colonies of white cockatoos and galahs which not only turned on an ear-splitting cacophony at dawn and dusk but crapped all over cars, caravans and washing lines. I saw one camper feeding the pests. She was welcome to them. With luck they would leave our trees for hers.

I could hardly wait to find more rock carvings. The Burrup Peninsula has at least 10 000 of them on jumbled boulders lying on scree slopes. Like the petroglyphs we had seen at Punda, near Newman, the etchings were likely to be in full sun, their smooth shiny surfaces darkened through iron oxide patination. Tourists are directed to one of the most prolific sites near the end of the road from Dampier to Hearson Cove. Here there are so many carvings that almost every boulder seems inscribed. Some later artists had pecked their work over earlier, less obvious images. Visitors can walk up little valleys between the hills of tumbled granitic stone and either climb up to search for carvings or see what can be taken in at ground level.

As at Punda, a creek of permanent water made sense of why the site had been occupied. Again, no one really has any idea of the age of these carvings, which encompass a staggering variety of images. As well as concentric circles and other symbolic shapes there are human figures, fish, whales, dolphins and turtles. Among the birds are waders in silhouette with long necks and curved beaks, some—as archaeologist Josephine Flood notes—with fish in their beaks. Land animals include kangaroos, lizards, snakes and dog-like animals with striped backs which Flood believes are undoubted drawings of the Tasmanian tiger or *thylacine*, which has been extinct in mainland Australia for at least 3000 years—a minimum age for these engravings.

In the valleys there are also shell middens, one of which was allegedly trashed by hordes of reporters following Prince Charles during a tour of the area some years ago. While climbing high on one rocky mound I heard Ros clap her hands in the way we do to alert snakes to our presence. Her cries of obvious distress had me bounding down the rocks like a geriatric mountain goat because I thought she might have trodden on a snake and been bitten. She had been attacked all right, but by wasps which had bitten her painfully on the right side of her face and ear. I was so relieved she hadn't been bitten by a snake that I was probably not solicitous enough about her predicament.

We had also taken expert local advice on where to find one of the most famous panels of carvings on the peninsula, known as 'the climbing men'. This small collection of etchings, strangely isolated from any other nearby, is in a small valley near the vast North West Gas Shelf Project plant which processes and freezes the natural gas brought by a network of underwater pipelines from the offshore drilling

platforms. After processing, the gas is chilled to minus 161°
Celsius and held in great circular underground storage
chambers, the domed roofs of which look like half-buried
alien flying saucers. This liquid gas is eventually shipped to
Japan in purpose-built tankers. The plant also supplies
80 per cent of Western Australia with natural gas, through
an extensive pipeline system, to industry and private
homes. (I was fascinated to learn that freezing the gas for
export to such a low temperature condenses it by a factor of
600. That means that the contents of one of the eight
tankers now on the Japanese run carries what would otherwise have to be transported by 600 similar ships!)

When we did locate the site of 'the climbing men', after
a modest rock scramble up a small hill, I was astonished to
turn around and see, just over a hill to the west, the gas
escape tower of the North West Shelf processing complex
flaring with burning gas. The ugly industrial complex was
perilously close. Unfortunately for photography, the climbing men were half in shadow, but nevertheless we could see
them clearly. Figures are depicted climbing on each side of
a vertical line. These are unique on the peninsula.
Josephine Flood speculates that they might represent
young men climbing a tree during an initiation ceremony.
Another panel to the left, in full sunlight, shows more
climbing men and heraldic looking designs that appeared to
me more like decorations on an Etruscan tomb than Aboriginal petroglyphs. The range of etched images on the
Burrup Peninsula is truly astonishing.

Unfortunately, the industrial development there has
disrupted significant areas of these ancient art galleries. In
the course of establishing the gas plant, Woodside Offshore
Petroleum Pty Ltd moved some 1793 engraved boulders

from their original locations and put them in a fenced enclosure. On a smaller but nevertheless regrettable scale, Dampier Salt disrupted a rich area of petroglyphs when they blasted an access road down to the coast. Now on company land, the remaining carvings can only be glimpsed momentarily through the windows of a bus which takes visitors on a paid tour of the salt gathering operation.

That is not the only desecration to be found on this raw, wild coastline. Within sight of the big gas plant, we drove west to the coast seeking another prehistoric human land-mark that had been described to us—the standing stones. It made the hair on the back of my neck prickle when I saw them outlined against the sky on top of the usual Burrup Peninsula mound of brown granitic rocks. Ros was also moved by the ambience of this strange place. Shards of narrow stone had been selected and wedged in an upright position, silhouetted against the clear blue sky on top of the ridge. There was no way they could have been a natural phenomenon. We looked down from the hill top to where a rough track ran down to a primitive boat ramp among the mangroves and decided to drive down to investigate. Just underneath the ridge of standing stones was a faded sign.

> Hereabouts in February 1868 a party of settlers from Roebourne shot and killed as many as 60 Yapurarra people in response to the killing of a European policeman in Nickol Bay. This incident has become known as the 'Flying Foam Massacre'.
>
> Plaque erected by the Ngarlura and Yapurarra descendants living in Roebourne and the Department of Aboriginal Sites.

No wonder my spine had tingled. The ancient vertical rock pinnacles on the skyline stood like silent sentinels, as though marking the site of that awful slaughter, although unseen hands had placed them long before. By unspoken accord we drove away from that place, around in a loop between two boulder-strewn hills with access to the sea.

In the late afternoon light we saw a little rock wallaby watching us warily before it bounded lightly up the stony hill with the ease and grace of its kind. Near where we had first seen it there were petroglyphs of two splendid bush turkeys, which we photographed. It was as though the wallaby had directed us to them.

The only way to see the salt mines—where Australia used to send its political prisoners (just joking)—was to do the tour in a rather rusty bus. Running around on salt continuously is not good for machinery. Like every resources industry in the Pilbara, the Dampier Salt operation, begun in 1968, is huge. The salt is mined horizontally from a vast tidal estuary which has been isolated from the open sea, and divided into evaporation pens with earth walls. It takes 65 tonnes of seawater to produce one tonne of high grade salt, and it is all taken care of by the sun and wind. On one hot summer day one million tonnes of seawater are evaporated back to God.

When the brine in the estuary gets concentrated and soupy enough, it is introduced to the final holding pens, called crystallisers. Once a year a bulldozer comes along and scrapes off the white salt left on the floor of the crystallisers into piles, then it is trucked to the so-called 'wet salt' stockpile and, eventually, to waiting ships at the Dampier Salt loading facility. The company also has another evaporation operation further south at Lake MacLeod and between them they produce some 5 million tonnes of salt for export each year, all enabled by the sun. Dampier Salt is principally owned by Rio Tinto, in conjunction with a consortium of Japanese companies.

Clever biological management, using brine shrimps and fish, keeps the holding ponds and estuary free of algae and unwanted nutrients and contamination. Just inside the gates separating the enclosed estuary from the open sea are thousands of fat mendicant milk fish, as well as cod, barramundi and bream. They swim around in the natural fish tank watched by closed circuit cameras in case crazed anglers should try to invade this forbidden fishing Mecca by day or night.

After having seen the corporate video and done the tour through gleaming white pens and piles and piles of salt, Ros and I had an insensate craving for potato chips.

Forty kilometres further up the coast as the crow flies is another busy deep water loading facility, Cape Lambert, at the tip of the Samson Peninsula. Yet another specially built railway, bearing long lines of trucks crammed with iron ore, wends its way from the Robe River Iron Ore mines at Pannawonica, only 150 kilometres to the south-west. We were a bit sated with large mining operations and were keen to visit the Samson Peninsula for another reason—the historic town of Cossack, site of the first European settlement in the Pilbara region.

The surveyor Francis Thomas Gregory (younger brother of Western Australia's Surveyor General and explorer, Sir Augustus Charles Gregory) explored this part of the Pilbara coastline in 1861 and his enthusiastic reports of good pastoral country caused the North-West's first settlers, Walter Padbury and his party, to land their stock at the mouth of the Harding River in May 1863. Others followed and the little settlement that sprang up along the shores of Butcher Inlet was first known as Tien Tsin Harbour after the barque which carried Padbury and his cattle to the area. Eight years later the Oriental sounding Tien Tsin changed to Cossack, when another ship, HMS *Cossack,* brought the state's governor Sir Frederick Weld there on a visit.

As the first port in the district, Cossack played a major part in the establishment of the town of Roebourne, and the discovery of significant pearling grounds close by soon gave Cossack a cosmopolitan character better suited to its first name—Tien Tsin—as Chinese, Malays, Filipinos and Japanese arrived to work on pearling luggers. Unlike Broome, alas no traces of Cossack's large Asian section remain, but the town really took off when the Pilbara gold rush began in the late 1880s and its main stone buildings were constructed. By the turn of the nineteenth century, however, with the gold rush over and the focus of pearling centred on Broome, Cossack's glory days were over. To further add to the town's woes, the harbour, the jewel in its crown, began to silt up and although various ventures like a leprosarium and turtle soup factory were tried, it was abandoned by the early 1950s.

Cossack is now a heritage site, and the most impressive of its nineteenth-century stone buildings is the Customs and Bond Store, with big, eye-catching, curved white stone arches facing the waterfront. The courthouse, museum and a stately home now doubling as a backpackers' hostel make an impressive streetscape. The old schoolhouse, out on its own, is appropriately located in Perseverance Street.

Restoration of the Cossack buildings is being carried out by staff and prisoners of the nearby Roebourne Regional Prison. As we arrived, a uniformed guard appeared with a van and a couple of highly tattooed Islanders who began unenthusiastically raking up leaves in front of the Courthouse. When we left they were sitting down by the old wharf fishing. And why not?

There is another connection between Cossack, or Tien Tsin, and early European contact with the Western Australian coast which I've found fascinating. The story began, for me, when I read a most unusual book by Gustave Rathe, *The Wreck of the Barque Stefano—Off the North West Cape of Australia in 1875*, brought to my attention by my brother Nicholas, who knew of our plans to visit the Pilbara.

The inhospitable coast of north-western Australia is peppered with thousands of wrecked ships, from the seventeenth century to the present day, of which the unfortunate *Stefano* is but one—and until recently not even marked on the map. Consider the date, though. Tien Tsin, later Cossack, was one of the few outposts of European settlement when *Stefano* was wrecked in 1875 on a hidden reef off Point Cloates just south of North West Cape. As we discovered, the survivors knew that Tien Tsin existed, and that there was a remote possibility that they might be able to hail a passing vessel to get there.

The unfortunate Dutch sailors who survived catastrophic shipwrecks in the seventeenth and eighteenth centuries knew they were on their own. The first written account of contacts with Australian Aborigines on the north-west coast was by William Dampier in 1699. It reflects a reasonably peaceable encounter compared with the bloody clashes with the Worora people of the Kimberley, experienced by nineteenth-century explorers like Phillip Parker King and George Grey.

To this day there are theories expounded that fair-haired Aborigines of the north-west may be a result of Dutch sailors having been taken into Aboriginal groups. Unexplained rock art paintings of European ships hundreds of kilometres inland have been cited as further evidence of such contacts, either painted by Dutch survivors themselves or by Aborigines who had seen their ships. But there is no direct physical or even oral evidence of this cultural interaction other than the enigmatic paintings we had been privileged to see.

That such interaction did take place is highly probable. On the night of 28 April 1656, the Dutch East Indies ship *Vergulde Drack,* voyaging from the Netherlands to Batavia, crashed into a reef off Western Australia's Ledge Point, some 100 kilometres north of present-day Perth. Of the 193 crew and passengers on board only 75 made it to shore. Seven of those survivors managed to make the 2500-kilometre voyage to Batavia in one of the ship's lifeboats. When they returned, no trace of any of the 68 who had been left behind could be found. In 1712 another Dutch East Indies ship *Zuytdorp*, its hold crammed with coins and bullion, simply disappeared—as ships often did in those days. In 1927 a stockman, Tom Pepper, discovered coins and wreckage under cliffs near the mouth of the Murchison River, north of Geraldton. In 1954 a young geologist, Philip Playford, identified the location of the wrecked *Zuytdorp* and the subsequent recovery of coins, bullion and other artefacts is now a well documented affair. Whether there were any survivors and what happened to them is completely unknown.

Which brings me back to the wreck of *Stefano* in 1875. This handsome barque was crewed by Croatian-speaking seafarers from the Dalmatian coast of the Balkans—an area with a proud maritime history. *Stefano* hit a submerged reef off Point Cloates and sank quickly. Only ten of their seventeen-man crew managed to struggle ashore. Of those castaways only two teenage boys, Miho Baccich and Ivan Jurich, survived. What makes this story unique is that the boys lived because they were taken into an Aboriginal group and travelled with them for four months before being rescued. That was remarkable enough. Fortunately for posterity, Miho Baccich—an exceptionally intelligent boy who became a captain at twenty-one—told his story in great detail to a Jesuit scholar soon after he arrived back on the Dalmatian coast. The priest, Father Stjepan Skurla, wrote it down as a first person narrative. So we not only have a gripping narrative of survival, but a contemporary account of how Aboriginal people lived, travelled and hunted.

Using supplies washed ashore from the wreck, and what little they could scrounge from the unfamiliar environment, the ten crewmen survived for two months. Their plan was to head south towards the Gascoyne River where they hoped they would find a European outpost. Before the boys' eight companions died, they had all had brief but amiable contact with an Aboriginal group who showed them where to find water on the beach and shared some shellfish and crabs they had gathered. They also handed over a map that had been luckily washed ashore from the ship, which showed the survivors where they were on the coast and identified Tien Tsin as a European settlement and possible source of rescue.

Although the narrator, Miho Baccich, refers to Aborigines (before joining them) as cannibals, it was the two boys who nearly indulged in that ultimate taboo. The full story can be read in Gustave Rathe's compelling narrative. Baccich tells of a ghastly moment on Christmas Day, of all days, when the second-last of their companions died in a cave in which they were sheltering. Maddened with hunger and thirst the two boys threw themselves on the body. Seeing this, their dying companion used his last breath to damn them to hell before expiring. This shocked the boys to such a degree that they slumped to the sand exhausted for the rest of the day. Then, in the relative cool of the evening, they attacked each other in their desperation, fighting over the last mouthfuls of fresh water. Their wretched, flailing, ineffectual combat lasted for several hours until both collapsed unconscious. They became conscious again later that evening and, as Baccich later said, 'more beautiful than the stars were the eyes staring down with compassionate intensity. I—we—had been found by the fierce, savage cannibals of this wild land!'

The Aboriginal group nursed the two boys back to health but had to move on to survive themselves. At all times they treated the two lads with consideration and sympathy. In the first few weeks the boys travelled with the women, but later graduated to hunt with the men. Realising that the Aborigines became irritated when they spoke in Croatian, the boys limited their conversations and tried to learn the language of their benefactors. Baccich, a keen observer, was able to recall for his Jesuit chronicler wonderful detail of how the tribe travelled, hunted, ate, fought—there was a clash with another group—and their ceremonial practices. The Aborigines managed to communicate to the two boys that they would try to link them up with a sailing ship with which they were familiar. Baccich knew that they were gradually moving up the coast towards North West Cape. Later he realised that some of the words, often repeated in this context, referred to Tien Tsin (*Cincin*) and Fremantle (*Pulimandur*). *Cialli*, another expression the boys could not fathom, was actually 'Charlie', the captain of the ship the Aborigines were hoping to meet.

Baccich, the narrator, is circumspect about his relationship with his fellow Dalmatian midshipman, Jurich. Thrown together by circumstances, they had no option but to cooperate. The dreadful fight on Christmas Day, when both were at death's door, was one indication of personal antipathy. Baccich was furious with Jurich on a later occasion when a full rigged sloop was actually sighted near North West Cape, but failed to respond to a large signal fire quickly kindled on top of a hill. Both boys screamed and cursed in their disappointment. But Jurich went further:

> Somehow, Jurich was beyond self-restraint. As we watched the tiny white ship disappear, one of the women crept up behind him and ladled water out of his container into hers. My despondent shipmate, without reflecting, grabbed the nearest weapon, a flat spear, and beat the poor woman so fiercely over the shoulders and head that she fell to the ground. 'My God, what have you done?' I shrieked. It was a despicable act... The native men quickly gathered around to hear the witnesses' account of what had happened.

The boys were in no doubt that they had seriously offended, but the reaction of the Aborigines could only be described as extremely civilised. Jurich was sent to Coventry for the rest of the day, and the next morning tribal elders—both men and women—gently explained to the boys that while teasing or even abuse might be tolerated, physical violence was not. It was, said Baccich later, 'a lecture on manners in the wilderness. And then all was forgiven. Nothing more was ever said or done.'

On 17 April, an old man—Bengo—said quietly, *Tanicballa Cialli komin* ('ship fellow Cialli is coming'). It had been a pre-determined meeting with Captain Charles Tuckey, bound for Tien Tsin from Fremantle, who regularly dropped off supplies of basic tucker at North West Cape to negotiate for Aboriginal divers to work in the fledgling pearling industry. The boys, who spoke no English, were rescued as their black companions always knew they would be. Baccich recalled with sadness that, in their excitement to reach the sloop *Jessie*, they hardly gave a backward glance to the Aborigines who had saved them and treated them so generously for four months. (However, he did make amends by calling back some months later, after living in Fremantle, to distribute gifts and properly thank his benefactors.)

Gustave Rathe, author of *The Wreck of the Barque Stefano*, is Baccich's grandson. On his return to the Balkans, Miho Baccich studied at a maritime academy and in 1879 got his master's ticket. He had a distinguished career as a mariner and businessman. Whether through circumstances or design, he did not keep in contact with his companion in adversity, Ivan Jurich. Rathe managed to find out that Jurich never went to sea again, but married and became a farmer. Miho Baccich's feelings for Australia were so strong that when his first daughter was born he wanted to name her 'Australia'. Fortunately his wife gently diverted Miho from his bright idea, and his daughter—Gustave Rathe's mother—was named Euxenia, a Greek word meaning 'hospitality' or, literally, 'high regard for the stranger'.

I regaled Ros with the basics of this unusual cross-cultural story as we lunched in the shade of a tree in the grounds of the Cossack–Tien Tsin Courthouse. Our next destination, Exmouth, at North West Cape, would link us again with the *Stefano* saga. Perhaps we would camp on the very beach from which young Baccich and Jurich were picked up by *Cialli*? As it happened, in the next few days we were to stumble across more recent evidence of this singular shipwreck.

The route down the coast and across to Exmouth and North West Cape is fairly bleak—a good illustration of why the Dutch didn't get too excited about the west coast of Australia when they happened upon it in the seventeenth century. They hoped the fabled south land would rival the Spice Islands in resources and perhaps even gold—but low sandy coastlines without shelter, water or even trees soon stifled enthusiasm. For North West Cape, riches eventually came in the twentieth century when the US and Australia signed an agreement in 1963 to build the United States Naval Communications Station—essentially a cold war operation. The complex was used to broadcast very low frequency communications to ships and submarines of the US and its allies in the Indian and Pacific oceans. The facility is still there, but is not as vital to US strategic interests in the satellite era as it once was. Its vast network of towers and aerials, though, still dominates the landscape at the tip of the cape, doubtless capable of frying the gonads of careless visitors if they made the mistake of getting too close. Now renamed the Harold E. Holt Navy Communications Centre, the once closely guarded and highly secret installation—safely away from the high-powered antennae —today presents a very user-friendly front with open gates and signs offering accommodation, access to a ten pin bowling alley and other tourist delights.

Our neighbours in the Rosemary Caravan Park in Karratha had warned us that it would get more windy as we went south, and they were right. The Cape Range National Park is located on the western coast of North West Cape with little protection against the stiff on-shore winds which batter it two days out of every three in September. On the third day the winds are just strong, instead of gale force. Ros and I christened it the Commonwealth Bay of national parks. (Commonwealth Bay, in Antarctica, which Sir Douglas Mawson chose as the base for his 1911–14 expedition, is the windiest place in the world, and was dubbed 'the home of the blizzard' by Mawson.) The camping areas in the Cape Range park are situated just behind low sand dunes which provide almost no shelter from the roaring westerlies that whip the drifting sand from them.

At Commonwealth Bay, Mawson and his men used to attempt to work outside the sanctuary of their hut when the wind dropped below 50 knots (90 kph). To do so they adopted the art of what they called 'hurricane walking' where, to stay on their feet, they had to lean into the wind at an angle of 45°. Unfortunately wind is not consistent enough to do this reliably, and there were many tumbles. Ros and I tried the technique out on the beach behind which we had camped, but after a face or two full of sand we gave up and retreated to The Manor which was already bucking and shuddering in the gale.

Ros hates wind. 'Never mind,' she said bravely, 'it will probably ease off after dark.' It got stronger. We lay in our beds as if in a yacht at sea as the freshening south-westerly tore at The Manor's canvas while its telescopic arms bent alarmingly. At one stage we considered abandoning ship and collapsing The Manor to save her—but the thought of spending the rest of the night sitting up in Penelope kept us in our warm beds. Next morning the wind did appear to be easing so we set off for a day's exploration of the Cape Range National Park.

As we drove along the coast from our site at Mesa Camp we could see great foaming breakers, their breaking crests hurled forward by the wind, crashing across Ningaloo Reef. The whole coastline, from the tip of North West Cape south for 150 kilometres, is a marine park. So what about the tourist brochures of happy snorkellers diving in a tranquil coral wonderland among photogenic fish? We did find a corner of a popular picnic spot, Turquoise Bay, that provided just enough shelter for me to wet a flipper, but it seemed far removed from the serene images in the glossy brochures.

CALM has constructed an excellent Visitor Centre at Cape Range, full of good information on the history of the area and displays of local fauna and flora. The resident ranger, Greg, was a helpful and pleasant bloke, who had been in Exmouth when Cyclone Vance crossed the coast on 22 March 1999. I said I thought Vance hadn't left. Greg thought I'd have noticed the difference if I'd been there in March. 'Officially we had winds as high as 267 kph in the town, but unofficially—there was no machinery left to measure it—we had gusts of 310 kph!'

One map on the wall showed the hundreds of ships wrecked off this part of the coast. I looked for *Stefano* but could not locate it. Greg told me the wreck of the Dalmatian barque had only been found by marine archaeologists from the Museum of Western Australia as recently as 1997, five years after the book *The Wreck of the Barque Stefano* was first published. Interestingly, photographs and paintings of *Stefano* in the book had helped identify the wreck, scattered remains of which were found on a coral reef not far from Point Cloates. That was why I could not see the name *Stefano* on the chart of known wrecks. I was delighted to hear about this and followed up Greg's suggestion to call in at the Exmouth CALM office to see a full report on the discovery, so rounding out my interest in the *Stefano* wreck and its aftermath.

On our way back round the tip of North West Cape to Exmouth to get the *Stefano* report we diverted briefly to drive up to the base of the Vlaming Head Lighthouse, constructed as late as 1912 as a guide to the neglected shipping along this savage coast. We saw two vaguely familiar figures gazing out to sea through their binoculars. Ian and Coralie, the bird watchers we had first met in Karajini National Park, were stalking bigger game on this occasion, and drew our attention to humpback whales breaching and besporting themselves a couple of kilometres off shore. I have to admit to being economical with the truth the last time I mentioned that Ian's great ambition was to cross a sighting of the lesser titted thripple banded finch off his list. He was actually looking for an emu bird. Now Ros and I had recently seen a photograph of this elusive rarity—which Ian told me he had eventually spotted. You would think an emu bird would be a decent size, perhaps not as bulky as a cassowary but, at the very least, as big as a wild duck. Not so. It is actually the rufous-crowned emu-wren, with rusty red plumage and a jaunty purple bib under its beak and so tiny that it can hardly be seen at all. It has a wispy little tail supposed to resemble some feathery feature of the emu. I think it is badly named.

Returning to our bleak and windswept Mesa Camp, we caught up with the cheerful news that even stronger winds were forecast that night. Gusts were already shaking The Manor and the ocean was a seething flurry of white caps. The weather news was delivered by a couple hunkered down next to us in a caravan. Robin and his wife had been waiting for four weeks for a lull to launch their little dinghy to go fishing, but the wind had been relentless. We were toying with the idea of going to Shark Bay, further down the coast, to see the wild dolphins that swim in to be fed by tourists at Monkey Mia. Ros had met campers in Broome who had been there earlier in the season and were still starry-eyed and quite emotional about their close encounter with these elegant creatures. However, they were at Shark Bay in July, when conditions must have been more settled. The photographs in the tourist brochures showed visitors up to their knees in calm water with glistening dolphins nosing about the shallows. It was now September and Robin said that the wind would be blowing even harder down there and that the further south down the coast we went, the stronger the winds were likely to be.

Neither Ros nor I was fond of wind. Robin said, 'Well, why don't you go inland instead? It's lovely in the Mid West at this time of the year. There are a couple of relatively new national parks to visit and scads of old gold mining towns to see. And don't forget the wildflower season is just starting. We can show you where to go, we know this area very well.'

The Bowdens have always maintained that one of the great luxuries of this kind of travel is the freedom to change our minds. We decided to drive 300 kilometres south to Carnarvon to collect our mail, then head inland along the Gascoyne River following Robin's mud map. To hell with the coast. And the more we thought about it, the less attractive our plans to get down to Perth were looking. Every time we turned on the radio we heard more forecasts of doom and disaster, with miserably cold temperatures, wind and rain. It was, after all, winter. We had become complacent in the benign Kimberley dry season and started to wonder why we had ever left it!

The decision to change our plans and head inland was cemented by the rising wind. By 1 am the gale was so strong Ros and I feared the shuddering canvas sides of The Manor would actually tear loose from their fastenings. I went out to try to reposition Penelope as a windbreak, but it had no effect. We slept fitfully as the whole camper bucked and reared, the four telescopic arms holding up the roof bending and flexing as they were designed to do. Perhaps we should have tried to steady The Manor on the windward side by putting out some guy ropes as a precaution. As our beds were extended out from each end of the camper, the canvas envelopes enclosing us flapped and banged while our beds heaved and pitched. At 3 am there was a tremendous crash that had both of us fully awake simultaneously.

'What the hell was that?' As I shone a torch around there was another crashing sound. It was the metal plate above the door (which folds away in travelling mode) suddenly being sprung out and then banging back into its position.

'This is crazy,' Ros said. 'We'd better get dressed in case something gives way and we have to get the roof down in a hurry.' We brewed coffee and sat at our inside table looking blearily at each other while the wind howled and rocked The Manor viciously. There are lots of splendid features about this style of camper, but it's not at its best in high winds—although perhaps I shouldn't complain. After all, nothing broke and we stayed snug. At the first glimmer of red on the eastern horizon we broke camp and were actually away before the sun rose.

Carnarvon, on the Gascoyne River, is an astonishing oasis of agriculture. Coming into the town from the north-west, there is a sudden transformation from sand dunes and scrub to banana plantations, great fields of corn and various fruit and vegetable crops. They call the Gascoyne 'the underground river' because the veritable cornucopia of produce appears beside what looks like a dry river bed. The water is there, but it has to be drilled for and pumped to the surface. Just behind our caravan park, where we stayed for one night to reprovision, we saw a whole field full of ripe tomato plants in two-metre high rows. There had been a glut of tomatoes and they were to be ploughed in, so we were told to help ourselves. They were superb specimens, full of flavour.

We were sorry to rush away from Carnarvon, which deserved to be better explored. The wind seemed to have dropped too. In fact, Carnarvon, just below the Tropic of Capricorn, boasts of having the most equable climate in Western Australia with 323 days of sunshine a year, an average maximum temperature of 31°C in January and 22°C in June. But with only a few weeks left for our expedition, we decided to trade the civilised coast for the wider and wilder horizons of the inland. We did take time to ride on a restored tramway that takes tourists along One Mile Jetty, originally built at the turn of the twentieth century to ferry ships' passengers and produce into town.

A relatively short run of 175 kilometres took us to Gascoyne Junction which, although the biggest town in the far-flung Shire of Upper Gascoyne, only has a service station—with associated shop and pub—a police station and the shire office. The villainous-looking garage proprietor charged me a 50 cent surcharge on my credit card 'to recover bank costs'. It was the first time ever in my experience anywhere in Australia that this had been tried on, but I needed the fuel and it seemed unwise to protest. We crossed the Gascoyne River and headed north another 50 kilometres to Kennedy Range National Park—which was only gazetted as recently as 1993.

We drove underneath the beetling brows of the eroded range that stretches for almost 200 kilometres in a north–south line. The western side, we read, is more benign, with permanent water, more wildlife and evidence of early Aboriginal activity. The eastern side, where the escarpment has been eroded into great cliffs and steep gorges, is arid but dramatic. There was no permanent ranger at the park, and the camping ground was fairly basic with a long-drop toilet and rings of stones to enclose camp fires. We nearly had it to ourselves, with only one other couple in residence. The escarpment towered over our heads and, after winding up The Manor to camping mode, we sat outside in windless tranquillity, enjoying a reflective ale while I barbecued some superb Carnarvon green prawns. We stayed beside the camp fire until well after 9 pm, under the stars and a gibbous moon, while our portable CD player delivered cellist Paul Tortelier playing unaccompanied Bach suites. I said to Ros:

'This sure beats having our arses blown off on the coast.'

In the morning light, the Kennedy Range escarpment looked like a moonscape. Ros said she thought some of the rocks looked as if they had been overcooked—dark and crumbling. There are extrusions of black lava, sometimes with a ring of sandstone sandwiched in the middle. We explored some of the nearby gorges. One featured remarkable honeycombed walls of sandstone. Another ended at a sheer rock face, obviously a waterfall in times of rain, but bone dry for us. It is astonishing where plants will grow. Among the black lava and scattered stones were hardy little bushes covered with pink flowers. A shower of falling pebbles made us look up, and we saw feral goats silhouetted against the sky standing nonchalantly, as goats do, right on the edge of the abyss regarding us disdainfully.

In the afternoon, plumes of dust in the distance revealed other visitors heading our way. In comparison with the night before, the camping ground was becoming alarmingly busy. A noisy but cheerful family settled down near us, a bit too close for our liking. But that paled into insignificance with the arrival of a couple of old blokes in a beaten-up caravan. They drove in at dusk and immediately fired up a very noisy generator—its clapped out exhaust amplified by the cliffs behind us. The entire camp ground uttered a collective groan, followed some hours later by a great cheer when they switched it off to go to bed. Why do people do this? They must know that they are hated and reviled by those who want to enjoy wilderness on its own terms.

A Tasmanian couple told us during the evening that the forecast was for rain. It had clouded over by the time we put our heads down and, as the camping ground was directly in front of a gorge watercourse, we decided to leave as early as we could in case the ground turned into red soup. It was just as well we did get away early because we heard later (when we met up with the Tasmanians at Mt Augustus) that the rain set in only hours after we left and poured out of the gorge into the camping ground stranding everyone there in muddy mush for 48 hours. They also said that they saw the bodies of two dead goats in the ravine near the dry—but by then wet—waterfall. Not 'as sure footed as a mountain goat' after all.

We had only driven about 40 kilometres when we passed a sign indicating that Sandiman Station was an historic homestead—established in 1884—and adding, why not drop in for a cuppa? As it was 9 am with our coffee synapses crackling, we did. The wife of the manager, Suzie Orr, came out to meet us and ask if we wanted toast or cake. We settled for her home-made butterfly cakes and a quick tour of the homestead which, Suzie said, had nearly been destroyed by Cyclone Vance, the same cyclone that creamed Exmouth. Vance broke all the usual meteorological rules by having maintained such intensity so far inland. Suzie's husband, Lindsay, had been on his own at the time and watched horrified as the roof of the historic homestead started to lift. Fortunately it stayed put but they lost several outbuildings and a blade off their windmill. It had been a near thing. Suzie said that the homestead—which they were renting as a B & B and a base from which to run four-wheel-drive tours up on to the Kennedy Range escarpment—had been abandoned for some years. She pointed to the shadowy outline of a small kangaroo on the concrete floor of an interior courtyard.

'A wallaby came in here to die and its decomposing body etched itself into the concrete.'

Suzie was concerned about the weather because Lindsay had just taken a tour of German tourists away for the day and if it rained, they could be isolated on the escarpment. Another complication was that if the tour could not be completed on schedule they were obliged to refund the visitors' money. A Toyota utility drove into the homestead, and a long, lanky bloke uncoiled from it, looking as though he should have slid off the back of a horse instead. We were introduced to Sandiman's owner, John 'Foxy' Fraser. After we exchanged pleasantries, Suzie asked him what the weather was going to do. 'Foxy' looked up at the cloudy sky and over to the west.

'No, it won't rain,' he said firmly. Then he paused thoughtfully, looked up at the gloomy sky again and added: 'But it might!'

We said our goodbyes and headed further inland towards Mt Augustus National Park—established only four years before Kennedy Range. A few raindrops spattered on Penelope's windscreen but we hoped we would outrun the weather by heading east. The country was sparse and stony except for lines of acacias and eucalypts along dry creek beds—only one was a wet crossing. Yet somehow this marginal country supports sheep and cattle and has done so since the nineteenth century. A pub, built on the Bangemall goldfields in 1896, still exists and is part of Cobra Station—so named because the station land 'snaked' over the landscape, including Mt Augustus and the Thomas River, for 120 kilometres. The present owners of Cobra Station are Seventh Day Adventists so neither fuel nor beer was available on Saturdays. We called by on a Tuesday and the hotel was doing a roaring trade. I broke the first rule of outback travel—always get fuel when you can. I thought I'd get a better deal at the Mt Augustus Outback Tourist Resort, where we planned to camp. We did, however, pick up some home-made marmalade at the shop as we had nearly finished Vera Yugolano's 'French' carrot-laced blend from Wittenoom.

Mt Augustus is advertised as 'the biggest rock in the world', eight kilometres long and rising 858 metres above the surrounding plain. Geologically it is three times as old as Uluru (Ayers Rock) and twice as big. Unlike Uluru which is a monolith (a single block of stone of uniform quality and considerable size), Mt Augustus is a monocline—an ancient stratum of granitic rock which tilted on its side through uplifting and folding over the last 1900 million years. Although bigger than Uluru, its impact is not as dramatic because its bulk is covered with small trees and other vegetation and it does not rise as abruptly from the plain. Nevertheless, it is a splendid sight, and we stopped to photograph it from a distance. At sunrise and sunset it is reputed to glow almost as red as Uluru.

The facilities supplied by the Mt Augustus Tourist Resort were fairly basic—a camping ground, shop and some cabins and, unfortunately for us, no diesel. They had run out but were expecting a tanker in two days' time—if it could get through from Meekatharra. Roads in these parts are closed at the slightest hint of rain, and there had been heavy falls in the previous 24 hours. I wished I'd seized my opportunity to fill up at Cobra Station. As we set up camp, Mt Augustus began to look like Hobart's Mt Wellington in a bad westerly, shrouded in dark clouds and rain squalls. The road we had just travelled over from Gascoyne Junction was already closed.

The title 'resort' seemed a bit overblown. Ros told of two peremptory signs in the women's toilet block:

PLEASE FEEL FREE TO USE THE TOILET BRUSH

IF YOU USE THE HOT WATER FOR WASHING DISHES DON'T EXPECT HOT SHOWERS

The bad weather blew away overnight and we woke to clear skies and sunshine, with Mt Augustus obligingly glowing red in the first rays of the sun as we had been led to expect, despite its covering of scrub. With fuel not due for at least two days, we had plenty of time to explore. Both Kennedy Range and Mt Augustus were named by the surveyor Francis Thomas Gregory on a journey of exploration in 1858. He named Kennedy Range after the then Governor of Western Australia, Arthur Edward Kennedy, and Mt Augustus after his explorer brother, Augustus Charles Gregory, then on his own expedition searching for the bodies of Dr Ludwig Leichhardt and his party who had been missing in central Australia for ten years. Francis Gregory was the first European to climb Mt Augustus on 3 June 1858, having seen it four days earlier from afar. The day before that he had camped at a place now called Cattle Pool, where he found evidence of an Aboriginal camp. Twenty years later he was followed by pastoralists who appreciated the permanent water there.

Ros and I walked along the banks of the Lyons River, the source of Cattle Pool, which teems with water fowl and other bird life including cormorants and budgerigars— and a very surprised, very large goanna. Higher on the bank

I found the chassis, cabin and engine of a Model T Ford. The date of manufacture, 1929, was stamped on the engine block. In its day, the trusty Model T was to farmers what Toyota four-wheel-drive utilities are today.

A road circling the base of Mt Augustus gives easy access to its various walks and climbs. I was in a high state of excitement because of a new genre of Aboriginal rock carving waiting to be seen. We followed signs to Ooramboo, on the south-east corner of the monocline, to a rock face with etchings that had not survived well over the thousands of years since they had been inscribed. There were no animals or representations of human figures, just wavy lines and some depictions of animal footprints etched into rock that had crumbled badly. A Museum of Western Australia plaque, presumably with useful information about the petroglyphs, was completely unreadable because sunshine and exposure had turned the metal surface a uniform dark brown. We saw a number of information plaques in this sad state, so I hope the museum staff revisit soon and fix them up.

Further west we walked up to a site called Mundee and were rewarded with the best engravings I saw on Mt Augustus. The site was spectacular enough, a great slab of stone straddling a small stream running down a rocky gully, surrounded by acacias and small eucalypts. The petroglyphs cannot be seen unless you scramble in under 'Flintstone Rock' and then wait for your eyes to become accustomed to the shadow. The etchings are beautifully clear, and run along in wavy lines and loops, strongly reminiscent of a John Olsen painting. There are also some circles and vertical stripes. Perhaps this had been a place of great significance. The stream runs under 'Flintstone

Rock' and there is only room for one at a time to view and photograph these small but most attractive engravings. Unfortunately the present Aboriginal custodians of the Burringurrah community have no knowledge in their Dreaming of the images carved by their Wadjari ancestors so long ago.

On our way back to the 'resort' we slowed down while an emu with six chicks shepherded his charges off the road and into the scrub—behaving more sensibly than emus usually do. Apparently emus creche their chicks, which are looked after by males. The female emu takes little interest in her offspring after laying her eggs. Maybe female emus aren't so stupid after all! Paul, the CALM ranger at Mt Augustus, said the males can be very aggressive while minding chicks. One had fluffed up his vestigial wings and charged his Landrover, refusing to back off.

We decided not to climb Mt Augustus because Ros didn't want an all-day walk, and in any case we were told a two-hour climb to a vantage point called Edney's Lookout on the eastern end of the mountain gave as good, if not a better, outlook. We had one more day's exploring available before the diesel fuel arrived.

The track to Edney's Lookout was well marked with small boulders of red granite and startlingly white quartz on each side of the path, as well as small cairns indicating twists and turns. At the start of the walk we met Ranger Paul, from CALM, who was doing a bit of track maintenance. He said that the splendid marking had been done by a ranger called Terry Bloomer in 1992, with the help of the Burringurrah Aboriginal Community. It was one of the best indicated tracks I have ever been on; it would have been easy to stray if it were not so well delineated. An added bonus was finding and photographing the unique Mt Augustus foxglove, which only grows on the higher slopes of the world's biggest rock. It has a pretty deep-blue flower, although Ros also found one with a paler hue.

The wind was whipping over the rock pinnacle that marked the top of Edney's Lookout, and we sat down behind a rock to eat our muesli bars, admire the 360° panoramic view and enjoy the visitors' log, kept in a rusty tin.

On 31 July 1999, Joanne from Northcliff, Western Australia, was so taken with the excellence of the experience that she wrote: 'May all people become aware of the beauty of our planet.' Her travelling companion, Jim, also from Northcliff, was less generous: 'Call a Royal Commission on CALM for their destruction of our forests in the south-west. Indict Court, Edwards, Shea and Tuckey for crimes against the environment and for treason against WA.'

Two days before our visit, on 24 August, Sandgropers Geoff and Lorraine were more focussed on the personal: 'The cardiac arrest or two is worth the pain when you get here.'

It reminded me of one of Paul the Ranger's better lines during his evening slide show when he was emphasising the importance of strong shoes or boots, and carrying at least two litres of water when walking on the mountain: 'I'm the only ranger here, and I can't carry people down by myself. So all I can do is walk up with a .22 and put you down.' I rather liked the concept of tourists being despatched like injured cattle.

Back at the car park Paul showed us a nesting grey falcon in one of the stately red river gums. Then, as we turned into the euphemistically named Mt Augustus Tourist Resort, we saw the welcome sight of the diesel tanker rumbling in. They only got diesel once a fortnight, and sometimes not a full load, because the working stations have priority over tourist operations. If it rained, the tanker didn't come at all.

ten

Wildflowers and Wild Places

We had not yet experienced a station stay, now becoming a popular element of outback travel, where tourists fly or drive to a remote property and are accommodated and have an intimate glimpse of life in rural Australia. Our map of the Mid West showed one such station, Erong Springs, about 150 kilometres south-west of Mt Augustus, advertising not only station tours including ancient Aboriginal carvings, but the intriguing Erong Ringing Rocks: 'Black granite boulders resound in different tones when struck with a hammer.' A quick phone call to the owners, Chris and Sue Graham, confirmed they did welcome campers and indeed they could take us on a station tour the following day.

On our way we crossed the meandering Gascoyne River once again and headed into flat stony country so arid that we wondered whether goats could survive in it let alone sheep. As we were to discover, feral goats flourish there, competing for meagre feed with the sheep which also manage to do surprisingly well.

We were welcomed by Sue Graham who showed us our camping spot on a little patch of struggling green grass shaded by luxuriant pepper trees. Not only did a station outbuilding offer flush toilets, but also hot showers after 5 pm when Sue fired up the boiler. Camp fires were allowed, so we realised we could use our camp oven and cook a damper for breadless days ahead. Chris was out crutching and drenching sheep because, although it was a dry year, for some unexplained reason they had a blowfly crisis worse than if the season had been wet. Such is the lot of the primary producer, but when Chris arrived back at the homestead in the late afternoon he seemed cheerful enough about it all. I suppose if you weren't you'd go mad.

Chris is a former New Zealand sheep farmer with a slight hint of the short flat vowel in his accent despite having spent most of his life in Australia. The Grahams have to take on extra jobs to survive. He and his son specialise in sinking and repairing bores and occasional piece work on other farms—as well as looking after their own property and hosting visitors like us.

The original settler there, Barney Murphy, built the first Erong Springs homestead in 1919 near where we were camped. Barney was a soldier settler and a much decorated Anzac who began his farming life living in a succession of rough timber shelters. A stockman's hut built in the 1930s, now in ruins, was very similar in design to the first substantial homestead Barney built for his wife. A classic outback dwelling, it had a square main section, divided into two small rooms, encircled by a large verandah on four sides, as wide as the house itself. This design ensured a shaded area near the house at all times of the day.

When I wanted a windbreak for our fire I was able to choose from a great variety of farm scrap nearby. The most convenient artefact for the job was a stainless steel kitchen sink. Ros photographed the cook at work so that it could truly be said that we travelled with everything including . . .

Unfortunately the full day station tour we had booked did not include the western side of the property where the Aboriginal rock carvings were, so Sue came over to our camp to suggest an elegant compromise. She would take us to the petroglyphs in the morning and Chris would take us on a shortened drive around the property in the afternoon to show how sheep farming worked in country so arid that we thought the stock must have had to develop an appetite for stones.

Sue rolled up punctually at 9 am in a battered Toyota 'Troopie'—about to turn over 300 000 very rugged kilometres—and we headed west along lightly marked tracks that I would have lost in minutes. She was extremely knowledgeable about the flora of the area and identified a host of desert plants, most of them qualified by whether sheep could eat them or not. Sue found a bush 'pear' for us, about the size and shape of a banana passionfruit, and cut it open. The seeds tasted foul, but allegedly are not when young—particularly after they've been baked in the ashes.

We stopped by a stand of sandalwood in a creek bed and sniffed its distinctive highly-scented aroma from a dry stick Sue snapped in half. Sandalwood (*Santalam spicatum*) is actually a parasite that grows from the roots of a variety of host plants. In arid areas it takes up to 90 years for the sandalwood's trunks to reach 125mm in diameter. The wood from the small, rather untidy looking trees with sparse irregular branches and dull grey-green leaves is highly prized in Asia for use in joss sticks for religious ceremonies. Sandalwood was first exported from Western

Australia in 1843. From 4 tonnes in the first year, exports leapt to 1335 tonnes by 1848 and earned an extraordinary 45 per cent of the young colony's export income. Even today, although the open slather boom and bust days of the 1930s are long gone, the state's 21 licensed 'pullers' contribute to an export industry worth $10 million a year. Sandalwood is pulled from the ground and nothing is wasted. The entire tree from its roots to leaves—even dead wood—is processed for export to South-East Asia. The rules and regulations of its harvesting are arcane and rooted, if I can be forgiven the expression, in history.

Sue told us that, as property owners, she and Chris were not well positioned to capitalise on the sandalwood growing on their station even if they wanted to. The whole industry is controlled by the omnipotent CALM. Essentially, Sue said, the property owners were at the bottom of the totem pole. If they did succeed in getting permission to 'pull' sandalwood growing on their land, they got the lowest price. A licensed contractor who came in to harvest it got a third more, and if CALM did the pulling they earned twice as much as anyone else. CALM administers the industry under the rules of the Sandalwood Export Committee, established in 1932!

The Grahams are keen conservationists, which we thought was just as well since the district's marginal land is managed through the state's Pastoral Board, which encumbers them with all kinds of draconian rules and regulations. For instance, they may not cut any timber on their land without permission. In the past farmers cut mulga trees for fence posts—but no more. There is a limit on the amount of stock they can run—even feral goats—and they are checked on every five years. Chris and Sue had been delighted to get a nice 'tick' after their last inspection for their land management.

Our next stop was by a natural 'Gnamma Hole Spring' which bubbled water to the surface continually and was surrounded by green reeds and lush grass. (I had wondered about the property name, Erong Springs.) The little oasis was surrounded by petroglyphs as it was a natural gathering point for ancient communities. Fortunately Sue had been fascinated by rock art ever since she arrived at Erong Springs seven years before and had been gradually noting and finding engravings over the years. Like the art at Mt Augustus, the petroglyphs are not representations of humans or animals, just meandering lines, perhaps representations of spear heads, animal footprints and concentric circles. One recurring motif was a small circle with lines trailing away from one side. At first sight it looked like a squid or octopus, but that was unlikely so far inland. All we could do was conjecture, because this rock art is so old that it is beyond the Dreaming of the local Aboriginal communities.

Sue had found several saucer-like depressions in rocks she was sure were places where women ground seeds for food. Occasionally she had seen rounded rocks which could have been grinding stones nearby, but were broken in several pieces. Sue thought that there may have been a custom of breaking a woman's individual grinding stone after she died. One site she showed us was extraordinary. There was a rounded depression on top of a rock, and in the middle of it was a complete grinding stone. For how many thousands of years had that stone been sitting there undisturbed? The previous owners of the property, Sue said, told her the grinding stone was in that position when they first saw it. Ros and I were most moved by this poignant evidence of the domestic activity of a lost people. As no one knows where it is, apart from the Grahams, there is a good chance it will remain there undisturbed.

We were joined at the homestead for lunch—lamb chops of course!—by another couple Meg and Bill, who themselves ran a farm stay property in the cool temperate south-west of Western Australia and who were joining us in the battered Troopie for Chris's afternoon tour. As we jolted along the stony farm tracks I asked Chris how he managed to round up his flock for shearing—or indeed the crutching and treatments for blowfly strike he was then carrying out. The short answer was water! Sheep have to drink, of course, and the bores are the only sources of water. Each bore is surrounded by a stock fence with a gate usually left open so the sheep can come and go. When Chris wants to round up his flock he shuts the gate and activates a cunning entry point—an opening with a sprung angled wire mesh in a V shape which the sheep have to push open with their bodies to get in. Once in they can't get out until Chris has done whatever he wants to do with them. If there is a wet season, more conventional mustering has to be organised.

When we reached the first windmill and watering point, there was only one feral ewe inside—and a big red kangaroo, which became exceedingly agitated as we approached and got one of its paws jammed in the fence. Chris, who wasn't looking forward to going inside the enclosure with him, was going to have to try to set him free without getting injured himself. But as he approached, the panic-stricken animal pulled itself free and jumped the mesh fence in a huge bound.

As we drove to the next bore, Chris told us of a recent discovery. Even though it had been as dry as the traditional dead dingo's donger, he had not been able to muster all his sheep. A helicopter pilot told him that he had noticed a patch of green on the side of a hill. Chris investigated and found a permanent spring on his property that he had not known was there! He had since put a fence around it and was hoping to gather in not only his sheep, but some feral goats. With the price of wool as low as it was there was better money in exporting live goats to the Middle East. The only problem was to trap the goats and make sure they were all billies.

'Muslim men will not eat anything female,' said Chris. 'They only want the billy goats which are the hardest to manage.' The billies were happily disease free but indestructible, Chris said. He was a fund of great goat stories, like the one about the road train full of billy goats waiting at the wharf to be loaded. One billy leapt off the third storey of the truck to the road below, straight down on its head, and bounced. Before anyone could get to it, the battered billy shook his head, got up and bounded away to freedom. It should have been killed outright.

'Another road train driver carrying goats for the Middle East trade is still cursing,' said Chris. 'This time a big billy leapt over the front section of the road train and crashed down on the roof of his cabin—then jumped down on to the bonnet and away, doing terrible things to his shiny paintwork.'

I was surprised to hear that Erong Springs, despite its arid, tough country, produced fine wool much prized in the market and comparing favourably with some of the best fine wool fleece from more benign cool temperate areas like Tasmania. When I said his sheep must include stones in their diet, Chris said it sometimes looked like that.

'In times of drought you can see both the goats and the sheep apparently trying to eat stones. They are actually moving small rocks aside to lick up seeds blown by the wind and trapped underneath them.'

We ended our tour by visiting a couple of Erong Springs gorges—one as white as snow with outcrops of opalite, a translucent jasper-like gemstone without the colours, and another with rocks as red as anything we had seen in Kari-jini National Park, but on a smaller scale. And yes, Chris did take us to the ringing rocks, which we did not hit with a hammer in the interests of conservation, but with small fragments of stone. Due to the random size of the rocks it was difficult to play a tune, but they did hold a note—some deeply resonant, others in the treble clef.

The computer age and the Internet had come to Erong Springs and greatly helped with forecasts, as well as other communication benefits. Chris said there was rain on the way, so as we had a number of creek crossings on back roads before reaching Meekatharra, 500 kilometres to the south-east, we headed off early the next morning—farewelled by Chris and Sue and a couple of hand-reared red kangaroos which refused to return completely to the wild and had come in from the bush for their morning ration of toast.

'Meeka' is an important service town for both the pastoral and mining industries on the Great Northern Highway, 760 kilometres from Perth—about halfway between the state's capital city and Port Hedland on the inland route. It was cold, windy and overcast when we got there, and rained briefly overnight, but by then we were temporarily back on the bitumen and didn't care. It was servicing time for Penelope, The Manor, our laundry and us. By pre-arrangement we had Penelope's oil changed, The Manor's bearings checked and our hair cut by an obliging hairdresser who came in on her day off, specially, after an SOS from Ripper's garage in response to a call from me in a phone box at Mt Augustus. Good friendly country town stuff. I also needed access to a phone to check my emails through my Apple PowerBook computer. This had been proving difficult and, as I said to a friend in an email, there had been times when I had to hire a motel room for ten minutes—carefully explaining why—to gain access to a phone plug. Unfortunately I made an error in the address and the message went astray. The person who received it was kind enough to bounce it back, adding:

> Sent to wrong address . . . try a new medication if you can only last ten minutes in a motel room. Regards . . .

Quite so.

We were conscious that, like the King's life, our expedition was coming peacefully to a close. In little more than a week's time we would have to leave Kalgoorlie for a lunge across the Nullarbor to be in Sydney five days later. We found ourselves travelling faster and more intensely, cherishing our bush camps and the wide open spaces we would soon have to forsake. Perhaps it had something to do with travelling down the map—the gravity factor in geography. This was a theory expressed to me by a diplomat friend when we were both stationed in New York in the late 1960s and when the cold war was still very much in evidence.

'Perhaps,' he said, looking thoughtfully into his glass of

Australian shiraz, 'Mercator's Projection has a lot to answer for. There is Australia, the great big empty continent, sitting there underneath the teeming millions in China and South-East Asia from which the dreaded Communism is seeping down the map like a bloodstain, threatening to leak into Australia. The gravity factor driving Australian foreign policy,' he opined triumphantly.

Because we were heading south we seemed to be falling more and more quickly towards Kalgoorlie and our return home, and after all the dirt road driving we had been doing it seemed odd to be barrelling down a first-class bitumen road. We were still following Robin's mud map and suggestions sketched out in faraway and bleakly windswept Mesa Camp on North West Cape. He advised driving down the Great North West Highway to Cue, and then cutting across back roads to the Mt Magnet–Geraldton Highway to Pindar in search of the spectacular wreath flowers said to be active at that time of the year.

The wide main street of Cue has a charming selection of turn of early twentieth century stone and timber buildings. Cue and its near neighbour Day Dawn were the centre of a vigorous gold mining industry that began in 1894 and petered out in the early 1950s when the difficulty of extracting ore from below 700 metres became uneconomic and dangerous. The extremely fine government buildings, well preserved today, are evidence of half a century of gold-driven prosperity. It has been said that with its gracious hotels and verandah-fronted shops, Cue would make a splendid set for a Western movie. One of the biggest gold operations, Big Bell, 30 kilometres to the north-east of Cue, had its own town in the 1930s, but little remains today. Underground mining was resumed there recently, however. Many of the Mid West's old gold operations are being re-examined in the twenty-first century as new technology and the all-important price of gold have brought activity back to old tailing dumps and previously abandoned underground workings.

We were back on dirt roads again, turning south-west from the Big Bell mine—access forbidden—down to yet another big rock, Walga Rock. Having just experienced the world's alleged biggest, Mt Augustus, we found Walga to be a modest monolith in comparison. Two kilometres long, at 50 metres it does not dominate the surrounding plain as do its bigger cousins. It looks, however, more like a mini-Uluru and is formed of a similar reddish granitic rock, although its flanks are more easily scaled. Camping is permitted around its base. We were there because of one of the best Aboriginal rock art galleries in the Mid West. Under a protective fold of granite which sheltered it, a vertical rock wall was an irresistible site for ancient artists. The 60-metre-long gallery is something of a jumble of paintings—not engravings—which have been painted over older works. Walga means ochre, or painting, in the Warragi language, and some drawings are so high that a type of scaffolding must have been used from which to paint them.

The most distinctive and unusual painting is a white ship with masts, rigging and ratlines, seven square portholes and four wavy lines underneath—which look at first glance to be some kind of script, but may be a representation of water. Why there should be the painting of a ship 325 kilometres from the sea remains a mystery. Not that there is any shortage of theories, ranging from a hoax to alleged evidence that Dutch sailors wrecked on the west coast in the sixteenth century were brought inland by Aboriginal tribes.

The respected archaeologist and expert in pre-historic Aboriginal art, Josephine Flood, has canvassed the various speculations. In 1926 two old desert Aborigines were recorded as saying that, 'a long time before', a girl in the tribe who had blonde hair and blue eyes had made the painting. As she had done so in a place restricted to initiated men, she had been killed. However, no evidence to support this story has turned up. Apart from the speculation that shipwrecked Dutch sailors might have been responsible—the ship does not represent a Dutch colonial vessel—it was thought an Afghan working on a nearby station in the 1920s might have been responsible, as the lines of 'writing' under the ship resemble Arabic script.

Flood was more interested in actual evidence. She said the white paint used to draw the ship had been analysed and came from the same source as the white pipe-clay used in other paintings at the site. That, at least, seems to marginalise the hoax theories. Flood herself thinks that the painting may represent an Aboriginal painter recording his first impression of a ship and the ocean.

Ros and I had the huge gallery to ourselves, and were able to study this enigmatic drawing, conveniently at eye level, while time stood still.

We were heading for the coast again. As Geraldton was 850 kilometres south from Exmouth, where we'd had our bums blown off, and only 320 kilometres north from Perth which we had decided not to visit because winter was in full frigid force, we wondered about the wisdom of this move. Basically we were driven by horticultural curiosity. Our Mid West guide, Robin of Mesa (Windy) Camp, had mentioned some weird wildflowers called wreath flowers and said that people came from all over the world and indeed Australia to see them. They looked like a funeral wreath, were quite remarkably large, rare and, unless conditions were right, might not flower at all in any one year. But he had heard there were some in the countryside near Mullewa, inland from Geraldton.

We were already in wildflower territory. Vast areas of white daisy-like flowers gave way to yellows, reds and blues—quite enchanting. We stopped beside the road and set up our lunch table in the middle of a clearing carpeted with wildflowers which stretched as far as we could see. By the time we bush camped we had almost come to take them for granted. No wonder wildflower-seeking tourists come from far and wide to Western Australia in early spring.

We had been told that Pindar, a small hamlet 130 kilometres east of Geraldton, was the Mecca of wreath flower pilgrims. We arrived there next morning at about nine, and found Pindar was fairly basic: a rusty railway line, seemingly derelict siding, the obligatory wheat silo and a handful of buildings. One, which advertised itself as a bed and breakfast stop, looked quite sinister with gables and narrow doors like the spooky Addams family home. Ros had little success in raising the dead, and we were unsure where to start looking for the wreath flowers. While she was still knocking on the funereal B & B door, I hailed a car which had come out of a side road.

'You wouldn't know where to find the wreath flowers I suppose?'

The faces of the four inside lit up. 'Do we ever. We saw

them yesterday. Here's a local mud map if you want it, but they are just over the railway line in a gravel pit to the left.'

A gravel pit? Just the kind of location wreath flowers revel in, we later discovered. They only grow in recently disturbed areas, and refuse to flower unless their environment is under stress. Strange flowers indeed. We joined a cluster of cars and campers in the gravel pit and went looking for these singular wildflowers. We did not have to look far. They were scattered all about as if someone had despoiled a cemetery. By this stage Ros had located them in a reference book. *Lechenaultia macrantha*, or fanflowers, are the largest of the Goodeniaceae family and, because of their penchant for mucked about country, are most often seen along tracks, road verges or areas recently graded. The flowers are yellow, suffused with red or pink on their edges and grow from a ground-hugging central leafy green core which gives them their remarkable similarity to a funeral wreath. Some of the larger ones were 50 centimetres in diameter!

The gravel pit, strangely, had an abundance of Western Australian wildflowers which were much photographed and enjoyed by visitors. The flowers looked as though they had been planted there deliberately, including native pomegranate, Mullewa roses and foxgloves. Of course they hadn't, but their profusion says a lot for the hardy nature of the plants. Although the gravel pit had been recently scoured, all the plants needed, even in that stony ground, was a bit of water and sunlight to burst forth. Western Australia has a staggering 7000 native plants and the vast majority of them are unique to the west. The gravel pit, with its cleared space, highlighted the infusion of wildflowers. But they were everywhere, in spaces between the scrub and trees, dotting the landscape with brilliant points of colour. It was as heady as a fireworks display. Ros was in her seventh heaven.

We needed to restock at Geraldton before looping south and west into more wildflower territory and tackling the interior of the arid Mid West again. This would be our last contact with the Indian Ocean before heading home and we hoped there would be no unpleasant surprises. Unfortunately our arrival coincided with a front boiling up from the Antarctic and we found ourselves in a waterfront caravan park to the north of Geraldton once again riding our bucking and rocking beds. This time The Manor was being buffeted not only by gusts of high wind but by horizontal rain squalls as well. The wind wasn't quite as severe as at Cape Range National Park, but dramatic enough. I woke at one point to see Ros lying on her bed fully dressed with her boots on ready for anything! At 1 am (never a good time for camping emergencies) one of the collapsible poles holding up The Manor's awning did just that, collapsed, broke partially free, flailed around madly in the wind and rain and had to be attended to. Silently singing the praises of all-purpose gaffer tape, I managed to subdue it until morning.

Our plans for sightseeing in Geraldton evaporated in the gusty gloom of the morning and we prepared to reprovision and flee inland again. We did manage a brief visit to the excellent Geraldton Maritime Museum which features relics recovered from various Dutch East India Company ships wrecked on the jagged reefs and treacherous waters of this part of the coast—principally *Batavia* (1629), *Zuytdorp* (1712) and *Zeewijk* (1727). No wonder Western Australians are bemused by the eastern states' preoccupation with the notion that the European discovery

of Australia began with Captain James Cook's visit to
Botany Bay in 1788.

So as not to retrace our route west (and in order to see
more wildflowers) we planned to run down the coast for 65
kilometres on Highway One, turn inland at Dongara, and
head for Perenjori via Mingenew and Morawa. There we
would take to the back roads again and head for White
Wells Station which offered camping and 263 000 hectares
of wildflowers. With the wind at our backs and rain squalls
decreasing as we headed away from the coast again, we
made good time to White Wells Station where even the
camping ground was spotted with yellow and white everlasting daisies. We did think kindly thoughts about
Geraldton after we enjoyed the absolutely fabulous green
prawns we bought there, and with which Ros did magic
things in a wok. Next morning, under clear skies again and
armed with a mud map supplied by White Wells' amiable,
chain-smoking caretaker Don, we megadosed on wildflowers, at one point photographing Penelope adrift in a
sea of pink and white flowers seemingly splashed on the
landscape by an impressionist painter. The Mid West wildflower mix comprises white, gold and pink everlastings,
billy buttons, wild pansies, purple vetch, flannel bush,
mulla mulla, acacia, lambs tails, *eremophila* (poverty bush),
parakeelya, daisies and blue pincushion.

White Wells is a sheep farm which specialises in fatten-
ing up fairly ordinary sheep for the Perth meat market.
The property was first farmed in 1879 by Franciscan
monks, who built tall whitewashed stone walls around
precious wells from which the station got its name. Unfortunately the recent rain had made the tracks too boggy to
reach them. Don said we could try if we wanted to, but if

we did he'd probably see us in a couple of weeks' time. White Wells is a popular wildflower destination for 'terrorists'—as Don dryly dubbed tourists—because it is only 40 kilometres from the Great Northern Highway and an easy day's drive from Perth on a sealed road.

We headed north again briefly on the Great Northern for 70 kilometres to Paynes Find which consists of a combined service station and pub on the highway and not much else. We knew of a small working gold battery nearby and had been told that the owners of the service station were not only renowned throughout the district for rudeness to their customers, but through sheer bastardry kept the existence of the working battery a closely guarded secret. All of which turned out to be true. This lot made Basil Fawlty look good. After filling up with diesel I went in to pay with a credit card, and to buy some chips and a Coke. I couldn't see the salt and vinegar packet I wanted and asked the woman behind the counter.

'We haven't got any.'

'What do you have then?'

'What you can see.'

Ros had no luck either. She wanted to know about the condition of the back road from Paynes Find to Sandstone, 234 kilometres to the north-west, and asked the same charming woman.

'It's open.'

I had included the cost of my Coke and chips on the credit card, and walked over to the fridge to get my drink. As I walked out I was challenged by the woman's husband and accused of not paying for it! Why do people like that take enterprises where they have to meet the public?

Our reception at the Paynes Find Gold Battery, one

kilometre east of the surly service station, was a welcome contrast in style. Elaine Taylor welcomed us into the small private mining museum attached to the battery and gave us a rundown on its history before taking us on a guided tour. The five-head ore crushing battery, still standing tall behind its covering of rusty corrugated iron, was built by the state government in 1911 to service prospectors recovering gold in the area. What is more, it is still working, and is used from time to time by twenty-first-century freelance prospectors to crush small quantities of gold-bearing ore that would not be accepted by bigger mining companies' batteries.

Thomas Payne was a prospector who had pegged out many claims in the district in the early 1900s. In fact, he had been so active that the place that now bears his name was originally known as Paynes New Find. Actually, the town was first called Carnation, so voted by a group of residents on 22 July 1911. But the government took no notice of this local exercise in democracy—perhaps they thought it a bit milksoppy—and labelled the speck on the map Paynes New Find. The 'new' was dropped within a few months.

Elaine Taylor told us that the battery's original 1911 machinery was still functioning, while some of the steel heads on the five hammers had, of course, been replaced over the years, worn down by pummelling the tough chunks of gold-bearing rock into powder. For good measure, Elaine showed us a video she had taken of a recent crushing, culminating in the pouring of liquid gold from a crucible heated in their small furnace. The process of extracting the particles of gold from a bed of mercury—the gold sticks to the denser metal—has remained unchanged since Thomas Payne brought his own ore to be crushed under the same hammers in 1911. A wonderful example of living, and working, history.

An added bonus, as we reluctantly tore ourselves away from Elaine's friendly and well-informed operation, was being able to buy some home-made quandong jam. And Ros could not resist buying some cleverly crafted earrings made from quandong nuts. Then, with only a few hours of daylight left, we had to find ourselves a spot to bush camp somewhere along the Paynes Find to Sandstone road.

The country we drove through was flat and quite well covered with bushy vegetation, mostly acacias with the occasional quandong tree. There were plenty of clear areas in between patches of vegetation, where we were able to drive off the road and park in idyllic circumstances on a carpet of yellow, pink and blue wildflowers offset by the startlingly red sandy soil. Within minutes we were enjoying a solar bush shower and a change of clothes. We felt clean and relaxed, and sat beside The Manor while we enjoyed a cuppa and listened to bird calls. There were plenty of dead acacia branches for firewood. I dug a pit fire for safety, and we barbecued thick chunks of rare porterhouse steak, so tender that they fell apart at the very sight of a table knife. Ros calculated that we probably only had time for three of these private bush camps before we reached Kalgoorlie—a salutary thought.

Very little traffic used this highway from Paynes Find to Sandstone. On a whim, next morning, when we pulled over for morning coffee, I put my folding chair in the middle of the wide, red dirt highway and drank it undisturbed.

The difficulty of getting fuel in remote places was

demonstrated again when we reached Sandstone, which is some 450 kilometres in from the west coast, and pretty remote from anywhere. Sandstone was in its gold mining heyday from 1908 to 1912 and some quite substantial stone buildings survive to this day—monuments to the unrealised optimism of that particular gold fever. We headed straight for a cluster of bowsers, opposite the pub, and waited. Nothing happened so I went to the obvious place to find out what was going on—the bar. Admittedly it was Sunday, but I was keen to top up my tanks.

'Bill's gone to play golf,' said the publican. 'He won't be back till after 5 pm.' By then we planned to be well on our way to Leinster, 200 kilometres away on the Goldfields Highway. I thought we'd probably make it, providing we didn't do too many side excursions, so we moved on. We caught a glimpse of the golf course on our way out of town. It didn't have a blade of grass on it!

I did burn up a bit of extra fuel driving the circuit of Sandstone's Heritage Trail—a legacy of the Bicentennial celebrations in 1988 and a Commonwealth and State grant to the Western Australian Heritage Committee. A well produced complimentary brochure—I picked it up at the pub—gave good information on the history of the area and a sketch map to locate the Reef-Oroya and Hacks Reef-Black Range gold mines (still being worked), as well as curiosities like London Bridge, a natural stone arch wide enough for horses and carts to drive underneath—indeed over the arch itself until erosion put paid to that. London Bridge was always a popular picnic spot and conveniently close to the underground brewery, tunnelled into a cliff face, which had the advantage of keeping the product cool in the days before refrigeration, and allowing a good fall for water, piped from a well on a higher level, to circulate through the brewery pipes and holding tanks. This unusual brewery was constructed in 1907 by an Irishman, J. V. Kearney. Unfortunately Kearney's boast that his beer was 'the best beer ever tasted on the goldfields' was not supported by Sandstone's thirsty miners who deemed it undrinkable by the time it was carted three kilometres or so to the town. It must have been pretty bad!

Speaking of pubs, some 25 kilometres from Leinster— a modern town supporting a nickel mine—is the Agnew Hotel, which a friend, Rod Ledingham, remembered fondly. He had emailed from Tasmania asking us to drop by and take a few photographs of the pub inside and outside if possible:

In 1971 I worked prospecting for nickel in the Agnew area with another geologist Ken Thorsen, who found gossan (the weathered remnants of sulphides) near Perseverance Bore on Leinster Station, and was the first, with a couple of drillers, to see the ore come out of a drill hole in the creek bed. It was black mud, and I thought it was oil, such was my total ignorance of what sulphides that have been pulverised with a big down hole hammer looked like. I took a sample and washed it. It sparkled like gold—'fool's gold'. We drilled into the massive sulphides for 36.5 metres then ran out of rods, so went to fetch a couple more from our camp, but we were waylaid by the Agnew pub on our way and got ever so slightly inebriated instead. It turned out to be the 'right stuff' and so I worked there for the next two years as a geologist.

Ken and I were hoping we would be invited back for the 25th anniversary bunfight, but no luck—I think they opened the mine in about 1978 and built Leinster Town where Leinster Station was.

The Agnew pub, at a distance, looked like something out of a Ma and Pa Kettle movie, its backyard littered with old machinery and rusting car bodies. A closer look confirmed the impression. I said to Ros that Rod mightn't recognise any changes at all from the 1970s. It was 11 am— in this land of hairy-chested miners, early enough to breast the bar. That wasn't an option even if we had wanted to, because the pub's doors were all firmly closed. I heard some sepulchral coughing from deep inside the derelict-looking hostelry but no one responded when I knocked on the door. The only other structure in view was the rusting poppet head of an abandoned mine across the potholed dirt road.

There was, however, an ancient phone box with one of those cylindrical dials you pull around with your finger. To my surprise it actually worked and I managed to ring Rod in Tasmania to tell him where we were standing. I also told him I didn't think we were going to be able to photograph the bar inside. It was unlikely to have changed, judging by the look of the outside.

Rod filled me in with a bit more background about the Agnew pub and its alcoholic publican, Billy Cock. There were many jolly sessions in the early 1970s with Billy, who matched customers drink for drink. He was so fond of booze that he moved his bed into the cellar to be even closer to the source of the sauce. Unfortunately he didn't pay for what he was drinking, or the bills for the four sheep stations he owned, nor did he keep adequate records of how much his patrons drank or paid. He went bankrupt and decided that the only solution was the final one.

Billy fortified himself for the last time, took his rifle and walked over to the Emu Mine that I could see from the telephone box. He sat on the edge of the vertical mine shaft and blew his brains out. At least one of his plans worked out efficiently. His body fell twenty or so metres down the shaft, the bottom of which was filled with water.

When Rod and his offsider, Leon Bonney, were called to the pub after Billy couldn't be found, they put two and two together and with the help of a reluctant local Aborigine tracked Billy's footsteps to the mine. They found the timber covering pulled back and a packet of cigarettes and a beer can on the edge of the shaft—and called the Leonora copper.

'He had a look down and asked Leon and me to keep an eye on the water in the shaft because he estimated Billy would float to the surface in a few days and we could let him know.

'Leon was a good welder so we returned to our camp, constructed a big grappling hook out of an iron bar and went back to try our luck.

'We hooked Billy first cast,' Rod told me cheerfully, 'and hauled him out. We laid out his body on a sheet of corrugated iron and then transferred him into the back of the police ute before all going back to the pub for a splendid wake—drinking Billy's booze, of course. We felt he would have wanted us to.

'At intervals people would stagger out and shake Billy's hand which was protruding from under the tarpaulin in the copper's ute, thanking him for his generosity and wishing him well in the hereafter.'

Rod said in retrospect it seemed an odd thing to do, but seemed perfectly natural at the time. He was most intrigued to hear that the pub was in a time warp and asked us, if we had time, whether we could drive into Leinster and take a few photos of the mining town he had never seen. The awful coughing could still be heard inside the pub, and I decided not to disturb whoever it was, who sounded extremely crook.

(We learned later that day the owner of the cough was most likely Billy Cock's brother Tommy, who had taken over the pub after his brother died and was still there.)

Leinster was a smartly laid out mining town for some 250 miners and their families. Judging by the number of prams and toddlers we saw being wheeled and carried to the town's supermarket and shopping centre, the average age of the community was probably under eight! There was a single men's quarters, but it was of modest proportions compared with the company houses set in attractive tree-lined streets. We noticed a golf course and Olympic-sized swimming pool. There was no pub, but there was sure to be a wet canteen somewhere. I doubted if the faded charms of Billy Cock's hostelry would lure many of the workers to Agnew. We were able to top up our water jerry cans from a source of public drinking water outside the health centre, and had lunch just out of town under the shade of a convenient acacia.

According to the gravity principle of dropping south down the map, we were closing fast on Leonora, a major town in this part of the world, with 2500 people and a mining industry still flourishing more than 100 years since the first gold rushes of the 1890s. We hoped to bush camp before we got there, but were thwarted by stock fences on the right of the road, and impregnable chain-link barriers safeguarding the gas pipeline buried on the other side. This pipeline, all the way from Dampier, supplies the Kalgoorlie–Boulder–Coolgardie mining, industrial and domestic market. Tentatively we nosed in across a cattle grid to what was clearly private land but were deterred from even asking permission—if we could have located the homestead—by a sign which said there was a program to rid the property of goats and shooting was likely to take place at any time.

We were almost to Leonora before we saw a side road leading off to the right, mercifully without fences. We continued until we saw a settlement and decided to ask permission to camp. This was just as well because the owners of the small farm, Bob and Annette, were not very well disposed to campers due to theft and damage to their property in the past. They warmed to us, fortunately, and asked us in for a drink. They had not been there very long but had bought the 23-acre property from a market gardener called Jack Straw (a great name for his profession), who had grown too old to carry on. Bob was a retired mechanic who just loved growing things. We were entertained in a large covered breezeway beside their caravan, surrounded by citrus trees bulging with fat juicy oranges, lemons and grapefruit. The fruit and vegetables were all sustained by bore water, of course, since the district gets very little rain. Bob said they felt they lived in a place called 'Elsewhere' because the district was never mentioned in forecasts on ABC Radio. 'Fine elsewhere' was as close as they ever got.

We mentioned we had dropped in at the Agnew pub, and Bob confirmed Rod Ledingham's story of Billy Cock's demise and said the coughing we had heard undoubtedly sprang from the emphysemic lungs of his brother Tommy. I got the strong impression that the winds of change were soon to blow over the Agnew pub. Bob offered us some stubbies of his home-brewed beer. I tend to agree with my late father who once said: 'Home-brewed beer is like farting—your own seems all right.' It seemed churlish to refuse, however, and Bob's brew turned out to be quite palatable.

Later, as we pitched our camp, the sky looked rather stormy. Perhaps 'Elsewhere' was going to get some rain after all. We did not enjoy our barbecued snags that night. The news on ABC Radio from East Timor was ghastly—the vote on independence had been taken, but there was anarchy and murder abroad in the land. The on-the-spot reports told of houses looted and burned, and pro-independence supporters being killed either by bush knives or gunfire. The remaining United Nations staff would probably have to get out and the whole dreadful business cast a pall over the evening. We went to bed early.

We called in next morning to say thanks to Bob and Annette, and Bob pressed a few more bottles of his home brew upon us. He told us to watch out for emus on the road. I asked why emus and not kangaroos? He said they were constructed differently—essentially just feathers and solid bone. 'Roos just dent your car. Emus destroy it.'

We were now well and truly into 'The Goldfields' region, where the landscape appeared to have been carpet bombed by B52s. Craters and heaps of old tailings—some of them a century old—dotted the countryside there. Every now and then fences and 'KEEP OUT' signs indicated a renewal of gold mining. Many of the old mines and tailing dumps were being worked over with new technology to glean gold that the old-fashioned processes left behind—the level of activity depending on the fluctuating world price of the yellow metal.

Leonora takes its name from Mt Leonora, named by the explorer John Forrest who passed that way in 1870 on his way to search for any trace of Ludwig Leichhardt's missing party, which headed out from Roma, in Queensland, on a transcontinental journey in 1848. Searching for Leichhardt became a holy grail of Australian exploration. No fewer than nine major searches were conducted for the missing German explorer in the 90 years following his disappearance. He had already been missing for 22 years when John Forrest named Mt Leonora in honour of the then Western Australian Governor's wife.

The first gold strikes near Leonora were pegged in 1896, but it was the famous Sons of Gwalia leases that shaped the area for the next 70 years. In 1894 a Welsh-born Coolgardie storekeeper, Thomas Tobias, went to Wales for a holiday and while there organised a syndicate of Welsh nationalists to finance a prospecting party in the Western Australian goldfields. The syndicate called itself Sons of Gwalia—an ancient term for Wales. Tobias was effectively diddled out of his gold strike by a fellow-countryman, George Hall, who bought the initial Sons of Gwalia mine outright for 5000 pounds. Effectively Tobias had sold out for a pittance and the operation became the largest underground mine outside the Golden Mile in Kalgoorlie–Boulder, closing in 1963 and producing over two million ounces of gold. That was not the end of the story. In 1982 a new company, Sons of Gwalia NL, resumed large mining operations in the open cut and underground which are still active.

Since the 1970s, heritage organisations and private individuals have worked hard to make the Sons of Gwalia mine and surrounds a memorial to early gold mining. There is a very good museum with restored mining equipment, but the jewel in the crown, in our view, is the restoration of authentic miners' cottages. Most are just basic timber frames covered with corrugated iron—and furnished with period furniture, mostly very simple items constructed out of packing cases and scrap timber. The houses must have been ovens in summer and freezing cold in winter. Each house has been notionally 'bought' at auction by individuals who promised to restore and furnish them. Visitors to Gwalia can tour the houses after buying a ticket at the Museum. Ros and I called into House No. 13, 'Jack's House', a tiny four-room dwelling restored by Beth Taylor and Geoff Hales. This was social history at its best, bringing the past to life through individual stories.

Noting the front step which was decorated with little coloured ceramic fragments embedded in the concrete— doubtless Jack's own pride and joy—we walked into his bedroom. Considering its size Jack must have been a small man. He was, as we discovered when we found a photograph of him in a newspaper clipping celebrating his 79th birthday in February 1972. Jack Longa, or Giovanni as he was christened in the Italian province of Bergamo in 1893, had come to Western Australia in the 1920s after fighting for Italy in World War I and then becoming a zinc miner. In Australia he started out as a sleeper cutter before tackling hard rock gold mining. He specialised in sinking shafts and his record of 111 feet in 11 shifts on the 24th level of the Ivanoe Shaft still stood, said the birthday article. Mind you, it was a wonder Giovanni Longa made old bones. He was discharged from company service in 1946—he was 53— when diagnosed as being 80 per cent affected with the lung disease silicosis. But there was Jack in 1972 turning on a five gallon keg of beer for his friends and saying he would up the ante by five gallons a year from then on. His friends calculated on that scale that his centenary would be a one hundred gallon party. The article referred to Jack's wife, son, four daughters and several grandchildren still living in Italy. Had Jack brought his family out to Gwalia there would have been plenty of Italians to talk to—thanks to the efforts of the future 31st President of the United States, Herbert Hoover. How's that again?

Hoover started out as a mining engineer and, in 1897, became a partner in a London-based mining company with interests in the Sons of Gwalia. His American employer who recommended him for the job was aware the job qualifications called for a man of thorough experience at least 35 years old. He was economical with the truth when he pointed out that Hoover was not yet 35. He was actually only 23! Hoover concealed his boyish looks by buying his first dress suit and growing a moustache. He passed muster in London and was sent to Western Australia to become mine manager at Gwalia.

With true Yankee free-enterprise spirit, Hoover realised, when he reached Western Australia, that gold mining at such a remote location as Leonora had to have its production costs pared to the bone. To achieve this he confronted the mining unions head on, minimising unproductive work practices and converting labour to a largely contract basis by importing cheap labour. Does this sound familiar?

In 1898 he reported to his principals in London:

I have a bunch of Italians coming up this week and will put them in the mine on contract work. If they are satisfactory I will secure enough of them to hold the property in case of a general strike, and . . . will reduce wages.

Hoover adroitly managed to introduce cheaper Italian labour and avert a general strike, thus being the midwife for the Italian community which was to characterise Gwalia for more than half a century. The future president of the US did not stay long at Gwalia, leaving for a position in China later in 1898. But he did return on a number of occasions in the next few years as a consulting engineer. So that was how Hoover saw the start of Jack (Giovanni) Longa's presence in that little timber and tin cottage now so well preserved for visitors like us to enjoy. And there are dozens of others like it.

The Museum at Gwalia has a splendid photograph of the moustached, dress-suited young Hoover who probably ordered the historic head frame and winder now relocated near the museum—the original mine office. Only metres away from this building is one face of the spectacular 290-metre-deep open cut, from the depths of which modern ore-carrying trucks bring ore from way beneath the surface. The open cut is as deep as it can be without collapsing the sides. The original Sons of Gwalia miners had the same problem and by 1963 had dug down below the open cut to 4000 feet (1219 metres), a depth yet to be equalled with modern underground mining techniques.

With mixed feelings we dropped faster and further south down the map to Kalgoorlie, a spectacular place, rich with history and with lots to see and do—but also our last leisurely stop on our outback excursion. After Kalgoorlie we would be hammering back to Sydney as fast as we decently could.

The twin cities of Kalgoorlie–Boulder were buzzing.

The Hannan Cup was on and horse racing fever had the streets bedecked with flags and posters. We could barely find a spot in a caravan park. Poor old Paddy Hannan, the Irish prospector from County Clare whose name adorns horse races, streets, mines and pubs—he even had a brand of beer named after him—never shared the fabulous wealth his gold strike in 1893 ushered in. Paddy had chanced upon the edge of one of the world's greatest gold lodes, soon dubbed 'The Golden Mile', and which has sustained Kalgoorlie and its satellite towns for more than a century. Even in those early days Paddy Hannan wouldn't have been able to make his fortune without massive corporate assistance, because the vast reserves of gold in the area are locked into an auriferous reef needing massive machinery and plant to crush and recover it. The old boy did pick up a few nuggets, but he was not a businessman. For many years Kalgoorlie was known simply as 'Hannans' or 'Hannan's Find'. (The name Kalgoorlie, by the way, comes from the Aboriginal word for a shrub, *kulgooluh*, the silky pear, common to the area.) In 1904, when he was 61, the government gave Paddy a pension of one hundred pounds a year, and he died in Victoria in 'humble circumstances'— usually a euphemism for poverty—in 1925.

By the turn of the twentieth century, Kalgoorlie–Boulder were substantial cities with grand public buildings and plenty of equally grand hotels—many of which survive to the present day. Both cities have handsome main streets bordered with splendid, brightly painted and heritage listed properties. For a time, some of Kalgoorlie's streets were literally paved with gold. What was thought by the early miners to be 'fool's gold' was put to one side and the discarded ore used by the council for road making until it was discovered that the ore was indeed gold bearing, but needed a different method of processing! Although the twin cities are dominated by the huge 'Super Pit' which is gradually consuming the entire 'Golden Mile' in its great open cut, a substantial part of the income of the wider district known as the Goldfields is now derived from nickel mines as well as the many gold shows.

Ros and I decided that bush camping had spoiled us for city caravan parks. On a 5 am visit to the loo she overheard a conversation between two women in pink dressing gowns and fluffy slippers on a similar mission. As Ros is rather contemptuous of my preoccupation with daily regularity (she firmly believes that if your bowels don't work one day they will almost certainly oblige on the next), she found it necessary to share her intelligence over breakfast.

First woman: I'm here because I take Nu-lax and you have to get up early. My doctor said it was very good. Do you use it too?

Second woman: Yes, I take Nu-lax too. But sometimes you have to go at 3 or 4 in the morning. It's OK at home, but in caravan parks . . .

First woman: This is right, yes. And if you don't go when you want to go, sometimes you can't go later.

I thanked Ros for her thoughtfulness in passing on that deeply moving conversation.

For quite illogical reasons—possibly because I am not a tidy person—I was becoming profoundly irritated by the campers next to us. They were so spic and span, and their car and caravan so pristine that it was difficult to believe they ever went anywhere. This fellow even had extra chrome on the hub caps of his car and van which glistened in the sunlight. Nor did they ever seem to DO anything. When the husband emerged in the morning (his wife stayed inside most of the time), he just sat in a folding chair under his canvas awning gazing vacantly about and trying to draw any passer-by into mundane conversation about the weather. What was worse, he kept looking at me as though he thought he knew me, but mercifully failed to make the connection between my battered face and one he had seen on his television screen. He was the sort of camper, I decided unkindly, who would wait until you were actually hitching up your trailer to come over and say: 'Moving on today are we?' (He did. I was speechless, but Ros said tartly, 'It certainly looks like it, doesn't it'.) Yet they were perfectly pleasant people, not doing me any harm at all.

I noticed a couple of local pigeons paying a great deal of attention to the gas bottles on the front of The Manor, screened by my folded out bed. The demented birds were actually building a nest over the valve of one bottle. It was not a good prospect for their future offspring. Even homing pigeons would have a problem coping with our travel habits, and their nest would have to survive the slipstream of 110 kph travel. We tried to dissuade them, but they wouldn't take any notice. Eventually I had to up-end a bucket over the top of the gas cylinder, but even then the birds didn't go away. They sat nearby, glared balefully, and swore at us in pigeon.

Kalgoorlie is a bloke's town, or so it seemed to us. A blackboard outside a hotel on Hannan Street, the main drag—so to speak—advertised these delights:

SKIMPIES

Lolly, Miss Nude Erotica, Shaye, Rachel, Sarah.

SKIMPIES

18 hours a day.

We didn't check out Kalgoorlie's famous Hay Street at night, but on our way to the supermarket we saw the staff of one cubicle-fronted brothel all cheerfully painting its elaborately decorated facade in the winter sunshine.

COME IN AND PLAY.

Isobel, Topaz, Sara, Yvette, Skye, Kaya, Mimi and Mikki.

EFTPOS.

A nice modern touch, I thought. Hard rock miners of yesteryear almost certainly paid with real gold.

The tour of Hannan's (who else!) North Mine had been recommended to us as a way of seeing how hard rock mining was done in the pick and shovel days, and we found it good value. It had been a genuine working mine, and visitors were issued with hard hats for the journey underground in a miner's cage suspended by a vintage cable and drum lifting mechanism. Our guide, Bill Williams, had been a hard rock miner in Zeehan, Tasmania, and could talk from direct experience of life underground. He showed us—and briefly powered up—one of the early pneumatic drills, accurately dubbed 'The Widow Maker'. Modern drills are damped down with water, but 'The

Widow Maker' just spewed rock dust back out into the shaft. Not only the operators but everyone else in the mine breathed that dust, and many miners had to be invalided out of the industry with wrecked lungs while they were still in their twenties. These dreadful contraptions also deafened the operators because ear protection was thought to be unnecessary. Walking through the tunnels—all hand cut—Bill showed us one section where the gold-bearing ore had been gouged out of a steep sloping section less than a metre wide, and extending for about twenty metres. How men could even fit into the space, let alone swing a drill or swing a pick, seemed impossible. But it was done.

The Goldfields could not have developed at all without water, which was piped 560 kilometres from the east coast by 1903—a huge engineering achievement for that time. Kalgoorlie is 360 metres above sea level, and the water had to be boosted on its journey by no fewer than eight steam operated pumping stations along the way. The whole scheme was designed by a brilliant engineer, C. Y. O'Connor. Kalgoorlie's green parks, gardens and sports fields are taken for granted by Goldfields residents today, but every now and then residents are reminded that their water supply is finite. In the summer of 1997, rationing had to be imposed by the Western Australian Water Corporation during two very hot spells. Householders grumbled when they were unable to water their gardens. To explain the difficulties of the logistics involved, the Corporation's chairman, Peter Jones, pointed out that during that hot January every man, woman and child in Kalgoorlie was using the equivalent of thirteen full baths of water each day! Recent discoveries of huge underground water reserves in Western Australia's artesian basin may soon ease the burden of pumping so much water so far.

We wished we had spent more time exploring Kalgoorlie, but that was how we felt about almost everywhere we had been in the previous three months. As we drove south towards Norseman to connect with the Eyre Highway and head east across the Nullarbor, I remarked to Ros how well wooded the country around Kalgoorlie was. I had always imagined it as empty, red sandy desert. There is red sand aplenty, but also a surprising number of substantial eucalypts as well as the ubiquitous acacias.

'That's even more remarkable when you think of what happened early last century,' Ros reminded me, 'when just about every tree of any size was cut down by tree felling gangs to fuel the boilers and furnaces for those early gold smelters.'

It was reassuring to think that so much regrowth had happened over the last 70 years. Although Australia is an old, eroded continent, much of its flora is hardy and, given half a chance, will not only survive but flourish.

We drove on, lost in our own thoughts. There was an unspoken realisation that our real journey had effectively ended in Kalgoorlie. All we had to do now was drive home over familiar territory.

I reflected on how incredibly ancient Australia's land forms were, with its flora—and indeed fauna—influenced by firestick farming by Aboriginal people for 40 000 years, perhaps longer. It was an unimaginable time scale compared with European history. Of all the things we had experienced in the previous three months, the memories of actually seeing those timeless Aboriginal rock paintings on the Kimberley coast and extraordinary petroglyphs in the Pilbara and Mid West were strongest in my mind. I would not forget those graceful, enigmatic Bradshaw figures with dangling amulets and ornate headgear, the white, wide, staring eyes of the haloed Wandjina spirits, their curiously mouthless faces implying a silent scream, and the mysterious climbing men, etched into the sun-baked rocks of the Burrup Peninsula.

But the most poignant and enduring image was that long abandoned grinding stone still sitting in the shaped depression in the rock at Erong Springs where a woman's hand had placed it ready to grind seeds, so unthinkably long ago.

Bibliography

Australian Gallery Directors Council, *Aboriginal Australia*, Australian Gallery Directors Council, 1981

Bain, Mary Albertus, *Full Fathom Five*, Artlook Books, Perth, 1983

Battye, J. S., *Western Australia: A history, from its discovery to the inauguration of the Commonwealth*, Oxford: Clarendon Press, 1924

Bligh, Arthur C. V., *The Golden Quest: The Roaring Days of West Australian Gold Rushes and Life in the Pearling Industry*, Hesperian Press, Carlisle WA, 1958

Burke & Wills, *The Burke and Wills Exploring Expedition*, Wilson and MacKinnon, Melbourne, 1862

Boulton, G., *Alexander Forrest—His Life and Times*, Melbourne University Press, Melbourne, 1958

Burt, Jocelyn, *The Kimberley—Australia's Unique NW Coast*, Houghton & Stoughton, 1989

Cusack, Michael & Susan, *Our Year In The Wilderness*, Australian Geographic Pty Ltd, Terrey Hills, 1989

Dampier, William, *A New Voyage Around the World*, Hummingbird Press, London 1998

Durack, Mary, *Kings In Grass Castles*, Constable & Co, Gt. Britain, 1959

Estensen, Miriam, *Discovery. The Quest for the Great South Land*, Allen & Unwin, Sydney, 1998

Flood, Josephine, *Archeology of the Dreamtime*, Sydney, Collins, 1983

Flood, Josephine, *The Riches of Ancient Australia*, University of Queensland Press, St Lucia, 1990

Forrest, Alexander, *North West Exploration*, Corkwood Press Limited Facsimile Edition, Bundaberg, 1997

Graham, Bruce, *Journals of Two Exhibitions . . . George Grey*, Friends of the Battye Library, Perth, 1991

Hall, Lincoln, *First Ascent*, Simon & Schuster, East Roseville, 1997

Horden, Marsden, *King of The Australian Coast*, Melbourne University Press, Carlton, 1997

Horden, Marsden, *Mariners are Warned*, Melbourne University Press, Carlton, 1989

Idriess, Ion, *Outlaws of the Leopolds*, Angus & Robertson, Sydney, 1952

Lancaster Brown, Peter, *Coast of Coral and Pearl*, Robert Hale, London, 1972

Marcus, J. (ed.), *First in Their Field—Women and Australian Anthropology*, Melbourne University Press, Carlton, 1993

McAlpine, Alistair, *Once a Jolly Bagman*, Weidenfeld & Nicholson, London, 1997

McGonnigal, David (ed.), *The Kimberley*, Australian Geographic, Terrey Hills, 1990

McGregor, A. & Chester, Q., *The Kimberley—Horizons of Stone*, Hodder & Stoughton, Sydney, 1992

Moon, R. & V., *The Kimberley—An Adventurer's Guide*, Kikarra Adventure Publications, Pearcedale, Vic., 1989

Mulvaney, D. J., *Encounters in Place*, University of Queensland Press, St Lucia, 1989

Nixon, Marion, *The Rivers Of Home*, Vanguard Press, Perth, 1978

Palmer, Alex, *Paynes Find*, SW Printing and Publishing Co., Bunbury WA, 1988

Rathe, Gustave, *The Wreck of the Barque Stefano off the North West Cape of Australia in 1875*, Farrar, Straus & Giroux, New York, 1992

Richards, Christopher, *There Were Three Ships—Camden Harbour Expedition 1864–65*, University of Western Australia Press, Nedlands, 1990

Rolls, Eric, *Sojourners*, University of Queensland Press, St Lucia, 1992

Thomas, Athol, *Bulls and Boabs*, St George Books, Perth, 1981

Walsh, Graham, *The Bradshaws—Ancient Rock Painting of NW WA*, Published for the Bradshaw Foundation by Edition Limitee, Switzerland, Geneva, 1994

Video—*The Kimberley, Land of the Wandjina*, ABC